— THE LEGACY OF —

BEEZER and BOOMER

— THE LEGACY OF —

BEEZER and BOOMER

LESSONS *on* LIVING *and* DYING
from MY CANINE BROTHERS

DOUG KOKTAVY

B BROTHERS PRESS
Denver, CO

BBROTHERSPRESS

3515 S. Tamarac Dr., Suite 200
Denver, CO 80237

This work is a memoir and is an accurate, truthful description of events I personally experienced. It is intended for informational purposes and reflects my personal decisions only. I am not offering any type of medical or veterinary advice. Readers are encouraged to consult with appropriate medical and veterinary specialists prior to electing any treatment choices of their own.

One name in the book has been changed by request to protect the individual's privacy. Otherwise, the story is told exactly as it happened, to the best of my recollection.

Presence Plan is a trademark owned by B Brothers Press.

Cover and interior designed by TLC Graphics, *TLCGraphics.com*
Cover by: Tamara Dever, Interior by: Erin Stark

Cover illustration, "One Morning in October," by John Weiss © 1986 John Weiss.
Licensed by The Greenwich Workshop, Inc. Fine art limited editions of the art of John Weiss are available from The Greenwich Workshop, Inc. *www.greenwichworkshop.com*

Interior illustrations by Chris Smith, *chrissmithart.com*

Photograph of the author on page 312 by Jay Simon. All other photographs are from the author's personal collection.

Cartoons by Shannon Parish, *http://ShannonParish.com*

B Brothers Press is a member of Green Press Initiative, which means we meet GPI's environmental criteria and support their efforts to reduce the social and environmental impacts of book publishing. For more information, please visit: *greenpressinitiative.org*

FSC
Mixed Sources

This book is printed on FSC (Forest Stewardship Council)-certified stock.

Printed in Canada. The interior of this book was printed on 100% post-consumer recycled paper.

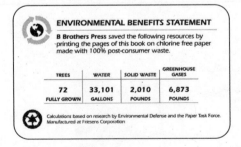

ENVIRONMENTAL BENEFITS STATEMENT

B Brothers Press saved the following resources by printing the pages of this book on chlorine free paper made with 100% post-consumer waste.

TREES	WATER	SOLID WASTE	GREENHOUSE GASES
72	33,101	2,010	6,873
FULLY GROWN	GALLONS	POUNDS	POUNDS

Calculations based on research by Environmental Defense and the Paper Task Force.
Manufactured at Friesens Corporation

To all those caring for a companion animal during its final journey.
May my story help lessen your fear and suffering.

Acknowledgments

I BEGAN WRITING A BOOK ABOUT MY EXPERIENCE CARING FOR A terminally ill pet when Beezer was first diagnosed. I'd never had a companion animal before and I was new at this. But all the books on terminal illnesses I could find dealt with pet loss *in the past tense*. In other words, after the pet had died. That wasn't my immediate problem in 2005. Coming to grips with massive uninvited change and loss of control while waiting for the final bit of earth beneath our feet to fall away into the abyss—well, that was another story.

The veterinarians, advisors and friends who supported me during this period of my life were incredibly helpful. Dr. Robert Goldstein and Dr. Robert Silver gave their all. Terri O'Hara, Sharon Callahan, David Koons, John Cooksey, Pat Lynn, and Carolina Rodriguez were especially supportive. Terri began as an animal communicator to the dogs and became a good friend to me. My many dear friends on the Yahoo groups—K9 Kidney Diet and Bone Cancer Dogs— lent much needed, selfless help. Thank you all for your generosity and friendship. In addition, Dave Lucey was the dogs' confidant over the years and today he continues to be a cherished friend to my shy Lab Coral. I am so appreciative of all of you.

Also I want to thank Leslie Bean, Ana Cilursu, Lisa Edwards-Filu, Liz Fowler, Amiee Ingram, Jody Weinberg and "Icky," Onalee Williams and "Dutch," and the staffs at Boulder's Natural Animal, Alameda East Veterinary Hospital, and Veterinary Referral Center of Colorado for their personalized caring. The Canine & Conditioning Rehabilitation Group helped prove to Boomer he was a gifted swimmer, no matter what. The Colorado State Parks system gets high praise for the magical dog parks at Cherry Creek State Park and Chatfield State Park. Whole Foods Market gets an honorable mention; it was there I converted its healthy people food into the special diets for my buddies. Thomas Hudson at Three Dog Bakery also gets kudos for his generous time and diet advice. Beezer and Boomer were frequent consumers. They also looked forward to the arrival of Mark Taylor, his UPS truck and his cookies. And speaking of treats, Citywide Banks kept Boomer's spirit's soaring with their magic cookie drawer and caring attitude. Thanks especially to Teresa Finnergy, Yvonne Valdez and Jessica Austin for treating Boomer as their most important bank customer.

As I began to write and tell Beezer's story, I joined the Colorado Independent Publishers Association (CIPA) and spent a couple of years sitting in the back of the room taking notes during the meetings. I have many thanks for my friends at CIPA. I also want to thank Argus Institute at Colorado State University Veterinary Teaching Hospital. Dr. Jane Shaw and her marvelous team, including Erin Allen, Gail Bishop, Del Rae Heiser, Lisa Hunter, and Carrie Katona, made me feel accepted and provided great ongoing support. Along with her veterinary wisdom, Dr. Shaw helped me to understand that this book had a place.

Writing a book proved to be one of the bigger mouthfuls that I had ever bitten off. About midpoint into the manuscript, I turned to a number of friends, colleagues, and acquaintances for a no-nonsense, honest review. Their thoughtful and careful comments were much appreciated. Every suggestion they made was seriously considered, with most implemented. I'm deeply honored by their sacrifice of time and willingness to be part of this project. My heartfelt thanks go out to each and every member of my Review Group: John Aberg, Leslie Bean, Daril Bentley, Louella Bryant, Betty Carmack, Ana Cilursu, Lisa Edwards-Filu, Mary Jo Fay, Michael and Lina Fedynyshyn, Debi Flocchini, Annette Frey, Julie Gall, Dr.

Martin Goldstein, Lori Hanson, Anne Harper-Andra, Dr. Nancy Kay, Laurel Lagoni, Dave Lucey, Sarah Lucey, Pat Lynn, Terri O'Hara, Carol Pluta, Karen Saunders, Andrea Schaller, Dr. Jane Shaw, Dr. Robert Silver, Karen Titus, Curt Todd, and Dr. Alice Villalobos. Many thanks to FedEx Office (formerly Kinko's) for turning out my manuscripts and review copies like clockwork. If I have overlooked anyone, I sincerely apologize.

After the first round of reviews and a few more drafts the manuscript was ready for some new eyes and some intense edits. I'd like to thank Daril Bentley for his grounding commentary. A big thank you goes to Louella Bryant, who spent hours reviewing the manuscript several times. Ellie, your comments, suggestions and professionalism were just over the top. I can't thank you enough for your in-depth commitment to making this project successful. Thank you as well to Karen Reddick, who added her great eagle eye and polish on the final draft.

I also have many thanks for my technical team. Artist Chris Smith did a masterful job with the illustrations, including several that were created simply by me explaining over the phone what the scene needed to look like. Scott Usher of the Greenwich Workshop and artist John Weiss really came through by allowing John's wonderful painting, *One Morning in October*, to be used on the book cover. Shannon Parish survived my numerous changes to create several memorable cartoon characters and scenes for the book and my website. Designer Steve Riecks' ongoing help with all the photos for the book was much appreciated. Tamara Dever and Erin Stark and the TLC Graphics team did a fantastic job of assembling all the pieces into a cover and interior design of which I am so proud. Thank you to all.

My biggest thank you goes to my editor, Barbara Munson. I dropped a great idea on Barb's desk in an incomprehensible state of chaos. Barb directed the writing, re-writing and endless editing and helped coax the book out of my heart with focused small writing projects. Barb's superb skills turned this into a better book than I could have imagined. I was very fortunate to find you and thank you from the bottom of my heart.

Any good circle wraps around until it comes back over itself. I'd like to thank Suzette and Marshall Fike for entrusting me with two of Cleopatra of the Nile's precious pups. Much appreciation for letting Beezer and Boomer share an earthly adventure with me.

Last, but not least, I'd like to thank the B Brothers themselves for something much bigger than a decade of "Fun with Fido" escapades. We had those, but the experience was so much more powerful. I learned to be humbled at the wisdom and nobility of animals and their willingness to share their knowledge with humans. For this, I am grateful to my beloved Labrador retrievers—and to companion animals everywhere.

Table of Contents

AUTHOR'S NOTE xv

~

PART ONE—EVENINGS WITH BEEZER

INTRODUCTION
3

CHAPTER ONE
Four-Legged Family Members
9

CHAPTER TWO
Let the Games Begin
13

CHAPTER THREE
The Illusion of Ego and Control
25

CHAPTER FOUR
*My Hair's on Fire
(and I'm Holding the Match)*
35

CHAPTER FIVE
Beginning the Long Journey
41

CHAPTER SIX
Evenings with Beezer
47

CHAPTER SEVEN
Anticipatory Grief
51

CHAPTER EIGHT
Leap of Faith
53

CHAPTER NINE
The Fork in the Road
57

CHAPTER TEN
Listening to the Animals
63

CHAPTER ELEVEN
The Teacher Becomes the Pupil
67

CHAPTER TWELVE
Are There Lessons Here?
71

CHAPTER THIRTEEN
Somebody's Inside That Fur
79

CHAPTER FOURTEEN
My Branch Office Is a Cage
83

CHAPTER FIFTEEN
The Daily Appreciation
91

CHAPTER SIXTEEN
A Milestone
95

CHAPTER SEVENTEEN
The Gift of Today
105

CHAPTER EIGHTEEN
The Circle of Life
111

CHAPTER NINETEEN
A New Version of Normal
115

CHAPTER TWENTY
*Honoring the Bonds
with Caregivers*
121

CHAPTER TWENTY-ONE
*Death, Dying and
Living with Balance*
123

CHAPTER TWENTY-TWO
The Gift of Being Wrong
129

CHAPTER TWENTY-THREE
The Paintbrush Incident
133

CHAPTER TWENTY-FOUR
Whose Master Am I Serving?
139

PART TWO — THE BIG DOG

CHAPTER TWENTY-FIVE
Boomer's Salute
145

CHAPTER TWENTY-SIX
Helping Others Helps Me
155

CHAPTER TWENTY-SEVEN
Melancholy Fall
165

CHAPTER TWENTY-EIGHT
A Dog's Life
173

CHAPTER TWENTY-NINE
A Christmas of Hidden Treasures
181

CHAPTER THIRTY
Fiduciary Duty
193

CHAPTER THIRTY-ONE
Three-Legged Dog
199

CHAPTER THIRTY-TWO
The Hang with Boomer Club
207

CHAPTER THIRTY-THREE
To Fear Is to Fuel
213

CHAPTER THIRTY-FOUR
Dealing with the Monsters
219

CHAPTER THIRTY-FIVE
Transforming into the Big Kahuna
229

CHAPTER THIRTY-SIX
Nooners with Boomer
237

CHAPTER THIRTY-SEVEN
Tightrope or Trailhead
245

CHAPTER THIRTY-EIGHT
Happy Birthday, Big Dog
253

CHAPTER THIRTY-NINE
Mets
257

CHAPTER FORTY
Hope vs. Hopelessness
263

CHAPTER FORTY-ONE
Lights, Camera, Action!
267

CHAPTER FORTY-TWO
The Farewell Tour
271

CHAPTER FORTY-THREE
*Surrender Does Not
Mean Defeat*
277

CHAPTER FORTY-FOUR
The Sunday Morning Picture
283

EPILOGUE 295

INDEX 299

Doug and the B Brothers at age five

Author's Note

I'M THE LAST PERSON YOU'D EXPECT TO TELL THIS STORY. I HAVE NO veterinary training and no social work or psychological counseling background. To the contrary, I grew up in an ice hockey family and now I'm a commercial law attorney wrapped in the daily micromanagement of ego and control. Historically, I'd be more readily identified with the beer-and-a-shot crowd than the *namaste* division of life. In retrospect, I probably needed these messages more than anyone.

My inward expedition takes place around my dogs' fatal illnesses. Beezer was diagnosed with kidney disease in 2004 and lived for nine months after that. Two years later Boomer tested positive for bone cancer. As my carefully constructed world collapsed, I looked everywhere but could find little help in dealing with all the issues I was facing: how to care for sick dogs, how to make decisions on their treatment and when to say goodbye. In the process I discovered the help I needed most was not for my dogs but for me. I was drowning in fear and guilt—fear of what lay ahead when the illnesses worsened; guilt about my possible neglect in caring for these wonderful animals.

It's been quite a journey. I blindly stumbled my way through, first shaking my fist at the universe and then embracing its messages. And in those lessons I also discovered why these treasured creatures are here and why they live such short lives compared to humans.

I'd like to say that these epiphanies came from some Tibetan monk I encountered on a vision quest to the Himalayas. *That* would be quite a story. No, my guides on life came in the form of two eighty-five-pound sibling Labrador retrievers.

I didn't get these lessons until my forty-seventh year, a time when my life seemed etched in stone, for better or worse. This old dog was able to learn new tricks from the most unlikely of sources and, truth be told, they were the only voices I'd allow to be heard. My best friends, my dogs.

I started writing this book when Beezer was dying. The story could have ended there and I would have been a wiser man. But then Boomer got sick and how was I now to write about yet another fatal illness? Wasn't one enough? In the soul-searching that transpired, I realized that their illnesses were just the catalysts to something more. There was a bigger story here. And so I plodded ahead with my writing, and herein lies the tale of two dogs dying and the rebirth of their brother Doug.

If you agree that pets are family members, you'll understand my crazy story. And if you have an aging pet or are going through a pet's fatal illness, I hope my experience helps in some small way to lessen the pain, dispel the fear, shed light on the process and provide a little peace. Most of all, I hope to encourage the realization that this isn't the worst of times; it is the richest of times.

DOUG KOKTAVY

PART ONE

Evenings with Beezer

Introduction

May 8, 2005

My Dearest Beezer,

It's been one tough week since your brother and I said goodbye to you. I've been lost at times. Mostly, I've been confused and out of sorts. You always knew how to take care of me and I miss that.

The day we said goodbye was so hard. You had fallen the night before and I know you were scared. So were Boomer and I. We three had gone to the veterinary ER and the doctor took you down the hall to check your blood while Boomer and I waited. I'll always remember how upset Boomer was when you left. He lay on the waiting room floor next to the closed door and kept his nose at the base, following you by smell. Boomer knew you were sick and I think he was concerned you wouldn't be coming back.

The doctor later had explained that your anemia was now pretty bad. That's why your back legs were failing. I was relieved that you weren't in danger that night. But I knew, down deep, that you would be in very grave trouble in just a few days.

We came home and I helped you up on the couch for snuggles. Then I sat there and did a lot of thinking. In the beginning, you, Brother and I had made a pact. Part of that agreement was that, as the disease progressed, you would never be hospitalized overnight. The hospital scared you and you let me know that it wasn't going to fix your insides. You kept telling me to trust you. What was important was being home, together. I didn't forget that.

Your desire was to live a quality life. You didn't want any extreme measures taken and you didn't want to wither away either. Your eyes always said *trust me*, and you smiled when we spoke about it. I think you were teaching me several lessons. It's funny…I had always been *your* mentor and guide; but, as we moved deeper into the process, I realized just the opposite: that I was the novice and you were my teacher. I did trust you.

Respecting your wishes was important to me. It was your life, after all. I thought back on the "practice sessions" of the past few months. You had gotten very sick several times, which made me think about our pact to say goodbye when the time was right. Then you would get better. I remembered that the last element of our pact was to give ourselves permission to change the plan if necessary. I was glad I was wrong those times, but thank you for the rehearsals. You were very wise to recognize I needed this practice.

Then it did come time to say goodbye. That Sunday morning was surprisingly calm. As I awoke with the sun rising, I saw you standing there next to the bed looking at me. You summoned the strength and lifted your front paws onto the bed, wanting to get up. I hustled over and lifted your rear end. Boomer jumped in as well. It was a brief moment in a time machine. Your head was on the pillow next to mine and your brother was sprawled by my feet. Many aimless nights over many aimless years it had been this way. I was appreciative of the moment but also melancholy at the rapidly failing light in this incredible picture. The picture I had enjoyed so many times and had assumed would simply go on and on.

We cuddled and, again, I ran the sequence of events during your illness over and over in my mind. I *still* could not let it rest. Surely there must be a solution. I was missing *something* in your treatment and needed to look at the records yet again. Review them for the umpteenth time. As a lawyer, I was trained to find loopholes and exceptions. I am surrounded by those things I can *prove*. Surely there must have been something I missed that would have made you better?

The doubts went on. Was today the right day for this final decision? Or did I have something to gain by gambling you could make it to Tuesday? And if so, then how about squeezing out Wednesday? What if I could actually help you to next weekend?

You see, my noble friend, I knew you would do everything you could to make me happy, as you had done for nine years. You always placed my welfare above your own. You would do your best to make it to next week, take a bit of pain, be scared, and lose more bodily control if it put a smile on my face. I knew you would gladly endure this agony, this indignity, for me, if your body allowed it. The better question was whether I was willing to pay the same price.

As we lay together in bed one last lazy Sunday morning, I etched in my mind forever the image of you and Brother, now snoozing back-to-back and head-to-head. Your two black coats melded together creating the illusion of one animal. I appreciated that you two could share this physical connection one more time. I'll always remember and treasure this Sunday morning picture.

We took one more walk to the park that final day. You were really tired and panting. Later I helped you into the car and we took a ride to get some hamburgers, which we all enjoyed. Then I started the phone calls.

One doctor, then another; they wouldn't let me off the hook. "This has to be your decision, Doug." One even pointed out that you were still managing to eat, which was a good sign.

No, I thought, I found vomit in the yard from yesterday. It's not eating if it doesn't stay down. In my mind, I overruled the doctors. They later told me this exercise was to test my resolve. I was finally glad the decision was up to me and only me. I was ready to pay the price of our love, to say the hardest goodbye.

I called back your vet who we'd made arrangements with to come over when it was time. "Today's the day," I said in tears, "I need you to come today." By far, this was the toughest sentence I have ever spoken. My mouth was in slow motion down to every last syllable. I wanted to take the words back, but, at the same time, I knew for your sake I couldn't take them back.

Then one very small miracle happened. After I said the words, a weight lifted off me. Not all of it, but enough to tell a difference. I actually felt a bit better on a terrible day. I think you helped me. You had trusted me enough to push on up to Sunday. I trusted you enough to let go. We were in sync, in agreement that the time was right.

Dr. Christenson said, "I can be there in forty-five minutes." She and I cried on the phone together. "I had to hear it from your own mouth, Doug," she added. "Beezer will be so very ill next week. You are making a compassionate and courageous decision."

I told her, "Don't worry if you're a bit late."

She arrived on time. We hugged and had another cry on the front porch and then she entered the house.

You were lying on your side on the floor next to your dog bed. Boomer was by your side as he always was. You had a strange, far-away look in your eyes. I lay down behind you and slid my right arm under your head. You rested your chin in the crook of my arm. I stroked your body with my left hand and felt so grateful we were at home for this passage.

The moment I feared most had arrived, but its presence meant I no longer had to fear the future. Amazingly, I felt a surge of energy, of courage. Was that coming from you?

The doctor gave you a shot to relax you. Within a minute or two you were asleep in my arms and dreaming. My arms were always there to protect you, dear Beezer, and especially on this day.

The doctor then prepared the final shot. I was whispering in your ear, "We'll always be together, we'll always be together, we'll always be together."

Just then, Boomer came over and started licking my face. I thought he was telling me that everything was going to be okay. Boomer told me something different a bit later.

The doctor then gave you the final shot. I could feel your breathing getting slower and shallower with each breath. Then I felt your breathing and your heart stop. Your gallant and dignified battle ended at 2:11 p.m. on Sunday, May 1, 2005.

I continued holding and stroking you while the doctor listened for your heartbeat. There was none. Boomer stayed close by and watched you depart. I was so very proud of both of you.

Then I got up and said goodbye to the doctor. I thanked her from all three of us. I placed a blanket on your bed and gently lifted you over to it. You looked peaceful.

Boomer and I let you lie in state for three hours. We wanted to give your soul time to leave, if such were the case, and I wanted to give Boomer time to say goodbye to your body his way.

One event that day lightened the mood. As I was cuddling next to your still body, my nose suddenly picked up a distinct odor suggestive of a problem. I raised a questioning eyebrow at Boomer. "Not me," he said. I managed a slight bodily shift calculated to reveal if somehow, in the focus of the moment, something had gone undetected. Relieved, but perplexed, I told Boomer, "It's not me either."

I got up and cautiously inspected your body. Lifting your tail, I was greeted by one final gesture on your part. I chuckled as I cleaned you up. Of course, there would be no "dirty shorts" at the funeral home. I noted that perhaps a sense of humor transcends death. "Way to go, Beezer," I said. Boomer just smiled.

I then loaded your body into the car. The guy from the funeral home had offered to come get you, but I'd have none of it. He had told me, "This isn't the way we do it." I told him, "Well, this *is* the way *we* do it." Boomer and I would be Honor Guard and transport your body. Boomer said it was really important to him.

We got to the funeral home around 6:00 p.m. Since it was Sunday, your body would have to be stored in a freezer overnight. The funeral guy, Scott, told us, "I need to put your dog in this plastic bag." I told him, "No, this is my dog and we would rather do it ourselves." I looked at Boomer and said, "Are you ready?" I then gently placed you in the bag and closed it.

Scott then said that he would get a helper and move your body down the hall to the freezer. I said, "No, this is my dog and we would rather do it ourselves." I looked at Boomer and said again, "Ready?"

I took Boomer by the leash and picked you up into the same loving arms that had adored you for nine years and thirty-five days. We walked about fifty feet and I placed you in the freezer. I kissed my fingers, briefly placed them on the bag and closed the door. We walked back to the car and went home.

That night was very quiet and surreal. Both of us seemed catatonic. More shock than tears. I was growing concerned about Boomer. Then, at 10:00 p.m., I noticed something that made me begin to cry again. He had crawled into your bed, curled up and gone to sleep. He stayed there all night, even refusing to come to bed with me when I offered. I hadn't realized it then, but Boomer had conducted his own ceremony in his own way. Good job, Boomer, I thought. I took my last sleeping pill, which had been saved for this night. It did the job and I crashed into a dreamless, empty void.

CHAPTER ONE

Four-Legged Family Members

EVERY NOW AND THEN SOMEONE COMES INTO YOUR LIFE AND LEAVES a huge impression. For me, it was two dogs—sibling Labrador retrievers. From the time they first came to live with me until the end, they never stopped being the complete and everlasting joys of my life.

I recall a scene from their first birthday as if it were yesterday. Suzette, my former legal secretary from whom I'd gotten the dogs, had decided to get all seven siblings together for a family reunion/birthday party. The dogs were romping all over her back yard and I stood on her deck surveying the mayhem below.

It was March 26, 1997. The weather could be wildly unpredictable that time of the year, especially in the mountains west of Boulder where the pups were born. Good fortune was with us that day and the weather was splendid. A Pendleton over a tee shirt and I was good to go. I recall the bluest of skies that make living in Colorado such a treat.

The party was in full swing. Everyone had come—six black males and one yellow female. The mom, Cleo, was there, monitoring the situation, but probably very glad she was no longer responsible for this lot. Even Dad Homer, a big yellow lab, came by for a while.

From the looks of them, Beezer and Boomer's siblings were developing into fine hunting dogs, as befits good Labradors. For us, a day of hunting would mean diving for tossed tennis balls at the reservoir, but those days were yet to come. Perhaps to the chagrin of the hunting crowd, I'd brought along multicolored, elastic-banded party hats. Suzette and I had managed to slip one on each of the dogs' heads, and, to our amazement, everyone left theirs on. Perhaps the over stimulation of the event, together with the image of all the other dogs with stupid hats, caused my two pups to forget that they were part of the hi-jinks. As I stood on the deck, a witness to the merriment unfolding, I had to swallow hard and force back a tear. I didn't realize it then, but my tough-guy armor had been given a big old dent that day.

The games began—fetch this, run there, pin the tail on the kitty— all the traditional stuff. Meanwhile, Boomer had methodically started picking minor fights with each of his siblings, and then with his mom and finally his dad. Conversely, Beezer seemed content to sit on the fringe of the action, observing. He even seemed a bit befuddled by the event. I'd come over and pet him from time to time. "It's a bunch of silly dogs, Beez," I'd say. He'd nod approvingly and snuggle in close to me for his own little birthday party.

The culmination of the event involved a large sheet cake I'd brought. All vanilla, as I knew chocolate was dangerous for dogs. Generous portions were cut for people and pooches alike, with the dog slabs being set on the ground. The silence was palpable as all the dogs descended on their birthday treats.

At one point, I closed my eyes and thought about what a surprisingly special year it had been…

———

I'D BEEN DEAD SET AGAINST GETTING A DOG. IT SEEMED LIKE A LOT OF work and I'd just begun practicing law on my own, in a downstairs office of our house. The whole idea of a dog seemed most illogical. But my wife, Carolina, had kept after me and kept after me. I resigned myself to the fact that this one-to-one vote would not end in a tie. So, when Suzette called and told us her dog was pregnant, Carolina said, "Let's get one of them," and I gave in.

The pups were born a few months later and we were able to visit while they were still nursing and living in the whelping box. Whatever reservations I'd had disappeared after seeing those adorable little creatures.

Suzette told us she and her husband were going to keep the yellow female, Nellie, and she allowed us the next choice. We got to pick from all six males. Suzette's husband helped by pointing out which of them seemed to be the "boss." I selected Boomer, although, I must confess, it was a bit like trying to select a treat in an ice cream shop. Some things just can't get goofed up.

We brought Boomer home when he was old enough and he immediately seemed at ease. At night, Carolina and I would lift him onto our bed to sleep. One night, I was startled out of a sound sleep due to a loud crash. I turned on the light and found that the pup had slipped off the bed and crashed to the floor. He was looking around with a bit of a dazed expression, but not even a whimper. No big deal, his brown eyes seemed to say.

I talked again to Suzette a couple of weeks later. Two dogs from the litter remained and needed homes. Would we be interested in a second dog? One of them was the shy, standoffish pup. Carolina was all for the idea. She remembered that one well. As a matter of fact, she had fallen for his eyes, she said. Even as an eight-week-old pup, Beezer had eyes that seemed to look beyond the person and directly into the soul. Carolina added that two dogs would keep each other company and make this experiment in dog rearing more interesting. That hunch proved to be the understatement of my life.

How happy I am today that I didn't stubbornly stick to my idea about no dog, then only one dog. What a different life I would have had if I'd insisted on getting my way. I am truly grateful to Carolina for her powers of persuasion.

Back to Suzette's we went. Little Beezer was sitting there patiently waiting for us, as if he'd known all along we would come back and get him.

During the drive home, Beezer sat on the floorboard of the truck with a puzzled look on his face. I talked to him all the way, reassuring him that this would be the only move he'd ever have to make in his life. I also pointed out that a grand surprise was waiting for him at home.

I'll never forget the expressions on both the dogs' faces when we walked in the front door. It was difficult to decide which dog was more excited (or was it me?). I carried Beezer in and set him down near Boomer, who had been sleeping in his bed. He opened his eyes and they saw each other. Instantly, Beezer ran over and an incredible whimpering, scrambling reunification occurred. I stood back, struck by the magic unfolding, and just appreciated the moment. I was overcome by the notion of how the whole was greater than the sum of the parts. That day I promised myself always to nurture and promote this sibling relationship.

Being able to facilitate these brothers spending their lives together remains one of my proudest accomplishments. That's not to say that the giving was all one-sided. This gift to Beezer and Boomer would come back to me many times over.

CHAPTER TWO

Let the Games Begin

HOW MUCH FUN WE'D HAD CAVORTING IN THE BACK YARD THAT FIRST summer! My ranch house is located on a cul de sac in a Denver residential area and the boys had a fenced-in back yard to romp in. Those two shiny black pups would later grow into handsome, sleek English Labs with muscular bodies, wide heads and relatively short legs. But as youngsters they were comical because their feet appeared to be attached directly to the bottoms of their torsos. We called them "fat little Tootsie Rolls with feet."

Carolina and I would later divorce, but that summer we were very happy raising the boys. She bought them a plastic kiddy pool. Boomer enjoyed splashing about and barking at the dinosaurs painted on the bottom of the pool as they shimmered in the sunshine. A fearsome pup he was indeed.

I particularly enjoyed watching them run around the backyard. Da boys were so short that their noses would slice through the grass, parting it in a V as they ran—like miniature snowplows pushing through green "snow." I'm not sure who had more fun on those days, the dogs or me.

They both earned nicknames early on. Since Boomer had been the alpha dog in the litter, I called him the Big Dog. He was clearly the John Elway of canines as he had won the genetic lottery.

Beezer on the other hand was less interested in horseplay. He was the runt of the litter, although he weighed the same as Boomer. Since he loved sitting in my lap, I later nicknamed him my eighty-five-pound Chihuahua. He was also Mr. Potato Head, a term of endearment I'd use when we were clowning around. He must have been tickled by the name because he would always lick my face when I called him that. What also set him apart from his brother was his bunny hop; when he was really happy he would buck and spin, just for the heck of it.

I had played ice hockey for years when I was younger, so I ended up naming them both for hockey players. In the 1950s and 1960s there was a guy named Bernie Geoffrion, who played for the Montreal Canadiens. When Geoffrion would whack a puck, there always was a booming sound and then the puck would hit the boards and there would be a second boom. So, his nickname became "Boom-Boom" Geoffrion and sometimes "Da Boomer." Beezer's namesake was from a goaltender named John Vanbiesbrouck, whose nickname was "Beezer." I'd thought it was perfect for my pup. I'd sometimes be watching an exciting hockey game on television when the commentator would shout, "And a great save by the Beezer!…And another by the Beezer!" And so on. Labrador Beezer, curled up on the couch with me, would always cock his head to the side as if to say, "Me? What save?"

Loving and cuddly by nature, the B Brothers were a bit snobby around other pooches. I think it was because they were pretty sure they were humans. "What a couple of *dogs*" their body language would communicate to the others. Swimming at nearby Chatfield Reservoir, a large state park about thirty minutes from home that had a dedicated off-leash area, Boomer took no crap from other dogs when it came to his tennis balls. A friendly fellow would come into the water and the Boom Boom would give a low, warning growl. Chasing balls became our cherished pastime. I would lob long ones out in the water for Boomer, but Beezer preferred the short ones. It isn't that he didn't want to swim that far…it was, why should he? Just throw another, Doug. So he'd get in two rounds to Boomer's one. Later, it was a puzzle to me, a paradox really, that Beezer had the weaker body yet Boomer couldn't hold a candle to Beezer's soul. Beez, I would learn soon enough, was a wise old spirit indeed.

Carolina and I never had to scold them. I think being puppies together kept their focus on each other and out of mischief. We did give them plenty of chew toys. My idea was if they had enough of their own toys, stuffed animals and bones, they'd leave our stuff alone. That even extended to food left out on the table. The two would even eat meals out of the same bowl at the same time, without ever a disagreement or growl. Boomer would happily scoot over to give his brother a bit more room. I've never heard of table manners between two dogs before and began to wonder what was up between those two at a very early stage.

Life was never dull. Although they usually were good about staying in the yard, one day, when they were older, temptation got the better of them and they took off on a major doggie trek. Our house was undergoing landscaping and temporary plastic fencing was tacked up along the side of the house. I was in my office. When I finally realized I hadn't seen or heard from the boys in a while, I looked out to see the fencing sagging. Gone! I knew right away what had happened. Boomer had seen the opportunity to split and Beezer, who would normally hang back, probably said to himself, "That's my brother; he'll get in trouble without me. I better go along."

I quickly jumped on my bike and headed down the greenbelt to the park, about a half-mile away. No Labs. Then I turned toward the bike path. "Did you see two black Labs?" I would ask everyone I saw. I knew I was going in the right direction when, without fail, they would point north and say, "They went that-a-way." Finally I spotted the escapees. We were now miles from home. Boomer wagged his tail happily when he saw me, but Beezer's face gave them away: "I knew this was a bad idea...*he* said it would be fun."

Another time, Beezer, still a pup, left me a special gift. I was downstairs working in my office and was on a lengthy conference call with other attorneys. It was a call during which I couldn't put the phone down and attend to *anything*. "Excuse me, I have to go see what my dog wants" would not cut it.

Behind me, I heard a puppy cautiously coming down the uncarpeted stairs. A minute or two later the Beez pattered into my office and came over to say hello. I reached down and petted him briefly. But I had to take notes and participate in the call, so he sat down at my feet and stared hard at me.

Not getting my attention even though he was fidgeting, he then got up, squatted and took a major league dump. I was still on the call as a thoroughly obnoxious odor filled the room. Beezer looked at his creation, sniffed once and scrunched up his face as if to say, "Eeeewww!" Then he turned and padded his way back up the flight of stairs. To my recollection, that phone call lasted an eternity.

Even when Beezer was older he didn't lose his timidity. I had been volunteering for the Safe Harbor Labrador Retriever Rescue. One day I got a call from them that there was a small black female Lab in Castle Rock, about an hour south of Denver, who needed transporting. I agreed to pick her up and keep her at my house until the foster person could come by for her. When this dog and I arrived, Beezer naturally decided to give her a sniff on her butt. But, perhaps a bit nervous, she immediately whipped around and bit his neck—hard. Instantly Beezer leaped skyward and jumped on my lap trembling. I had to shrug and give him a little advice. "That's what happens with girls," I said.

Dear Mr. Beezer,

Do you remember those early days? We got to spend all our time together, even when I was working. After breakfast, I'd walk downstairs to my office to begin my day. It didn't take long before you were negotiating the stairs on your own and joining me in the office. It was here where I first noticed a sharp contrast between your personality and Boomer's. You and I certainly shared a special relationship. Boomer developed into a very busy dog. He would have UPS trucks, neighborhood kids and a multitude of activities to monitor from the front door. Squirrels, blowing leaves and normal back yard perimeter patrol added to his administrative responsibilities. He was the Dog on Duty—the DOD.

You, Mr. Beezer, on the other hand, were the classic shop dog. We used to laugh when we'd see this scenario on TV…a small-town service station invariably had an unleashed hound lying around the shop lazily monitoring the operation. Your interest, even as a pup, was to become my white-collar shop dog.

This was a surprise. I hadn't counted on your daily presence in my office. Heck, I hadn't even considered that you would become such a loyal office mate. The spontaneity of this gift, and its development over the years, made your time spent in the office all the more important.

I was in the process of finding a way to make my solo law practice profitable and my workdays were sometimes stressful. Before you two came, I had been employed by someone else for ten years, dealing with the pressures and challenges of being a young lawyer in a law firm. Unhappy with the law firm experience and working for other lawyers, one day I called it quits. This new business venture had coincided with your arrival.

Being my own boss allowed me a tremendous amount of freedom. It was scary, but I enjoyed being 100 percent responsible for my own success or failure. I had to solve my own problems and had no one to rely on but myself.

I found your daily dedication to the office strangely mellowing, contrasting with my fast-paced, specialized creditor's rights practice. While I represented banks and automobile finance companies when accounts went into default, you were constantly by my side. I would be on an important—maybe even tense—conference call with someone, and then after the call, could reach down and stroke your sleek black coat for a few minutes. There was a positive, light-hearted energy about you. Even then, I understood what a powerful asset you were to the office, although at the time I didn't know how you did it.

To get to my office, you boys had to maneuver the stairs to the basement and pass through the outer office where my coworkers, Dave—also an attorney—and Rhonda, my paralegal assistant, had their desks. Both of you soon learned that extra pats and praise were available here. But you, Beezer, would usually head right for my office in the back and plunk down at my feet.

Each day became an opportunity to figure out ways to have fun and be silly while working hard. Sometimes we got in some really good pranks. I recall one day when I answered the phone to a cold call...

"Could I speak to the person responsible for your health care decisions?" the woman asked.

In my best deadpan business voice, I replied, "That would be Mr. Beezer, but he's busy taking a nap."

It seemed an eternity as I listened for a response from the woman and somehow kept from laughing. I did look down at you and you gazed up at me, smiled, and I could have sworn you winked.

You, Mr. Beezer, also had an uncanny knack for timing that the most gifted comedian would be proud of. Boomer loved his menagerie of stuffed animals and would carry them around. We called them his friends. You never had much use for this type of toy. Occasionally, though, you'd pick one up and walk around with it. The funny thing was the way you'd carry it. Your teeth would grip the smallest, outermost tip of the friend—usually an ear or tail. Your tenuous hold would cause the animal to sway back and forth from your mouth as you walked. It seemed that on the most stressful working days you would decide to walk slowly, deliberately into the basement with a teddy bear dangling from your mouth, a glint in your eye. You were a real ham. Your cartoon antics reminded me of an old man with an unfiltered cigarette in his mouth—talking, smoking, chewing gum all at the same time.

I'll never forget those days, Mr. Beez.

⌒

I'D OFTEN MARVEL AT THE WAY THESE LITTERMATES DID THINGS IN UNIson. When they slept, they would curl up in the exact same position, like two bookends. When I later installed a doggie door, they both had to go out the door together. Of course, the door was meant for only one at a time and more often than not they'd get stuck, literally. The more they pushed forward, the more stuck they got. A real Three Stooges act.

Any outing, even a short walk or car ride, became a grand adventure. The sparkle it brought to their eyes made those excursions all the more special for me. Puzzling, though, was the formation they used every time when I walked them on leashes. We would typically head down the street from our house toward the neighborhood park. Beezer and Boomer would lead the way like a couple of draft horses, veering, crashing and bouncing off each other. Then something strange would happen. If Boomer had started out on the right, he'd tuck behind Beezer and take up position on his left. This formation adjustment took place at the beginning of the walk and, if necessary, again during the walk.

I know this sounds insignificant. It is. But, I began to notice the pattern from the very first time I walked the dogs. Since I was baffled, and being a good attorney, I'd remind myself before our walks to observe the formation. Was this a pattern or just my imagination? I kept a mental record. Days turned into weeks, and weeks turned into seasons. Boomer would always move around to walk on Beezer's left. There had to be a reason why he did this, but I was clueless.

I began a series of tests. Maybe it was Beezer's eyesight. Sure, I thought, his left eye is weaker than his right. Boomer knows this and walks on his left to protect Beezer's blind spot. So I'd test Beezer's peripheral vision at home when I'd happen to be well on his left. A slow movement with my hand. To my surprise, Beez always moved his head to the left to see what I was doing. After numerous tests I pronounced his eyesight fit.

Maybe then it was Beezer's hearing. His left ear hears less than his right. Boomer knows this and walks on his left to protect him because of a hearing loss. So I'd test Beezer's hearing when I'd find myself well on his left at home. "Beezer," I'd whisper, lower and lower with each test. Every time, he'd turn his head left and look at me as if saying, "What?"

Eventually, I pronounced Beezer's hearing fit as well. What else could it be? I supposed the behavior could have been prompted by smell, but it seemed most unlikely that Beezer had had a stinky right side for all this time. I was out of senses to test. It had to be something else. The 100 percent nature of the occurrence ruled out randomness. I finally just gave up trying to solve the mystery and chuckled. "You guys understand it—I guess that's all that matters," I said. Years later, I would get my answer.

SATURDAYS WERE ALWAYS THE DOGS' FAVORITE DAYS. THEY WERE SO good at spotting the clues: I wouldn't go downstairs to the office, people weren't arriving for work, and a decidedly low-key atmosphere existed while I enjoyed my morning paper. Exactly why I'd even try to sit down on the couch to read is a silly mystery unto itself. They would have no part of it.

First the boys would prance back and forth with their ears at alert. Next, I'd be serenaded by a low moaning that sounded like a ship in a fogbank, which could, on any other day, indicate gastric distress. But not today, not on a Saturday. The final straw would be a series of increasingly forceful tandem nuzzles under my forearms, which would rattle the newspaper and culminate in a coordinated launching onto the couch and into me. That's it, I thought—I can't fool them.

"Should we go for a dog walk to the reservoir?" I'd ask, feigning nonchalance. What would happen next mimicked a jailbreak in a two-man prison. Boomer levitated straight up. Beezer, the conservative one, began his bunny hop routine.

We would then jump into the car for the ten-minute ride to Doggie Disneyland, known to humans as Cherry Creek Reservoir. At this massive dog park the dogs always enjoyed running, playing in a meandering stream and visiting with the other dogs. The dog park easily accommodated our ninety-minute loop without covering the same ground twice.

One Saturday, we were about halfway through our walk; Beezer was about twenty feet in front of me on a horse trail, immersed in the tall grass, occupied by the smells of the day, and Boomer was nowhere to be seen, off on his own adventure. Beezer and I intercepted a small band of dogs, including a huge black male poodle. All the dogs gave Beezer the appropriate hello sniff and continued on their way—except this poodle.

For some reason, this guy had it in for Beezer. He puffed up his chest, making himself seem even larger than he was, arched his back and stepped in front of Beezer on the path. Not wanting a confrontation, Beezer turned off course slightly. The giant poodle then adjusted his course to again cross in front of him, thrusting his chest in Beezer's face. This he repeated several times and I could see the frustration building on my dog's face. "Mellow out, man, I'm just here to have fun," Beezer was saying. But the poodle seemed committed to a confrontation.

Time to step in, I thought. Then my peripheral vision picked up a black blur on my left moving at warp speed. It was Boomer. He arrived on the scene before I completed one step in Beezer's direction. I expected Boomer's parachute to "pop" at the last second and bring this dragster to a stop. This didn't happen.

Boomer sped up, lowered his head and drilled the poodle at full speed. The poor dog was knocked ass over teakettle, flying several feet straight up in the air. End of problem.

Naturally, the giant poodle's owner immediately appeared. She was an attractive young woman aghast at the unprovoked attack on her angelic little cupcake. Somehow, I was able to apologize to her and avoid laughing. My hands sprang up to cover my face, hiding an ear-to-ear grin, and my stomach was ordered to stifle the impending explosion of laughter. Then Beezer, Boomer and I made eye contact with looks that exclaimed, "This is really fun!" while we made a hasty retreat and scooted onto another path. It was a grand day indeed!

But this picture of seemingly endless fun and games with my guys only tells half the story. Even though both Carolina and I thoroughly enjoyed the boys throughout their early years, our marriage was foundering. When the dogs were five, we separated. For the sake of expediency, I moved out of the house and into an apartment nearby. Initially in the divorce settlement, Carolina stayed in the house where my office was and also kept both dogs—I hadn't wanted to separate them. But being apart from them was terrible. Every night I'd hole up in my deathly quiet apartment and wait for the morning to come—the time when I could return to work in my office and back to my buddies. After nearly a year, I finally got to move back to the house, which had been my childhood home, and Carolina moved to a place of her own.

After that, the carefree days of the B Brothers moved on in time unabated by problems. I was aware of their advancing age but I always felt serious issues would only arise at some undefined moment well into the future. Time has a funny way of impeaching careless thought.

CHAPTER THREE

The Illusion of Ego and Control

O VER THE NEXT YEARS FOLLOWING THE DIVORCE, HAVING THE B
Brothers in my life was therapeutic and even blissful. Every day
brought something to laugh about and feel grateful for. The boys
had turned into handsome, muscular dogs with shiny black hair with
just a hint of curl. People would tell me it was hard to tell them apart.
But, much as a parent can distinguish between his identical twins, I
had no problem with my two family members.

In December 2003, when the Labs were seven, I got a call from
Suzette. I hadn't heard from her in years. Her news was that two of
Beezer and Boomer's littermates had gotten sick from kidney disease

and had died. She wanted to let me know so I could take action. I slowly put the phone down and felt my first twinge of concern.

I immediately called the animal hospital in Denver where I had been taking the boys their entire lives and told the doctor about their siblings. We made an appointment for the next day and I took the boys in for blood and urine tests. Boomer checked out fine, but Beezer had a bit of protein loss in his urine.

"We'll keep an eye on it and check it again in one year," the vet told us. The protein loss could mean nothing. No need for concern. No change in diet was discussed, no supplements, no medication. In fact, no other action of any type was recommended. That didn't sound too alarming, I thought. We went back home, comfortable in the knowledge that I'd done all that was necessary. Beezer and Boomer were in the prime of their lives. I never gave it another thought.

But, eight months later, the story was very different.

My Dearest Beez,

That day in the vet's office was so difficult. I know you must have felt it too, even though you never let on. It hadn't been a year since your last blood test. We were sitting in the small, cold waiting room. Your brother was at home so it was just you and me. My arms were around you and I quietly wept into your warm fur. I was terrified for what was about to come.

You'd just had another round of urine and blood tests. I was more than a little concerned when your vet said we'd have to see one of their internists. I sat in disbelieving silence as those words echoed around my head. Nobody gets sent to a specialist because everything is *okay*, I thought. We sat in the room for what seemed like hours, waiting for the internist.

"Please don't be sick, Lovie," I pleaded into your fur. "Please don't be sick."

I had begun to notice a change in you a couple of weeks before. You'd always taken great pleasure in eating, but now that had changed and your appetite had been increasingly off. I'd give you and Boomer a bowl of kibble in the morning and a can of mixed vegetables in the evening. Then, for some reason, you were eating less and less of your mixed veggies and then refusing them altogether. I was really puzzled when you started to refuse your morning kibble. So here we were for more tests. But this *had* to be something minor, right?

The internist came in and very matter-of-factly told me that you had a form of kidney disease known as glomerulonephritis. The filtration part of your kidneys wasn't working properly, which allowed protein to leak out. She thought we had caught it early and assured me that your numbers were very low, which was good. However, she said, this was a progressive, fatal disease. She prescribed several medications and a prescription diet.

The doctor's words shook me to the core. I thought about Suzette's call. Was this the beginning of the end, as it had been for his siblings? The vet explained the disease but I never really understood the physiology; all I understood was that you were dying. As I cried, you looked me straight in the face and, with those brown eyes that talked to my soul, said, "What can I do to take your pain away?" Your selflessness was noble and courageous and, ironically, I drew strength from *you*.

⁓

OVER THE NEXT FEW MONTHS, MY MOOD SWUNG BACK AND FORTH LIKE a rope on a tree branch. I frankly was not coping well. One moment I'd be hopeless and in tears; the next moment, I'd be defiant.

"Together, we'll beat this thing," I'd declared to Beezer, while faithfully giving him his medications the doctor had prescribed. I also was now researching alternative treatments. I recalled how I'd used an East-meets-West approach when I'd had a serious knee injury from hockey a year or two before. I'd had traditional physical therapy prescribed by my orthopedist, but I added acupuncture to the mix. My knee healed in record time. I decided to look into it for Beezer.

On the Internet I found a doctor nearby who practiced acupuncture in addition to traditional western veterinary medicine. We went to see Dr. Hannah Christensen and she told us that acupuncture could help support organ function and wasn't just limited to joint problems, like my knee. I figured, what the heck, let's try it.

Dr. Christensen gave us a Chinese herb, jin gu shen qi san, to add into Beezer's food. I liked the name. It sounded mystical. I had visions of some ancient, robed Chinese veterinarian dispensing miracle cures made from roots and leaves, and was buoyed with hope and confident that this two-pronged attack would resolve his symptoms. I mean, we caught it early, right? And from here on out we'd work this problem just like every other problem that we solved in the office. It would be tough, but we were used to that. Beezer would be by my side for many years to come.

And then Beezer *was* showing signs of improvement! By October 2004, just three months later, his appetite had returned to normal. His November blood test showed that the level of creatinine, a protein found in muscles and blood and excreted in the urine, was dropping. This was a good sign, too. Creatinine levels in the blood provide a measure of kidney function. It was the creatinine that had been the alarming indicator since August. I began to relax.

I also got cocky. Every problem, I reminded myself, no matter what, can be solved if I just worked hard enough at it. I'd learned that as a kid, on hockey rinks. I later reinforced it in my law practice and it kept me going during the difficult years following my divorce. Kidney disease was a challenge, but we'd outwork it.

So I brushed away my doubts and moved forward. We had a fun Thanksgiving with my mother, Louise, my sister, Kris, and her family and looked forward to a happy Christmas season. We were faithfully following the two doctors' regimens—diet, meds and acupuncture—and we were beating kidney disease.

But two days before Christmas, we were again in the cold little examining room at the same veterinarian hospital where we'd gotten the bad news in August. I began to choke up just by being in that room. We hadn't even seen the doctor yet. In fact, *nothing* had happened yet, at least nothing outside of my mind and my heart. I knew Beezer was very puzzled by the whole thing. He cocked his head and gave me a quizzical look, as if to say, "Dude?"

His appetite had been off again for about a week. My initial response had been to explain it away—this isn't happening. First of all, the November blood test clearly indicated he was getting better. (I found out later that ups and downs in blood test numbers can happen with kidney disease.) He'd had the best that both eastern and western medicine could offer. We had outworked the problem. It was just a stomachache or something easily explained. I wished away whatever the problem was.

But a week went by after his new symptoms and there was no improvement. In fact, Beezer's appetite was getting worse. So back we went to the hospital for another full run of blood and urine tests. Once again in the examination room, we waited for the internist to arrive. I was lying on the concrete floor with my arms around Beezer, my face once again buried in his fur. I couldn't talk. I didn't have to. He stayed right next to me, a rock. I silently thanked my beloved friend for putting his health issues aside that day to help *me*. I would have asked for his forgiveness for my weakness, but I knew it was not necessary.

The internist came in and said that Beezer's tests were the worst yet. The creatinine number that had been decreasing last month was now at an all-time high. Related numbers were worse as well.

"Most dogs with numbers like these have about ninety days to live. Now's the time to try any exotic ideas you have for treatment," she said. I crumpled onto my dog, tears streaming down my face. When the internist asked me a question, I looked up at her, but no words came out of my mouth.

"Why don't you go get a box of Kleenex," the doctor told her assistant.

I heard, "exotic ideas you have for treatment...," but her words after that simply went in one ear and out the other. I had no idea what she meant. "I can give you the name of a homeopathic vet in New York whom I have worked with in the past," she continued. "There really isn't anything more we can do for you."

That was it, then. I'd taken both dogs to this animal hospital all their lives. Now, they were sending Beezer home to die? I couldn't even begin to understand, let alone control, the myriad emotions I felt.

Finally I choked out a few words. "There has to be something we can do," I pleaded. The assistant came back into the room and handed me the whole box of tissues.

"I can't let my Beezer..." My voice grew lower, slower, and I failed to finish the sentence.

The doctor cleared her throat, pulled out a pad of paper and drew a picture of Beezer's kidneys. "They are progressively ceasing to function," she explained patiently. Something called the glomeruli were supposed to act like a sieve and keep protein from leaking out into the urine. Beezer's sieve was not working well and getting worse all the time. She explained there was nothing that could be done to stop or reverse this process.

A vet tech then brought in a bag of intravenous solution and a stand. She briskly set up the bag and attached it to a plastic tube and then connected a long needle to the end. Then the vet inserted the needle at the base of Beezer's neck in the area between his shoulder blades and turned a valve on the bag, which began a steady, slow flow of liquid. "We call this a subcutaneous, or sub-Q, treatment. This fluid will help hydrate Beezer and flush out the toxins in his body," she said. It was kind of like a poor man's dialysis machine.

The vet reached for Beezer and tried to demonstrate how I would do this at home. "You just pull up on the hide and insert the needle under the skin, but on top of the muscle." I felt certain my swollen eyes and blank stare adequately communicated my level of incomprehension. I responded with silence as if to drive home the point.

"We'll send you home with a case of fluid, lines and needles," she continued. "You'll have to give Beezer one bag, three times a week." My brain immediately sent an emergency override re-transmit message to my ears.

"I can't do this, Doctor," I said. "You want me to take Beezer home and stab him three times a week?"

I wasn't in any condition to engage in a discussion or make a cogent point, let alone win an argument. I continued to make eye contact with my boy, looking as deeply into his eyes as he did into mine. That was how we talked. Verbal discussions were for fun. Silent eye contact was for meaning. I told Beezer I couldn't breathe. Beezer told me he was there for me. Our unblinking eyes continued to focus on each other to the exclusion of all else. A vague buzzing in my ears indicated the vet was continuing the conversation. She then shook my hand, wished us well and left the room. That was it.

In the past, I'd seen people leave the vet's office in tears and obvious pain. "I'm sure glad I'm not in their shoes," I'd say to myself as I'd consciously avoid eye contact. That day the young woman at the checkout desk understood. Her normal cheerful attitude was subdued and businesslike. I paid my bill, gathered my prescriptions and somberly headed to the door with my beloved pal. Walking out, I glanced at a full waiting room. Everybody was looking down or away from me. All their dogs had been pulled close. I could hear the clock ticking and I understood what these strangers were thinking. Today, the bell tolled for me.

～

As we headed home, for the first time in my life, I felt helpless. Somebody has got to be kidding! I couldn't insert a needle into Beezer's body! It wasn't that I didn't want to, I just couldn't. I figured doing it right, sticking myself, or killing Beezer accidentally were all three even-money propositions. Somebody needed to come up with an idea that I could actually accomplish.

All I wanted to do was get home. Boomer was waiting by the front door with a look of concern. "What the heck happened?" he telegraphed to me when he saw my face.

I sat in stunned silence, not moving. I hadn't faced a loss like this since my father had died some twenty-five years earlier. I'd been only twenty-two at the time and never got a chance to say goodbye. Even my divorce, which hurt so badly, didn't compare with this.

My mom called me later in the day. I hadn't told her that Beezer had gotten worse over the past week. I'm just not the kind of guy who talks easily to family about his problems or emotions. She was chatting away, happily making plans for Christmas. We were all supposed to go to my sister's house for the day to be with my nieces, Brittany and Ashley, and nephew, Alex. But I couldn't think of anything more difficult than putting a smile on my face and participating in Christmas. I didn't have anything to *celebrate*. Quite the contrary, I felt I'd ruin it for everyone. All I wanted was to be by myself. I told my mom I just wasn't able to come. Then I closed the drapes, turned off the phone and cried until I didn't have any tears left.

I sat there for what seemed like hours, thinking about how unfair the situation was. I felt cheated. Mostly, I felt fear—deep, numb-to-the-bone fear. Along with trying to handle the sub-Q, the bigger fear was how could I watch my best friend die a slow death? What would happen to me during this process? And after? How could I work in my office without my Beezer? My life was going to change whether I was ready or not.

⌒

I THOUGHT I WAS USED TO CHANGE. I'D DECIDED TO START MY OWN law practice in 1995, about ten years after I became licensed, and return to my creditor law roots. I find this area of law simpler, less judgmental and a far better business model than litigation. Someone borrows money and fails to pay it back. Nobody is at fault, and both sides are simply required to live up to the agreement.

My pressure comes from the inherent stress of being self-employed. I didn't plan in advance to start my own office; it just happened. I wasn't sure whether I'd be good at it or not. I worried about bills and all the things that any other business owner worries about. Of course, as time goes by, I feel less stress. The longer I am profitable, the less likely it is that my business will fail. One of my greatest joys is being an entrepreneur and not having to be dependent on anyone else.

But now, with Beezer newly diagnosed with kidney disease, I was one half notch above incompetent in the office. I told Dave and Rhonda, "You two are going to have to step up and help. Do not assume I know what is going on or that I am aware of the deadlines. I am struggling. A few of my grenades might be missing pins." I knew I could count on *their* competency and support in getting through this.

I figured I could at least handle some of the administrative tasks, though, and set out to help *them*. But I couldn't even focus on that mindless work. I ended up filing two or three ten-day requests for extensions of time with the courts, and these were for the simplest of matters. Then I was calling my long-time clients about putting off deadlines and ended up telling them about the crisis in my life.

Do you mind if we push off such and such? I assumed that they would appreciate the call, the honesty. In all likelihood, they were probably shaking their heads over my melodrama. It's a good thing they weren't around when I gave Beezer his first sub-Q injection.

My Hair's on Fire (and I'm Holding the Match)

I SURVEYED THE MEDICAL SUPPLIES IN FRONT OF ME WITH ALL THE enthusiasm of a death row inmate. Sure, I'd seen the sub-Q procedure done at the vet's, but the experience had been woefully inadequate to prepare me for today's task. Beezer and I were now sitting on the living room floor, he in his dog bed, me right beside him. I had a full IV bag of saline plus a hollow rubber tube about five feet long to connect to the bag and a rather gruesome looking needle to connect to the end of the tube. In my mind, the needle resembled something used to hold railroad trestles in place. I would have to assemble the three pieces, then stick the needle into Beezer and drain the bag into my buddy. I could only imagine the thoughts going through Beezer's head as he watched his moist-eyed, shaking "doctor" begin the procedure.

I felt like I was about to perform brain surgery from a textbook—a textbook written in Chinese. I looked around for Boomer, hoping for a bit of encouragement from the Big Dog. He was nowhere to be seen. Smart dog, that Boomer. No sense sticking around the bank when your accomplice has a leaky water pistol and his mask on backward.

Step #1 was to find an IV stand. I walked around the house and examined its contents. A floor lamp was briefly considered but eliminated due to probable top-heaviness. My best option was a high-backed bar stool. I took a clothes hanger and twisted the hook out and then fastened the hanger upside down to the top of the stool. Step #2 was then hooking the line into the bag, bleeding the line into the sink, and then attaching the bag to the hanger. This step was accomplished a bit clumsily, but successfully. Step #3 was attaching the needle to the line. This was easy, but I felt my chest tightening as I was now out of easy steps.

I sat down next to Beezer and began to pet him. All I could think about was how much I loved him—and how scared I was. What if I did it wrong? What if I hurt him? How would I live with that? He was only nine. He should have been romping through the park, not getting poked by his best friend.

I practiced making the little pouch on Beezer's back, below his neck. Over and over I created it and let go. The Beez was doing everything he could to help, lying quietly with his head resting on his front paws. The problem was me. I looked at my watch and discovered my dilly-dallying pouch preparation was approaching a half hour. Finally, I reached over and grabbed the line and needle, pulled off the cover, made one more pouch and inserted the needle. To my relief, Beezer didn't even flinch. I reached over and flipped the line open. Nothing happened. I continued to stare at the top of the line and watched as intermittent drops fell slowly from the bag into the reservoir for their journey through the line. It was well over an hour by the time this tortoise crossed the finish line.

THERE HAD BEEN NO CHRISTMAS FOR US THAT YEAR. I DECLINED EVEN a modest appearance at my sister's house on Christmas day. New Year's Eve was equally uneventful. I had been invited to a party at Matt and Pamela's, my good friends who throw a heck of a shindig. I called Matt and explained the circumstances. He said he understood. I stayed home that night and cried. I want to make it clear that neither Beezer nor Boomer was crying. Just me. My world was beginning to collapse inward.

During the next five weeks I pulled myself together enough to rally a defense against this disease. I was determined to lick it and promised Beezer as much. Picture trying to bail the water out of the Titanic with a bucket. The shocking part was that I actually *had* convinced myself that I could dry out the mighty vessel if I moved enough liquid.

I decided to contact every veterinarian I could think of, no matter what part of the country they were in. I was determined to find the doctor that would cure Beezer. First, I called my friend Amiee who lives in Boston. She contacted her uncle, Robert Goldstein, DVM, who is a holistic veterinarian in Connecticut. I was surprised to learn that Dr. Goldstein, and many other vets, for that matter, routinely consult on out-of-state cases via telephone. I gathered Beezer's medical records, faxed them to his office, and arranged for a telephone conference two days later.

Amiee had also sent me a book written by her other uncle, Martin Goldstein, DVM, also a holistic vet. His book, *The Nature of Animal Healing: The Definitive Holistic Medicine Guide to Caring for Your Dog and Cat*, was helpful and had a state-by-state index of other holistic vets. Maybe I could find a local vet?

The book led me to Robert Silver, DVM, a holistic veterinarian who practices in Boulder. I was able to arrange a telephone conference with him the next day. Our initial phone conversation was encouraging. I even recapped the entire situation to him in a lengthy follow-up call. Unfortunately, Dr. Silver said, he would be traveling outside the country for a month beginning in January. He'd be available for Beezer in February.

In between my personal infantry charges, I'd lie down with Beezer and cuddle. I could see the confusion in his soft brown eyes. For years he had brought nothing but happiness to my life. Now he was watching my heart break and he must have been thinking it centered around him. I know he was bewildered by how I was acting. I know I was scaring him. I had to try and hide my fear and put on a front of courage.

I didn't realize it right away, but this time period was the start of an interesting paradox. Beezer continued to be a happy dog. He wanted to spend time with Boomer and me, and he enjoyed walks immensely. I never noticed any letdown in energy or spirit. He was living in peace. Conversely, I was living in increasing self-inflicted pain. My hair wasn't on fire, not yet, but I had a can of gas in one hand and a book of matches in the other.

During this time, I traded a few e-mails and telephone calls with a homeopathic vet referred to me—yet another player in a brand new game.

I was raised a decidedly western-medicine kind of guy. The bigger the hospital, the better the chance of success. My confidence was raised exponentially if the hospital had a large, expensive machine that took fancy pictures and made interesting sounds. But that attitude would soon change.

I figured advice from the homeopath was as good a place to start as any. The homeopath said he could devise a treatment plan. However, he said, I would have to discontinue all other treatment. I was too distraught to even consider this move. It was just too great a leap of faith for me to place 100 percent exclusive reliance in my dog's survival on a stranger's voice on the telephone. I thanked this doctor for his time and moved on.

The supplements I was giving Beezer that Dr. Robert Goldstein recommended included specially made Chinese herbs specific to kidney disease, liquids to be dispensed several times a day through droppers, and powders to be mixed in Beezer's food. Meanwhile, I had been continuing the traditional care at the Denver hospital and acupuncture with Dr. Christensen. My days began and ended with Beezer's medical care. In between, I tried, halfheartedly, to practice law and make a living.

As the days wore on, I could feel my health beginning to slip. I usually went to the gym every day, but I hadn't been after December 23. I wasn't eating. I wasn't sleeping. This neglect was especially strange since I had been in good enough shape to complete four triathlons the summer before.

Now, though I appeared positive and upbeat, inside I was a mess. I was facing a battle it didn't look like I could win. I knew only one way to deal with a situation like this—fight back. As I went through the days, tormenting over my next moves, I kept playing over and over in my head the words of Vince Lombardi: "Winning isn't everything, it's the only thing." I wasn't about to quit.

I also recalled the lessons of my youth learned on the hockey rink. Many had been taught me by my father, who had been both my coach and my mentor. I was good at hockey simply because I worked harder than the person next to me. I wasn't any better, any smarter, any faster; I just wanted it more. The desire produced the result. Therefore, the control of the result lay in the amount of the desire. This philosophy worked in hockey and later in everything I did that I cared about. These principles had taken a new form now. I'd *control* this disease by simply diverting resources and energy from other tasks to Beezer's disease, much like a general calling in reinforcements for his troops. The counterattack I had in mind would make General Patton proud.

The disease had other ideas. The mid-January blood and urine tests came back and the creatinine level was the highest ever. Beezer was getting worse, not better, and this despite the new supplementation regimen and a 110 percent commitment from me. I'd never experienced failure on this level before. My whole life was set up around solving problems. I controlled events. I controlled outcomes. Now all my efforts were coming up short. I began to see that this building crisis was revealing a deep misunderstanding about my place in the universe. If I had thought I controlled the world around me, apparently I was wrong. In that case, who was I and where did

I even belong? January 2005 was a long, lonely, lost month for me. I desperately needed a compass to help me figure out this dilemma… and by late in the month I had found one.

CHAPTER FIVE

Beginning the Long Journey

I WAS NOW SPENDING HOURS HUNCHED OVER THE KEYBOARD OF MY computer as I hunted for any piece of information about kidney disease, treatments and what felt like the never-ending quest for the Holy Grail. One day I stumbled across a search reference to a Yahoo.com group dedicated to treatment of dogs suffering from kidney disease. This particular group had about two thousand members from all over the world with the common connection that their dogs were sick and they wanted to do something about it. I was instantly interested. I filled out a membership application form, e-mailed it to the moderator of the group and waited for a reply.

The Yahoo kidney disease group is technically a listserv. It functions like an electronic bulletin board with automatic e-mails. To post a message, a member accesses the site and then is directed to a message area. There the member can post a question or comment to the group, which is then sent to everyone on the list. Any member can respond to the inquiry. The list also provides an extensive database with details on diet, supplements, treatment and more. It is truly one-stop shopping, if kidney disease is your topic. For Beezer and me, the Yahoo kidney group was a godsend.

The list also gave me a safe place to talk with similarly situated people. I say safe because I could vent my feelings with impunity. We all felt the same about our dogs. The concept that "it's just a dog" is the antithesis of this cyber community of souls in pain.

I immediately was inundated with dietary information. I learned that to help a kidney ailing dog live longer, the gurus in the group advocated a home-cooked diet made up primarily of egg whites and glutinous rice (similar to sushi rice). The goal, they said, was to reduce phosphorus in the diet while maintaining a dog's normal protein and caloric requirements. This concept proved to be both perplexing and challenging since reducing phosphorus typically meant reducing protein. I decided to give it a shot anyway. It would take me weeks to distill the dietary goals into a simple formula I could apply correctly with my dog. That meant Beezer became the test-kitchen guinea pig.

Ironically, most commercial prescription kidney disease diets end up with radically reduced amounts of protein. The kidney group would often refer to the book *Home-Prepared Dog & Cat Diets*, by Donald R. Strombeck, DVM, PhD, to fine-tune the traditional commercial approach. After all, Mom's homemade chicken soup is always superior to anything in a can, right?

I also learned that kidneys are made up of small filters called *nephrons*. Once destroyed, there is no way to fix, grow or restore a lost one. Therefore, the goal of treatment in kidney disease is to slow the loss of these nephrons. Then I discovered that some products in protein, when consumed, cause toxicity to these filters. The commercial decreased-protein diet came about because of this effect. However, carnivores require protein to live. So a difficult balancing act evolves. The kidney group provided excellent ideas to harmonize this problem.

Meat protein is the main culprit, I learned. Most meat contains high amounts of phosphorus. The phosphorus causes a type of crystallization that damages the nephrons. The kidney group members would routinely suggest ways they had found helpful to reduce the amount of phosphorus in the diet while maintaining a healthy level of protein. This was fascinating. I discovered meat charts in the archives of files posted earlier on the list and found that the ratio of phosphorus (bad) to protein (good) was almost 10:1. I no longer had the latitude to feed Beezer 1 gram of protein at a "cost" of 10 mgs of phosphorus. I had to reduce phosphorus intake by 75 percent. It was like trying to feed Beezer a dollar's worth of food every day, but I could only spend a quarter.

I became a "phosphorus accountant." Calculator at my side, food charts and worksheets in hand, I set out to control every little morsel that the dog ate. Egg whites became our staple because of their high "biologic value." High biologic value means little of the protein requires processing by the kidneys. The ratio of phosphorus to protein in egg whites is about 1:1. I guess body builders have known something all along.

Once you have this strategy down, you have to entice the dog to eat. Not so easy for kidney dogs. I now knew that kidney disease is progressive and results in increasing toxicity levels in the body. The toxins go to the stomach, which is the central repository for all the gunk. An increasingly acidic stomachache decreases the animal's desire to eat. It's like a flu that just never goes away. Many days I'd work up a healthy homemade meal, add proper supplements—all of this would take about an hour—and call Beezer to the table. Many days, he'd give it a sniff and look at me as if to say, "You gotta be kidding," and walk off. Eating, or lack thereof, was always a frequent point of consternation on the kidney group list and at my house.

SINCE I WAS SPENDING SO MUCH TIME ON THEIR WEBSITE, I BEGAN TO categorize and label the list members by how much experience I thought they might have. Everyone signed their messages with a first name and reference to their dog, like Primo or Fuzzer Bear or Kodiak. It was soon clear that some of these kind souls had animals that had already passed, but they remained online and available to help. I fell into the obvious category of "newbie." Clueless, scared and overwhelmed were the common denominators of a newbie post (usually someone with a newly diagnosed dog), and nearly every day there were new newbies. I began to sign my posts from Doug and the B Brothers.

The second category, the "paramedics," were the members who seemed to be online all the time. A newbie would post a message expressing frustration or fear and a paramedic would immediately pop up to talk the newbie through the crisis. I called "9-1-1 online" many times during those early days and will be forever grateful for their prompt replies.

The most interesting category was the people who managed to keep their dogs alive and well for months, and even years, after diagnosis. These people could do various calculations in their heads and had all the dietary supplements fine tuned. *Their* dogs always ate their concoctions and they seemed to control kidney disease rather easily. I called them the "wizards." The wizards never posted problems; quite the contrary, the wizards posted progress reports, which were as routine as a July weather forecast in Arizona: hot, dry and clear—day after day. Their dogs were sailing along. I *really* wanted to become a wizard.

Another group was smaller in number but very interesting in content. These people would write about the disease as being some type of journey. When I first would read these posts, I wasn't sure if they meant the dog's journey, the human's, or both. They'd speak of balance, harmony, peacefulness and a certain order to the events unfolding. I called them the "philosophers." At the time I didn't have the foggiest idea what the philosophers were talking about.

It didn't take long to realize that I could have been taking affirmative dietary steps with Beezer as far back as a year earlier, when I got that first urine test suggesting kidney disease. I could have added CoQ10, B Complex, and omega 3. I also could have decreased phosphorus and begun home cooking. Now I felt to blame—I began kicking myself for such stupidity. In my mind, Beezer was getting sicker because I'd failed to take proper action a year ago. Guilt crept into my life like an insidious viper.

But it didn't end there. My self-imposed angst now also included a huge dose of guilt's evil twin, fear. It would be no exaggeration to say I was now terrified of what might happen with Beezer tomorrow or the next day. I kept thinking of my life without him. And that little voice in my head swung back and forth easily between fear and guilt. Sometimes the voice would give me a daily double: "You screwed this up a year ago, which means you get to sign Beezer's death warrant tomorrow." This warfare was getting exhausting. I'd wonder which raging battle was more intense—the fight for Beezer's life I was now participating in or the fight in my head and my heart.

Boomer's advance is thwarted by Beezer's well-considered defense.

Beezer getting ready for sub-Q and our "Evenings with Beezer" session.

Synchronized water retrieval.

CHAPTER SIX

Evenings with Beezer

I MANAGED TO CONQUER THE SUB-Q PROCESS I'D BEEN DREADING AND actually came up with an innovative solution for an IV stand. The kidney group had commented on the importance of gravity to the endeavor. It turns out, the higher the bag is placed, the better the result. This was very helpful information.

The initial barstool sub-Q station was subsequently moved into the kitchen, where I hung the bag from an upper level cabinet pull. This elevated the bag to over six feet and improved flow immensely. However, it was uncomfortable sitting on the kitchen floor for any length of time. So I kept looking.

My living room has a rectangular vaulted ceiling with an indented lip and holds a swag light with a rope where the ceiling ends. One of the corners of the vault happened to be directly over my black leather couch. I sawed the ends off one of my many hockey sticks—I had quit playing hockey after the knee injury and now had no better use for the sticks—and placed the shaft into the corner creating a hypotenuse. I now had an ideal way to attach a bag of fluid to the hockey stick and suspend the bag eight feet over my couch. The Beez and I could lounge on the couch and effortlessly do our sub-Q regimen.

The dogs would watch with curiosity as I'd assemble a bag and then hang it from the stick. I'd drape the line over the back of the couch so all I had to do was gather my patient and get comfy. To my great relief, the Beezer was a willing partner. He'd shuffle over to the couch and jump up exactly where I'd tap the cushion, curl up and lay his head down. His brother never stuck around. Boomer would take one look and either go outside or over to his dog bed. At first, I thought he was afraid. Over time, as I quit being so tense during the procedure, I realized that Boomer saw this as a very special time for Beezer and me. He'd step aside for now. A noble gesture from my other special dog.

I quickly grew accomplished at placing the needle under Beezer's hide. I discovered the opening in the needle was not at the very tip, but slightly to one side of the narrow barb. If the opening was face down toward the muscle, the flow was diminished. Therefore, a slight twisting once inserted would allow me to regulate the speed of the flow. My queasiness quickly passed as I realized the procedure was completely pain free for the dog. I even started relaxing. I went out of my way during these hours to avoid any activity that might distract us or take away from the intimacy of the experience.

With Beezer now more than a month past diagnosis, all normalcy was gone from our lives. Before the illness, my day typically started with a workout at the gym down the street and then home for office work. Sometimes Beezer, Boomer and I would go for a walk to the park. Generally, though, my days centered around me. A new type of normal had come into my life with Beezer's kidney disease.

Since I lived alone, all the typical household chores as well as Beezer's care fell to me. I'd awake early and begin the daily feeding ritual and vitamin and supplement regimen. The length of time this would take was always a mystery. Then the occasional walk became mandatory on a daily basis. There was both a midday regimen and an entire evening ritual. Somewhere along the way, per the vet, the one bag of sub-Q three times a week became one-half bag two times a day. As Beezer's illness progressed, his morning and evening treatments were slowly, steadily eating up the day. In between, I'd squeeze in running my law practice and trying to meet expectations. I completely quit going to the gym again and told myself I didn't really miss it.

Every day, however, I could count on one oasis of time where I could sit and relax, close my eyes and just be in the moment. It was during those evenings of sub-Q treatments on the couch where Beezer curled up next to me, no TV, no phones. Much like filling a tank with gas, I'd have to keep my hand on the dispensing nozzle and make sure the "tank" didn't get up and walk away. The placement of the needle in the back of the neck allowed my hand to move to Beezer's ears, the top of his head, his muzzle, all the soft places we enjoyed so much. It was our quiet time and I now looked forward to them.

Since these evenings also seemed a good time for chats with my dog, and my idle chatter soon evolved into reflective conversations, I decided to record these ramblings. Perhaps some important thought would come out of them. Who knew? I bought a handheld tape recorder and dictated into it as we did the sub-Q ritual on the couch...

"It is Wednesday, February 2, 2005, and I am starting my recordings with my best friend, Beezer the Wonderdog, my eight-year-old Labrador retriever. He will be nine in just about two months. The vet has told me that this wonderful creature, whom I adore so much and who is completely devoted to me, has ninety days to live. We are just over thirty days into that period.

"This animal trusts me so much to allow me to put a needle in him. He gets on the couch as if to tell me, 'Do what you need to. It's okay.' But I am just so scared right now...scared that this wonderful animal that I have been so lucky to have is going to be departing from me soon. I am going to miss him so much. I just want him to live as long as possible...sometimes I want it for him and sometimes I want it for me. I know, I know!

"Let me talk a bit about Beezer. I am stroking his body, trying to give him assurance that no matter what, I will always be there for him. He is listening to me. He is one of the gentlest animals I know. I can never recall a moment where he lashed out in anger or frustration; he has never bitten another animal or a human being nor even growled in anger.

"Beezer's life has always been one of trust, affection and devotion. I wish he could live forever, but it is not to be, and I have spent the last five weeks trying to make some sense out of all of this.

"I need to hit the pause button now…

"Ah, it helped to get that little bit of crying out because the next emotion I am feeling right now is gratitude. I am so grateful for this time, this evening with my Beez. Rather than going to the gym or going to a movie or working longer in the office, I have this tremendous opportunity to tell this dog that he means so much to me, and how he is in my thoughts but also in my touch. If it weren't for the kidney disease, I would not have this opportunity and instead of having the first night of evenings spent with Beezer, I would be off doing whatever it is I would do on a Wednesday.

"There is something very important in that last thought. Something Beezer may be trying to teach me, as I gaze into his big brown eyes, about the gift of being alive. I am going to try as hard as I can to listen to Beezer, but I don't know how many more Wednesdays I have left with him. He would not mind if I went to the gym or the movies, or even worked a bit longer. He would not mind at all. Because he loves me unconditionally. But he does say, 'Please use this time wisely because when it is all used up, it is gone.'"

CHAPTER SEVEN

Anticipatory Grief

A S I SPECULATED ABOUT BEEZER'S DYING, I FELT PULLED FORWARD in time. This was a place I was trying to avoid—it was an unknown to me. I had dealt with *death* before. Death was final. It was present. It was a body lying there in front of me. I just hadn't dealt with *dying*.

Certainly I wasn't the first person who ever went through this dilemma with his pets. One thing attorneys are good at is finding information, so I set out to get answers. In my search I'd found books and articles online on how to bring up a puppy or train a dog, and I read many wonderful shaggy dog stories. Then I'd hit a big gap. The information trail picked up again with the topic of grieving for a pet who had died. There was nothing in between—during the difficult time that I was in now, facing the loss, not knowing what to do, and feeling alone—I needed some help with Beezer's *dying*, both for him and for me.

So, I picked up the yellow pages and jotted down the phone number of a couple of area hospices for terminally ill people. Of course! This was exactly what I needed. At one hospice I explained to the woman who answered the phone the difficulties I was having. She remarked, "You are dealing with *anticipatory grief.*" I sat back in my chair and pondered her response. I'd never heard those two words used together. It made sense. Grieving before something even happens. Yes, I thought, that was exactly what was going on.

I asked if I could make an appointment with a counselor. I'd bring my checkbook. *Finally,* I thought, *someone* who understood what I was going through. To my astonishment, she said, "We are here for people. This is just a dog. We can't help you."

I called a couple more hospices. Same result. I didn't want to *bring* Beezer there—I just wanted some support. I was greatly offended and considered getting angry but decided to let go of my frustration. I had bigger fish to fry. Fine, I thought, I'll do it myself! I'm done with these people.

I looked at my dogs and felt a bit of comfort wash over me. So this is the way it was going to be. There would be no cavalry. There would be no relief, not even a guide with a map showing how to get out of the dark forest. We were on our own. We'd find our own way out of the woods and we'd do it by relying on each other and the friends we'd made up to now. I would keep copious notes and assemble them eventually into a guidebook for others. The boys and I would create a map for other lost souls, those who understood it's not just a dog; it's a family member.

I put away the phone book and ordered several books on hospice care from the Internet. "I'm going to need both of you to help me," I said to the guys. "We can do this if we work together." Like three teammates on a hockey team, all working in unison. I really did feel like we were a team and together could accomplish anything.

CHAPTER EIGHT

Leap of Faith

THAT POSITIVE FEELING LASTED ABOUT A DAY. I JUST COULD NOT KEEP my emotions in check. At any given moment, I was either defiantly angry about my predicament or a basket case. Lack of sleep was getting to me. Out of frustration and fear, I even scolded Beezer when he wouldn't eat—something I had never done before.

Ironically I had been the picture of good health just last summer. My cardiovascular fitness had always been a source of pride. But, since my dad had died young of a heart attack, I was determined to do everything I could not to place myself at further risk and follow in his footsteps. I saw a cardiologist regularly and he was always very impressed with my treadmill and cholesterol tests and my low blood pressure. Dr. Flanagan would say, "Just keep doing what you're doing, Doug."

By the end of January, this picture of health was unraveling. I still was getting no exercise. I was experiencing an increasing level of distraction, which was headed toward outright confusion. In early February I began to have vision problems. Then the dizziness started.

On February 9, I almost blacked out. Okay, you idiot, I told myself, you have to do something about this! I called Dr. Flanagan's office, but he was on vacation. During our last visit he had given me the name of an internist, but I hadn't followed up. Now I called this doctor and asked if I could get in to see him. "Sure," the receptionist said. "How about next month?"

Well, that wasn't going to work. I needed to see somebody *today*. I even half-heartedly considered the emergency room. Trying a different tack with the receptionist, I said, "Could I drop by and just get my blood pressure checked? I feel kinda funny." She told me to come on in.

I drove over to the doctor's office, hoping for the best. An assistant ushered me into a spare room and sat me on a chair. A young man came in with a portable blood pressure sleeve and took my pressure. Obviously puzzled, he took it a second time. "Hang on for a minute," he said. "Let me get another machine."

When he came back with a new device, I was instantly alarmed. This one had wheels and a nurse was now with him. They whispered and took my blood pressure again. "Are you okay?" the nurse asked. She said my blood pressure was dangerously high. I was instructed not to move and they would recheck it again in fifteen minutes. They left the room.

That's just great, I thought. I wasn't particularly surprised at the direction things were going, but a deep sense of disappointment came over me. I was giving myself a heart attack. "Wonderful crisis management, Douglas," I muttered.

The nurse came back in fifteen minutes and took my pressure. Now it was worse than the first two times. She said the situation was serious and the doctor would have to make time to see me. Of course, I didn't have an appointment and people would have to drop what they were doing to attend to my needs. So I added embarrassment to the growing list of emotions I felt.

They moved me to a treatment room and the doctor came in and introduced himself. He was tall, lean and looked none too happy to see me. He quickly asked me a few questions about my circumstances, handed me a magazine and told me to have a seat in the waiting room.

Standing over me, he sharply instructed, "You have thirty minutes to bring your pressure down or we'll have to consider extraordinary action."

"You mean the hospital?" I asked sheepishly.

"You have thirty minutes," the doctor snapped, and then he turned and walked out the door, leaving me alone.

I had a long, lonely talk with myself in that waiting room. My six-week plan of action had been a spectacular failure. The worst possible alternative now would be for me to get sick. I decided I'd better relax and try to get through this day.

I closed my eyes, released all my emotions, and practiced slow, deep breathing. I tried not to think about anything to do with Beezer's illness. I talked to my body and asked it to release the stress. I promised my body I'd make some changes if it could help me out now. I listened to myself breathe and blocked out everything else.

Thirty minutes later I was back in the treatment room with the doctor. He took my blood pressure. Higher than it should be, but markedly improved. He remarked that this reading was normal for a person under a high amount of stress. It would do no harm as long as the high pressure was temporary. He gave me a prescription for a few sleeping pills. We made an appointment for a follow-up visit and I went back home.

As I drove home, it began to sink in. The course I had charted was flawed. I was heading straight into the rapids and was losing the ability to navigate. I needed to make a correction, now. "Shape up, Douglas," I yelled.

A great deal of responsibility rested on my shoulders. I had to be healthy to discharge those duties. It was time to change or I would end up in the hospital…and the Beez would die without me.

Okay, I thought, even though I was trying everything in my ego-based, proven game-winning strategy notebook, nothing was working. Beezer was getting worse. I had a strong hunch that I needed to do something fast. That something would have to be radical. The only thing left was leaping, not stepping, out of my comfort zone into new and uncharted territory. I recalled the movie *Indiana Jones and the Last Crusade*. Most mirages show something that isn't there, but one scene in the movie depicted just the opposite. The illusion was that a bridge *wasn't* there, and, in fact, it was. Indiana Jones just had to step out into the void to find it and then see it. The bridge only revealed itself after this leap of faith.

In real life, a leap of faith holds together logically if you have supreme confidence that you have tried and exhausted every other alternative. And so I took that leap of faith. I knew not where I would land, but I knew I had to place my trust in something other than Doug. I took a deep breath and stepped forward.

CHAPTER NINE

The Fork in the Road

"**I**'M HAVING A HARD TIME HERE," I HEARD MYSELF EXPLAINING ON the phone to Dr. Robert Goldstein in Connecticut. I couldn't believe I was actually making a call like this. But he had a remarkable empathy for my circumstance. I could hear my voice crack as I told him I was afraid that Beezer was dying, and, despite the new supplement and herbal program, he might not be getting better.

Dr. Goldstein asked me if I'd ever considered contacting an animal communicator. I said I didn't know what he was talking about. He said that certain people have the ability to communicate with animals, much like a telepathic person can do with humans, and they can find out how a dog is feeling. It may be possible to get feedback on what the dog wants in situations like this where the dog is ill and the owner isn't sure how to best help the pet. If I'd like, he could give me a name to call.

On any other day, in any other set of circumstances, I'd have laughed out loud. "Put your money in a shredder because at least you'll have confetti," I probably would have said. I'm sure I would have privately snickered at such a weak-minded person who believed in such foolishness. But it wasn't any other day. Whatever coping mechanism I had been calling upon was failing miserably. I asked for the name.

The next week, I was talking to my business and life coach, David Koons, during our weekly telephone session, and was complaining how unfair my situation was. My outburst had been precipitated by an e-mail I had just received from a friend on the kidney group list: "This has to be one of the most difficult things I have gone through in my life," she wrote. "Misha is not only a dog, she is part of our family." The e-mail took me back to the beginning of my days struggling with Beezer's illness.

"Why me? Why Beezer?" I lamented to David. "He is such a loving and gentle soul. What did we do to deserve this?" A perceptive fellow, David had me repeat the following sentence: "Everything happens for a reason and that reason helps me grow."

I vacillated between frustration and curiosity as I pondered those simple words. I knew I needed to be open to change, but was I to venture down *this* path? I'd known David a long time, but I wasn't sure he could solve my problems with a riddle. On the other hand, my life had unraveled pretty significantly over the past couple months. People who knew me for decades were also becoming increasingly concerned about my health. I'd spent years solving problems for friends, family members and clients. Now, they were telling me the Rock was crumbling before their eyes.

But, "Things happen for a reason, and the reason helps me grow"? You have got to be kidding me. I was way too busy for some new-age nonsense. And I really wasn't in any mood to hold hands and sing *Kumbaya*. Under any other setting, I never, in a hundred years, would have sat down and let someone preach me this malarkey. But something else nagged at me as I pondered David's words. If I went this route—took this leap of faith—did I have the courage to look so hard in the mirror? What would I find?

In the end, I decided at least to go through the exercise of considering the phrase. What possible *reason* justified Beezer's illness? Why would any higher power choose this fate for my buddy? How his illness might "help me grow" would be a lesson for another day. I had to deal with part one of the equation first.

My logical side said that Beezer's illness could simply be a coincidence. A statistical probability, much like a late night telephone call in which the police regret to inform you about an automobile accident. You know, just one of those unfathomable things. But, what if I was wrong?

If Beezer's illness was coincidental—bearing no particular meaning—then it was pointless to look further. Forget "things happen for a reason." Beezer had drawn a short straw and would be dead very soon. It was just one of those things. I called this option the Rule of Coincidence.

Of course, this option would mean assembling the speakers and guest list for the pity party. "I Got Screwed, Again" would be the topic in the Maple Room, "Life Isn't Fair" in the Oak Room, and the keynote address would be, "What Did I Do to Deserve This?" The Rule of Coincidence option was straightforward and required little reflection.

I certainly was no astute observer of life. "Clueless" perhaps is a better term. What if I were missing something important? I wanted to be available for each and every lesson Beezer had for me. I wanted to attach as much importance to his life as the universe intended. Beezer might lose his life to kidney disease, but perhaps there was some hidden agenda that I was unaware of. This real fear—of missing something important—pushed me forward. And I knew I had to hurry—Beezer might not be around much longer. Whatever lessons were available would require my immediate commitment. My instincts told me to act like a lawyer, prevent a default judgment from entering and cover my bases, just in case.

I continued with my little exercise. What if things really *do* happen for a reason? Even seemingly bad things? Was I willing to dig this deeply? It was as if I was at a fork in the road and I had to make a choice between going to the left or the right. Which one should I choose?

The logical attorney piped in. On one hand, said the lawyer with forefinger raised to make a point, if I applied the Rule of Coincidence, the left fork, then I'd better be sure I wanted to go this way. No going back. I'd still have great memories of Beezer, but whatever important lessons associated with this final disease there might be would go unlearned. Of course, the fatal kidney disease guaranteed

I couldn't change my mind later. I wasn't confident about this path—it seemed very risky.

On the other hand, looking for the *reason* that Beezer and I were experiencing this illness would involve much less risk on my part. If I took the right fork and found nothing, I'd be comforted by the thought that at least I tried. This might help with guilt later on. If I found a reason and didn't like this fork, I could always later retreat to the left fork and the Rule of Coincidence. But, maybe, just maybe, there was a grand lesson that was unfolding. One where I was only available, as pupil, for the most unlikely of teachers, my Beezer.

Besides, I would be letting down my buddy by not being available for him. Well, I couldn't do that. I'd always been there for my team-mates even back when I was a kid on the hockey rink some forty years ago. I wasn't turning my back on my buddy now.

There really *was* just one decision. I made a pact with Beez that I'd follow the right fork wherever it led. It was time to venture down the Rabbit Hole with pick and shovel in hand. I had no idea where to dig, but I decided to accept the challenge. I was afraid of missing this opportunity, so I committed to exploring whether Beezer had contracted a fatal disease *for a reason*. I'd leave no stone unturned. I also made an agreement with myself to remain judgmentally neutral. I didn't have to believe or disbelieve what I was doing. I was just doing. I didn't have to prove or disprove it. I was merely exploring. This seemed safe. I agreed that an approach based on *"what if* this were true" might reveal much more than "here is what I can prove."

This line of reasoning also made sense. Proof and control had gotten me nowhere over the past months. I was watching sand pass through the hourglass. The only logical thing was to make an immediate, radical course change. Even if that course change was seemingly illogical.

Once I accepted the axiom that things happen for a reason, it was time to begin examining why Beezer was experiencing fatal kidney disease. I needed to embrace what I feared the most, which involved my purposeful setting aside of the very foundations of my life. I lived in a world of proof, control and ego. I absolutely believed that I could solve any problem if I worked harder. I was about to impeach this belief.

Doug and the Beez
during early kidney
disease treatment.

Beezer, Boomer,
and sister Nellie.

Beezer and Nell.

CHAPTER TEN

Listening to the Animals

MAKING THE FIRST CALL TO AN ANIMAL COMMUNICATOR TURNED out to be a lot easier than I'd anticipated. Since I'd received referrals from both Dr. Goldstein and Dr. Silver, the idea held some degree of substance. I would keep an open mind. I felt that the answer to my problem didn't lie in having proof; hence, I didn't ask for proof from the communicators I contacted—like asking them to tell me over the phone what color food bowl the dog ate from—that sort of thing. I decided I'd just go with it.

After all, what did I know? Over a period of many years we humans have lost our intuitive connection (through technology, our own self-importance, whatever). Look at the 2004 tsunami. People rushed down to the beach to take pictures of the receding ocean. The animals ran the other way to higher ground. Who has it figured out? I decided that calling for help from animal communicators was worth a try…it's about *what if* this is true. I didn't need proof.

I decided to call both a local animal communicator, Terri O'Hara, who was recommended by Dr. Silver, and a communicator in California whom Dr. Goldstein mentioned. I figured why not talk to two? This was how I handled all my decisions: if one is good, two is better. That certainly was my philosophy with the dogs' medical care.

First I called Sharon Callahan, the California animal communicator. It turned out she often handles her conversations with her "clients" by phone. When I asked her about her work, she explained that she was given the ability to commune with animals in a unique way. "When I attune to an animal, I experience an actual merging of myself and the animal. In this merged state, I am able to feel what the animal feels and experience what it experiences. So the animal is not actually 'telling' me something in the way that we usually perceive of 'telling,' but it is more that the animal allows my soul to merge with its soul." I scratched my head, not sure how this was going to work, but in my new "leap of faith" mode, I was ready to give it a try.

I had previously sent Sharon a photo of the boys and, during our first phone call, gathered both dogs in the living room while we talked and introduced them to her. I turned on the tape recorder and she started with some general questions directed to me, mostly about my concerns and issues with Beezer. Later she communicated directly with the dogs and was able to tell me some of the things they were thinking. I was amazed by how she could do this.

For background information, I told her that Beezer's illness was creating chaos in how I look at things. I said I was trying not to micromanage the situation into the ground. But I did want to understand this process of sickness and dying and be able to deal with it better. Telling her about my law practice at home, I explained that it was nice to be self-reliant, working on my own, making my own decisions, but I could see that relying on just myself had left me in a situation where, if I am faced with a problem I can't solve, the well is dry. I also told her about my new philosophy to apply "What if this were true?" to Beezer's terminal illness.

What happened next was astounding. Sharon telepathically dialed in to Beezer and he communicated some eye-opening words of wisdom, which she said he had been trying to tell me on his own. She said he told her that I should live in the present—if I could do that, I wouldn't have fear about his dying—or about anything. I wouldn't have guilt. He knew I wasn't dealing with dying well and wanted me to understand how natural it was. He said that dying wasn't sad for dogs. Great words of wisdom from such an unlikely source. I mulled over that for the next few days.

Later in the week I called Terri O'Hara. During our first phone session I got confirmation on Beezer's message. If I had been a bit doubtful about animal communicators' abilities, they were laid to rest after Terri's conversation. She told me things she could not have known about my dogs. She also explained that truth would come forward if I would just allow the boys to talk to me, and then listen. We all have the ability to communicate with animals, she said, if we would open to the idea and slow down enough to hear and sense the animals with our hearts, not our minds. That's how animals communicate—heart to heart.

After we hung up, I got to thinking that maybe there was something to this. Maybe I really do communicate with my dogs. Perhaps not as clearly as an animal communicator can, but to some degree. It is not that farfetched. I do not think anyone would argue if you suggested that animals have senses that human beings do not. The sense of smell in dogs is well documented.

Certainly on a rudimentary level, the dogs and I communicated every day. I always had a good idea about what they were telling me, like wanting to go to the park, get a bone, go to bed. Why is it so hard to imagine that a person might be gifted in such a way that his or her communication skills are two, three, ten times better than mine? I'm not talking about speech with words and sentences but some sort of subconscious, extra-sensory communication. And, though it's hard to imagine this control-driven, analyzing, got-to-have-proof guy would ever be open to this, I was soon to discover that the souls of my dogs had been reaching out to my own.

I'd really laugh
at how carefully
Boomer would cradle
his friends;
they'd last forever.

Hamming it up for a car ride.

The full crew
at water's edge,
waiting for the
adventure to begin.

CHAPTER ELEVEN

The Teacher Becomes the Pupil

Dear Beez,

I am recalling one of the special moments we had together during your illness. Your breakfast was over and the mess in the kitchen was cleaned up. It was a quiet Sunday morning. Your brother was over by the door in his pet bed sleeping soundly. Sun streamed in from the skylight. I could hear the water flowing from the little decorative stream out front. You were sitting in your bed, staring intently at me in a way that only you and I understood.

I thought about the day before. My lifelong friend John had spirited me out of the house and taken me to see an eye-opening movie called *What the Bleep Do I Know?!* It was about a new way to look at reality, quantum physics really, and it got me thinking. Up till now, your illness had created one specific reality in my mind. This reality involved death and fear. Was it possible to attach a different meaning and significance to your illness, which would make me feel better? I looked deep into your eyes and asked you what you thought.

Your response came directly into my soul. I believe you were saying not to be afraid. It sounded like a mantra: *Living in fear is to live in the future. Fear is always an emotional response to a conditional future event. It may or may not happen, and if it does happen, it will be sometime down the road. So to live in fear is to live in the future.*

Wow.

I kept staring into your eyes, asking for more. You also said: *Living with guilt is to live in the past. The guilt was water under the bridge and I should just let it go.* I thought about that for a minute. When you were diagnosed with the kidney problem, I failed to take any action. You quickly corrected me. I *had* taken action. I took you and Boomer to the vet. My decision had come from a place of caring, you reminded me. The fact that I had additional information later on didn't affect the past. I had made the best decision possible with information available at that time. You assured me there was nothing to feel guilty about.

"Is there anything more?" I asked. I heard: *To live in fear or guilt means missing out on the gift of today.* Over and over my mind heard the phrase: *Just trust me and I'll show you.*

I felt a great weight begin to lift. I moved forward to embrace you. Just then, you lifted a front paw in an offer to shake hands. "Of course," I responded.

Then it hit me. I was witnessing you teaching *me* about living and dying. Lessons I'd been unable to learn on my own. Circumstances I'd been unable to deal with singularly. What if it had always been meant to happen this way? What if you *had* been sent to earth to teach me these lessons, as the animal communicators had suggested.

But what had I taught you? To shake hands. The realization traveled through me like electricity. I turned red and covered my face with my hands. Good God, I'd assumed all along that, as a human, I was the superior being. What if even that wasn't the case? Teaching you to shake hands wasn't much of a contribution to the collective experience, especially given the curriculum that you were offering.

Horrified, I began to apologize profusely to you. I leaned on your shoulder, overwhelmed. You had a bit of a "gotcha" look on your face. *Stick with me, young man,* you said, *and I'll teach you much.*

BOOMER WOKE UP JUST THEN AND LIFTED HIS HEAD TO SEE WHAT THE commotion was about. Thump, thump, thump went Boomer's tail onto his bed. Thump, thump, thump as if giving his approval to Beezer's tutorial on life.

I sat there for a while, trying to assimilate what I had just witnessed. My world wasn't at all how I had perceived it even one month ago. In fact, my world was rather upside down. I sat back and just embraced the experience. The teacher had become the pupil. That knowledge changed everything, and I was eager for more lessons.

Boomer surveys
his new yard.

Boomer
chewing on his
brother's ear.

Welcome home,
Beezer.

CHAPTER TWELVE

Are There Lessons Here?

B EEZER AND I WERE SITTING ON THE COUCH FOR ANOTHER SUB-Q session. Boomer was off snoozing somewhere. The Beez and I were both doing a lot better—I was more relaxed and we were working hard on acceptance, working hard on trust. I was trying hard to embrace Beezer's message to not worry, to enjoy today. But I knew I had to dig as deeply as possible to make the lesson stick.

Of course he was right. None of us knows what is going to happen tomorrow and even if we did, the events are out of our control. I knew that—at least my mind knew that. But maybe one of the purposes of Beezer's life was for me to experience his illness and open up my heart to new ideas, new ways of thinking. If that were the case, what an incredible meaning his life would have in addition to the superficial, yet critically important, one that we just enjoy each other's company.

If this were true, what a deeper gift. From where I was in my life, Beezer was the only one able to teach me these lessons. What a wonderful act of selflessness. The emotions I felt then did not involve sadness, but deep gratitude, respect and appreciation for the Beez.

I knew now I had to make some changes. I had managed my life in such a way that I did not trust anyone other than myself. Perhaps part of the crisis I had been going through was the realization that life can be so much more fulfilling than what I had been experiencing. Until now this little animal and his brother were the only ones that I had ever really trusted to take care of my emotional needs.

And Beezer was doing a great job of that now, but how would I meet my emotional needs when he was gone?

This dog was helping me learn to trust the people closest to me, even if it involved hurt. I wasn't able to manage my life, so I controlled being hurt. Life just did not work that way without closing off part of myself. And I think some of what I had been going through over the past six weeks was that a lot of the emotions I had locked away for so long were now exploding uncontrollably and I did not know what to do with them.

What was also becoming clear, thanks to Beezer with Terri's and Sharon's help, was that, for humans, life is *supposed* to involve pain. However, suffering occurs when self-judgment is added to pain. The fear and guilt I had been feeling were examples of turning pain into suffering. But now I saw that pain and suffering are two distinctly different concepts and not synonymous. More importantly, I saw that feeling pain doesn't necessarily require suffering. It then follows that pain is inevitable, but suffering is optional. Another lesson from the Beez.

I also recalled how, in our first conversation with Terri, Beezer had said I was going to write a book about this whole experience. I'd responded, "I am? I'm a frigging lawyer, I don't write books!" More confirmation that I could be wrong on many counts.

⌒

EVEN THOUGH I CONTINUED TO FEEL OUT OF SORTS, THE SUB-Q SESSIONS were becoming more and more fulfilling and even enjoyable. I think it was because they promoted such a display of mutual love. Beezer allowed me things because he trusted me. He was sharing the fact that today was a special day and he was happy to be alive, I could see that now. He wagged his tail as proof.

Again I talked to David Koons about my feelings regarding Beezer's prognosis. "When you're in fear, worry and doubt, you're not in faith," had been his reply. I needed to trust that the universe understands, he said, and remember that, when our purpose on earth is finished, we die.

And I saw that I had not been in faith. I had to try harder to understand Beezer's purpose in whatever time I had left with him and try, try, try to get faith in the universe. And, if everything happens for a reason, I needed to look at the gifts—even the gift of Beezer getting sick.

What *was* the gift of his getting sick, really? I was trying to put my arms around this important revelation, but it seemed to hover just out of reach.

⌐

I WAS NOW DEALING WITH BEEZER'S LACK OF APPETITE ON A DAILY BASIS. He hated the various powdered supplements sprinkled in his food so I bought empty capsules and, while watching television, painstakingly filled them up with the powder.

But getting Beezer to take all his pills became its own little adventure. I was never very good at the toss-the-dry-pill-down-the-throat routine that many veteran dog owners have mastered. Beezer and I finally settled on a little known marriage of baby food and basic hockey techniques. I'd take a spoonful of baby food and place it on the tips of three fingers. I'd then submerge a number of pills into the gooey stuff. I'd have my patient sit and I'd straddle him from behind. Then I'd coax his mouth open, slide the fingers in and use the forefinger of the free hand to slap-shot the mix to the back of his mouth. Hockey 101 to the rescue.

Meals were becoming smaller and more frequent, and I was still trying to become a wizard. I created a worksheet with my daily goals for calories, protein and limits on phosphorus. I contacted baby food companies, doggie treat manufacturers and any other relevant food company that could give me per-serving amounts for these items. I then recorded the information in one of the numerous three-ring notebooks full of health and dietary information I'd created to manage Beezer's illness.

A real wizard, however, would be able to entice a sick dog to eat. I knew some people on the kidney group list who could. I was only so-so in this area. Keeping the meals small meant I wouldn't feel too bad if he decided to spray it back out at me or refuse it altogether. Beezer got a lot of rice, egg whites, grilled chicken and asparagus. I'd prowl the prepared-food counter at Whole Foods Market, a large natural and organic supermarket nearby, looking for fresh greens, mashed or sweet potatoes—anything for variety. I'd also thin a bit of baby food as gravy for a top dressing and play around with condiments like barbeque sauce. I don't think the salt was particularly good for him, but somehow eliminating salt didn't seem at the top of the list of priorities.

A constant challenge was that what worked today might not work tomorrow but could work again another day. The solution was to keep one-of-everything in the house. Egg whites and glutinous rice still continued to drive the bus. Some days I would try anything to get Beezer to eat—with his disease, it was better to eat the wrong thing than nothing.

Drinking enough water is critical for a kidney dog, but after a while he wouldn't drink from his bowl. Instead he would go outside and eat snow. It was really important to keep him hydrated and the snow helped. But in Denver, even in the winter, you could never count on there being a lot of it. Some January and February days are in the fifties or sixties. But Beezer wanted snow. So I went out and bought one of those crank-type snow cone toys that shaves ice cubes into snow. I'd spend mornings in the kitchen, cranking a polar bear until I produced enough snow for Beezer's needs. I left out the flavoring.

Throughout this ordeal, leave it to Boomer to inhale anything Beezer wouldn't eat. Beezer would watch him with a bit of sadness as if to say, "I wish I could eat like my brother."

Did all this food prep cut into my day? Did the costs put a huge crimp in my budget? You bet. But nothing was as important as doing all I could for my best friend. Aside from work, I had no other responsibilities. What else would I spend my time and money on?

AT THE END OF FEBRUARY, I GOT TO DUST OFF MY EGO-DRIVEN WORK skills and also get out of the house for a while. I had an important meeting with my largest bank client in downtown Denver, an invitation to speak to a group of senior officers about the new bankruptcy laws that would take effect later that year. Ironically, a half hour before, I had been at home, so frustrated about Beezer's illness and his refusal to eat that I'd sat down and cried. I couldn't help but contrast that new Doug and the older version, who never, ever cried. Now, here I was, back at work, in my element, on stage to speak as an expert in my field.

I was ushered into a very plush conference room and seated at the head of an elegant table. It was the kind of table that spoke to me with the firm instruction: "Don't even think about setting that cup down without a coaster." It had been some time since I'd had a suit and tie on and the whole setting seemed like a familiar, comfortable memory coming back to me. The officers came into the room and seated themselves around me. One of the vice presidents introduced me to the group and gave an overview of the topics on the agenda and then gave me the floor. All eyes turned to me. I was loaded for bear.

This is the type of work I like and I'm good at. My clients were counting on me. I was in control. Since graduating from the University of Denver Law School and getting my license, I'd had several different career calls—all in different areas of the law. After early years in creditor work, I spent eight years in a criminal and personal injury litigation practice. Plaintiff work is difficult because you are always dealing with negligence. Who is at fault? Sadly, the defendant with the deepest pockets is made culpable. This type of practice is very judgmental and I increasingly found the area less desirable. By contrast, a creditor practice, while difficult, is judgmentally neutral. You sign the promissory note and you deal with the consequences. Fault and blame seldom enter the picture.

At the bank that day, I deftly went through the different points of the anticipated new law and instructed the officers on how it would affect them. I had already developed strategies to deal with each change. We had a question and answer session and then called it a day. I ended the meeting by reminding the officers that my firm could "solve their problems."

My mood was decidedly upbeat on the drive back. It didn't take long to realize why. I had spent the last hour stoking the ego fire and reminding that part of me how important I was and how very in control I was of events and my own life. I thought long and hard about the imminent contradiction about to occur when I returned to the Beez and his kidney disease. It was like living in two mutually exclusive worlds. I thought back to my musings on faith. I *cannot* solve this problem and it is shattering my belief system. I had created a life where, yes, I was living in faith, but my only faith was in myself.

I was just beginning to see how I had been imprinting these control lessons from my work life onto Beezer: he *will* get better, I can outwork it! I always could outwork the problems, even as a kid. During a game, on the ice when I'd get creamed, I'd get up and hit 'em harder and then hit 'em again even harder. Since I now worked for myself, my income, my livelihood was solely dependent on me and the people I directed. I was single and went out of my way to keep it that way. I enjoyed triathlons; I trained on my own, and the joy I got out of the events was largely from my own efforts. I had created a life where I had excluded the rest of the universe from being involved.

Perhaps my ego was so big that I thought I could solve everybody's problems, and to keep feeding this monster I took on more and more of them. Perhaps I even invited people to bring me their problems. But this tendency had created my current crisis of faith because I was faced with a problem beyond my ability to solve. I just *could not* solve this problem. I was always very understanding or tolerant of other people's shortcomings and mistakes, but I was brutally critical of my own errors—real, perceived or imaginary.

That night in bed with the boys I made up a story about two little black dogs and Mr. Doug. At the end of the story, as we were falling asleep, the last sentence was, "And they lived happily ever after." I willed it to be true.

Last week's ultrasound didn't dampen Beezer's spirit when it came to the dog park.

The Big Dog, my Boomer.

The Beez.

CHAPTER THIRTEEN

Somebody's Inside that Fur

I WAS SITTING WITH DR. SILVER, NOW BEEZER'S PRIMARY DOCTOR, IN his Boulder office a few days later, reviewing Beezer's newest protocol. I liked Rob a lot. He was smart, caring and had no intention of waving a white flag at kidney disease. I silently noted the importance of having a guy like that on the team. It didn't hurt that he also had a black Labrador, a well-mannered office dog named Bean.

One of Rob's good qualities was listening and discussing options. It was important for me to express my beliefs and opinions in a productive manner. I was Beezer's advocate, a role I considered so important. Beezer's voice would be heard through mine. This meeting was a good time to discuss goals and limitations related to the days ahead and to try to clearly sort out my feelings regarding Beezer's time left.

Over the past month I'd received much wisdom from unconventional sources—I was now calling the animal communicators Terri and Sharon once a week or so. Both had their own unique talents and perspectives on what was happening with Beez and me and how our lives fit into the bigger picture. I also was in touch with my life coach weekly. Having Dr. Silver's feedback was a nice balance.

As we talked that day, I saw that many issues, like trying to get Beezer to eat, fell into a gray area where my response had to be, "I don't know." For now, the challenge was simply to identify whatever obvious markers existed on both sides of the ball.

One area was clear. I *had* to make decisions that would benefit Beezer. Whenever he told me it was "time," then I'd act in his best interest and let him go. We were so close, I was pretty sure I'd know when that was and that assurance really helped. I did not want a situation where I was keeping Beezer alive because *I* couldn't let go. Dr. Silver agreed with me.

I told him I also didn't want Beezer to suffer or be in pain. That was equally unfair. Fortunately, kidney disease is relatively painless. It wasn't like Beezer had something gruesomely painful, like bone cancer. I knew about that pain from having recently read up on canine cancer. Also, cancer treatment is more cut and dry and would have made choices much clearer. Still, I wanted to discuss potential pain issues and be clear on that point.

I commented about the role that finances play in treatment decisions for other people. I had the financial means to try different options and use several doctors, and I was grateful to be able to go the extra distance in Beezer's treatment. But I realized many people are not so fortunate. Choosing between treatment for a four-pawed family member and paying next month's rent could create a real dilemma, and of course its offspring, guilt. I concluded that whatever they could do for their pets out of caring and love would be just right.

Dr. Silver outlined a treatment goal focusing on quality of life. He offered some ideas on supporting other body systems that might help to slow the progression of the disease. That's what holistic medicine was about, I had learned—treating the whole dog, not just the disease. Overall, we agreed that the main goal would be to keep Beezer feeling as good as he could for as long as we could.

I added that I didn't want Beezer to become an experiment. Somebody existed inside that black fur. I wanted to make decisions respectful of that recognition. This resolution led to my first fledgling attempts to really understand what Beezer's wishes *were*. It wasn't *my* body or *my* life; it was his. I wasn't sure how to go about this perplexing task, but it was helpful to acknowledge its existence.

Finally, we discussed Beezer's last day. I think it was then that the absolute finality of this situation became clear. He was going to die. Trying to envision that day, when I might have to euthanize him, really hit home. How would I want that day to unfold? I'd heard troubling stories over the years about frantic dashes to the emergency hospital when a critically ill dog had crashed. These circumstances seemed to take place at the most inopportune times, late at night, holiday weekends and so forth. The final minutes meant new surroundings, new faces, confusion, chaos and fear. I found this scenario most disconcerting. An important goal then was that Beezer would pass at home, if possible. Hopefully, the Beez would be in his bed with both his brother and me beside him. Rob agreed.

Getting clear about what was important to me—and both dogs—helped a lot. Having even a rudimental game plan would help with decision making in the coming difficult days. And now I had no doubt that they were coming.

CHAPTER FOURTEEN

My Branch Office
Is a Cage

I T WAS NOW MARCH, SEVENTY-FIVE DAYS PAST DIAGNOSIS. ALTHOUGH Beezer wasn't eating well, I continued to dole out and occasionally force down the nutrients he needed. He was still energetic and as loving as ever. Our walks and park visits continued. Without fail, after those idyllic trips, I would have to chastise myself for fantasizing, however briefly, that there was a chance he was getting better.

But now we had so many treatment options to consider. None was a clear winner. In a modern day version of kids' see-saw, I wrestled with the question: should I give Beezer in-patient IV treatment? This was a stronger version of sub-Q. The consensus from the kidney group was that the in-patient IV treatment was the best way to go. The thought was that the dog needed to be given these fluids over periods of four consecutive days to cleanse out the impurities efficiently—kidney dialysis, for all practical purposes.

But this in-patient regimen had me squarely at odds with my gut feeling about leaving the Beez overnight. The animal communication sessions had confirmed what my heart was telling me about this. In one conversation, Terri had said Beezer was conveying his wishes, he had been very clear and I needed to listen. He didn't want to stay overnight—he knew it wouldn't change the final outcome. And yes, on one level, I had accepted the fact that a lengthy period of one year or more without significant problems was not in the cards. Beezer's numbers pointed to a short life left and my gut told me that things would move at a rapid pace regardless of my actions. On the other hand, here I was in direct contact with people who were experiencing exactly this type of success after multi-day in-patient IV treatment. Should I comply with Beezer's wishes?

Every day brought more decisions and a heightened sense of urgency. Broaching the subject of the overnight treatments with Dr. Silver, I told him I thought the IV might be helpful but I wasn't willing to hospitalize Beezer overnight. Furthermore, I wasn't willing to drop him off for the day and pick him up later. Whatever treatment had to be done would be with me at Beezer's side. Could he accommodate my wishes? Rob instantly offered a plan.

He said that, along with the standard treatment IV, he wanted to add something called a Myer's Cocktail, a vitamin and mineral intravenous treatment. He suggested that I bring Beezer up to Boulder in the morning, stay with him all day, and then bring him home at night. We'd repeat this once a week for four weeks.

Whatever would make the Beez feel better and give us an opportunity for more quality time sounded like a good plan. But I wasn't kidding myself. I was aware that the treatment was just as much for me. I needed to feel like I had done my part. I didn't want the situation to deteriorate and feel guilty later on that I hadn't done everything in my power to help my buddy. I told Rob we'd come up the next day.

That morning we got up before sunrise. We had to be at the vet's by 7:30, which meant we'd leave home about 6:30. I petted Boomer and explained to him that his brother and I were going to Boulder but would be back that evening. He would be in charge of the house.

As usual, the staff was happy to see Beezer. He greeted everyone and exchanged pleasantries before we headed into the back. Adjacent to the procedure room was a smaller room with two six-foot-long dog runs. The vet tech and I got a few blankets and made Beezer a bed in one of the runs. The Beez amicably agreed to having his front paw shaved and an IV inserted. We carefully lifted him off the procedure table and led him back to the dog run. We got him inside and he immediately lay down, being the very good boy he is. A full bag of orange-colored water was set up and the lines were connected. Dr. Silver popped in and injected a few extras into the bag and the pump was started. It was 8:00 a.m. and the Beez was on the clock.

My next task was to create my work area. First, I set up my shorty lawn chair right next to Beezer's door, which was propped open. This allowed me to reach in while working and pet Beezer with my right hand. I also brought up my captain's briefcase along with several files. The large briefcase doubled nicely as a small desk and I was able to dictate assorted letters and memos throughout the day. My cell phone allowed me to contact the office and return telephone calls.

I also brought along a stack of children's books from the library and would take frequent work breaks to read Beezer a story. I know he got a kick out of story time because he would get a most contented look on his face as I'd read to him about small trains trying hard, cows that went "moo" and mischievous little monkeys. Occasionally, I'd get a call on my cell phone during story time. I'd wink at Beezer as I'd briefly slip my attorney hat back on. I was pleased by how easily I could jump between these two distinct worlds. All in all, I got in a surprisingly solid day of work.

That first IV treatment took until well after 6:00 p.m. We loaded back up and drove home to greet Mr. Boomer. I was astonished at the agitation awaiting me in my other canine pal. Boomer sniffed his brother and began a barking fit. He ran out the doggie door to the back yard where the outburst continued into the evening. Later, at bedtime, Boomer refused to take his customary place at the foot of the bed. It was then I realized my error and began apologizing.

Boomer's reaction was a clear reminder to me about the deep connection between these two brothers. I'd inadvertently stepped on Boomer's paws by excluding him from the day's treatment. Boomer was left at home to wonder what happened to his brother and fret over whether Beezer would return. I felt bad about placing my Big Dog in that position and vowed not to make that mistake again.

I said to Boomer, "I understand that you want to be with your brother for his treatment. I made a mistake and I'm sorry." I got a big kiss from the Big Dog and we put that issue to rest. Every vet trip from that day forward would include Boomer as well. It was either the three of us or none of us. Fortunately, I had assembled a vet team that understood and appreciated my particular requirements. I was very grateful to have these kind and caring professionals at my side.

And so, when we returned to Boulder the following three weeks for the remaining IV treatments, Boomer was invited as well. I brought a few of his stuffed animal friends as Boomer would be spending the day in the dog run lying at his brother's side. I think Beezer found a bit of comfort in having his brother there for him. I know I did.

A FEW WEEKS LATER, WE HAD JUST COME BACK FROM THE RESERVOIR AND Beezer was drying off, lying on the couch with me. I had two wet dogs around the house for all of Saturday, typical for March. Stinky wet dogs. I loved every minute of it. "Are you sleeping?" I asked the Beez. Out cold. Wow, what a cool animal, once again telling me, "I am not afraid, today is a glorious day."

Maybe that *was* the key…no matter what, today *is* a good day. Next week's intense IV would be the fourth week, and the doctor was going to recheck the numbers. I had given it a lot of thought. I did not believe the numbers were going to improve much. In fact, I had a hunch the numbers were going to deteriorate. But Beezer was just doing magnificently; his spirits were high, his love of life still strong. His body, however, was showing signs of atrophy. His spine was starting to protrude and he was just at the very beginning of getting skinny. What could I expect? He had a fatal disease and there was nothing I could do about that. But, perhaps the intense IVs, if they were having any effect, were improving his quality of life for the short term.

The one positive thing I *could* say was that Boomer and I, as Beezer worsened, were going to go through this metamorphosis together and we would both learn to take care of each other. I was trying to listen to Boomer's needs as well. Boomer also was included in the animal communication sessions at times and made it clear how he felt. It is such a paradox that humans, advanced in our ability to deal with so many things, are primitive when it comes to dying and any threat of major change. We are sent into tailspins. We always ask, what is next? What happens next? But *this* human was finally beginning to see that Beezer's life and even his illness had purpose and meaning and perhaps could supply the answers to these age-old questions.

My Dearest Doug,

I'm so proud that you have chosen to travel this road. I feel your pain as I watch you and live with you. It is necessary for your growth; indeed, this earthly journey was planned long ago. The fact that the script is unfolding as intended does not make it easier. But I have so much faith in you and your willingness to face what you fear. We spoke of this long ago in the Old Place. You just don't remember.

You see, my dearest brother, it wasn't by accident or happenstance that Boomer and I came into your life. It was planned long ago, at a time when our spirits mingled. It was understood that you would live your human life exactly as you have. In due course, Boomer and I would join you for an adventure here. The bond we share is, in part, due to our earthly love and affection, but it is also derived from the time we spent together so long ago. We animals remember this place. Our memory allows us to face death with grace and fearlessness. Conversely, you humans have forgotten the Old Place. This makes you fearful of the other side of the circle. Boomer's and my journey here was intended, in part, to remind you that fear is an illusion.

I will not be getting better from my illness. I don't know how much time I have left, but I do know the time is short. Down deep, you realize this as well. Part of your learning, my brother through time, is for you to make decisions about how you spend what time is left.

I want you to embrace my end of life process with the same dignity and resolution that I am doing. Do not be angry, resentful or fearful. All is unfolding as intended.

Your life as an attorney is a perfect example. In your legal life, you have an immense capacity to manage things and obtain desired results through organization and hard work. The paradox you now face, with me, is that you control nothing. You are learning that your considerable business skills have no meaning on this journey.

You are also learning that you cannot control what is taking place with my body. It never was yours to control. Your concept of resolving my illness was nothing more than an illusion.

Your fledgling acceptance of this idea makes my mission much easier. I feel less pressure, less need to take care of you. I can focus on staying healthy as long as I can and staying in the moment with you and Boomer. This release of pressure allows us to focus on our love and trust. These emotions then create a positive energy field for all three of us.

Remember, when this journey was planned long ago, you were given the ability to decline. The free choice had to be yours today. That's why you have no recollection of the plan now. The lesson is only learned when the pupil arrives voluntarily.

My dearest Douglas, you need to have trust in the process. Release the need to manage every moment and, instead, concentrate on enjoying every moment. I want you to understand that surrender simply means to render back to the universe that which you can't do yourself. Somewhere along the way, you humans have lost that meaning. You think that surrender means defeat. Nothing could be further from the truth. Surrender has nothing to do with winning or losing. We aren't on a hockey rink or in a courtroom.

This isn't easy for you. It's not supposed to be. I'd much rather that you spend today with me instead of searching on the computer and telephone for a cure. It's not in there.

The cure is in your heart. This isn't the worst of times, it's the richest of times. Put away your lists and cuddle up with me.

It's time to have fun. It's time for one more walk, one more adventure. The fun will expand when you focus on the good times. Conversely, the disease will expand when you focus on my kidneys.

Stay available for these lessons, dear brother. Please stop being so hard on yourself. I see the guilt you impose on yourself because you can't heal my body. You create doubt over your self-value because you don't have a solution to circumstances decided long ago by the universe.

I'll keep talking to you through my eyes in days ahead. I try to reach you in your sleep, but your human side has such a constant chatter that my voice is often unheard. You don't yet understand why you are taking these small steps. Soon you will.

So many humans become fearful when their animals grow old. The difficulty arises because the human sees our birth, our life and then our death. The cycle is painful and reminds them of their own mortality. Your purpose is to add to the dialogue by telling this story. It is why the three of us are together. Both before, in the Old Place; on earth now; and much later, on the other side of the circle.

It's not about the body, it's all about the soul.

With all my love and affection, Beezer

CHAPTER FIFTEEN

The Daily Appreciation

I READ SOMEWHERE THAT A PET SOMETIMES WILL HANG ON PAST ITS time because the human isn't ready to let go. I grew concerned that Beezer would linger on for me. I decided we needed to talk about that.

We had story time every evening before we went to sleep, which seemed like the logical time to work in this discussion. Usually I'd lie in bed next to the boys and ramble on about the continuing adventures of Mr. Doug and the little black dogs. Beezer would smile, snuggle closer and drift off to sleep. Boomer would remark, "The story would be better with popcorn," before nodding off himself. I found a strange tranquility during this nightly ritual, especially given my upside-down daytime posture.

That night I finished the story and then whispered to Beezer that he had my permission and blessing to transition on his own. "I don't want you pushing beyond your time because of my selfish need for you to hang on," I told him.

During another evening's conversation, I asked Beezer if he was going to leave on his own. His eyes twinkled and I felt him say, "No, I think you are going to have to help me."

Feeling strangely composed, I looked deep into his eyes and replied, "You know, my friend, you really would be taking me off the hook when the time is right."

Beez responded, "That probably will not be our journey. You are not supposed to get off the hook."

It was late in the evening, completely quiet, and I was focused on my dog to the exclusion of all else. It was then I was sure I was communicating with my buddy. No, I couldn't hear him with my ears. And it wasn't exactly conversation, either. I'd hear concepts and feelings with my heart. What I got was as close to proof as I needed. I trusted that the new information my heart was transmitting to my brain was from the entity inside the fur, my most valued friend in life.

I then told him I didn't want to get off the hook, but I quickly realized that the other scenario—where Beezer is left alone—opened a whole new can of worms. I might come home one day and discover that my friend had left. So we needed to talk about *that*, too. I didn't want any unfinished business or regret after it was too late to say goodbye. Thinking back on the regrets I'd had when my father passed away unexpectedly, I realized I *needed* that chance to say goodbye.

So our story times then expanded into some heavy-duty philosophical discussions. Each exchange was different, yet the same. I would tell both dogs how much they meant to me and how lucky I was to have them in my life. I always thanked them for that. We would recap whatever adventure we'd had that day. Sometimes we would talk about the fun times in our past. Parks and swims and grilled ribs come to mind. Sometimes we'd talk about the difficult times. I'd always end up shedding tears as I'd go over the details of the illness. I'd ask for input on how to spend what time we had left together. Then we'd always end on a positive note by expressing our mutual love and deep appreciation for each other. I'd then turn out the lights.

It was during these daily appreciations that I first explained to the dogs what the phrase "fatal disease" meant. It also was the first time I admitted that I wouldn't be able to change the outcome. Speaking out loud in these sessions was cleansing and healing for me. Frankly, at times I wasn't sure if I was talking to the dogs or talking to myself, or maybe both.

The key was that the conversation was limited to the three of us. No computer friends, no vets, no outsiders. The power was greatest when confined to the smallest area. I'd get another reminder of that concept very soon.

Earlier in the evening I spoke to Sharon Callahan about Beezer constantly following me around. As the Beez and I sat on the couch, with Boomer nearby, Sharon tuned into their thoughts. She asked Beezer how he was doing.

"He says that he doesn't know how long he's going to be able to stay with you, Doug. And what he's trying to tell you is that he wants to spend every moment that he has left with you if he can. And he says he has to keep his eye on you too because you tend to go off in your mind and do your own thing. So sometimes he has to bring you back to earth a little bit. He says staring usually works, and Boomer says you shouldn't get so mushy about it."

"That is too funny," I said. "Do either of the dogs feel like Beezer's insides are getting better, worse, staying the same? What are their takes on it?"

"Beezer seems to feel that he's holding his own. And that's what I'm sensing, too. That it's holding stable. Beezer feels very tentative about how much time he has left. I mean, he just doesn't know, which is why he follows you around like that, because if he has only a short time he sure wants to make the best of it. The biggest regret people will have after the fact is that they ran around too much doing all kinds of treatments and things and didn't just spend time enjoying their beloved animal."

One of my vets had told me that same thing. I needed to keep reminding myself that just spending time could be the biggest piece of the puzzle. We were nearing a marker that would affirm this precise thought.

CHAPTER SIXTEEN

A Milestone

I AWOKE, LET OUT A LONG, SLOW EXHALE AND LOOKED OVER AT THE B Brothers. They were both happily yipping through doggie dreams. Today was the fellas' ninth birthday and the three of us were together. We had been given the scary ninety-day warning on December 23. That period had expired four days ago. Beezer had to be given a lot of the credit and I was happy and relieved that we'd made it this far.

I lay in bed and savored the moment. The sun was just coming up. Boomer was down at the foot of the bed, keeping watch through his eyelids as only he could do. The Beezer had gotten off the bed during the night and sauntered over to his own dog bed a few feet away. I noticed that for the past couple of weeks he had been doing this and it was unusual.

Sharon explained it to me this way: "I know it can be hard but it's actually a very normal part of the process. It does indicate to me that he is moving closer toward his transition because what happens is that the body energy system becomes more fragile. They actually will have a harder time sleeping close to people or their animal friends because the intensity and energy is just too hard to deal with. It's good that he is regulating things for himself in a way that works, but it is an indication that his time is getting closer."

The order of business for their birthday included an early morning telephone call again with Sharon. I had been working on a variation of our typical "How ya feeling" communication sessions. Today, in addition to checking in with them, I'd prepared a formal list of questions for Sharon to direct to the boys. I envisioned myself as an investigative reporter for a newspaper and I had to interview two Labrador retrievers. As I dialed Sharon's number, I noticed my spirits lifting. It was their day—we would make sure it was a fun one.

"How is Mr. B?" Sharon asked.

"He's a happy dog today. We just got finished with our sub-Q. We did have a little change yesterday, though. About an hour after he had his breakfast, he threw it all up. And that's a first. And obviously, for the body, it's not a good thing."

"You know, Doug, throwing up for Beezer was a kind of a non-event. It's hard to get him to even think about it. He feels good now. So you know there's also the possibility it was just a one-time thing."

"That's the answer I wanted to hear," I said. "Because today is their birthday, I have a few special questions to ask them. First, what was life like having a littermate growing up together? Do they understand they are brothers?"

"They both say in unison, 'It's the best,'" Sharon said. "Boomer understands that very few dogs ever get the chance to grow up with a brother or sister. Beezer agrees with that and says that it adds a richness to life that both of them know wouldn't be there otherwise. You know, dogs can recognize this brotherly connection even after years of separation, although it's confusing at first, just like with people.

"Beezer and Boomer are both very aware that they have been privileged to be able to live together. Boomer says he knows that when his time comes, Beezer will be there for him, too, just in a different way. Boomer says that's what brothers do.

"This is interesting…they both think there's actually three brothers and you're one of them, Doug. Beezer says it's three brothers together. He says that you've never made him feel like a child or a dog; that you've always made him feel like a brother, like an equal. Boomer says, 'Yeah, that's true.'"

"Do their memories go back to when they were puppies?" I asked.

"Beezer's memory goes back to even before he was born. And in some ways these two dogs feel like two halves of one, like twin souls or something. I mean, they're very different, but they're complementary different."

I thought of how the two would lie together sometimes on the bed, back to back, like one big slumbering dog.

"So they really *are* brothers," she continued, "beyond the sense of just having been born of the same litter, I mean. They feel that they're brothers because they were brothers in the other place even before they came."

"That reminds me of when we first got the boys," I said. "We picked up Boomer and came home and about a week later, we decided to go back for another pup…a companion for him. And that seemingly random event brought Beezer into my life."

"Boomer says he told you to do that."

"You know, I believe he did!" We both had to laugh over that one. The old Doug would not have believed that could be feasible, but things had changed.

"What else do the dogs say about me?"

"Beezer says you have a really, really big heart, not just toward him, but for everyone that you love—and for nature, and for making things good in the world. He says that you don't like people or animals to be taken advantage of, and not only do you have a big heart, but it keeps getting bigger and more open. Boomer says, 'Yeah, that's true,' and they both say that one of the things that they love the most about you is being in bed because they like the way you smell. They say—this is very interesting—they both say that you can tell a person's character by how they smell."

I had to smile hearing that.

"Have I managed Beezer's illness correctly and within both of their wishes?" I asked next.

"They don't really understand the concept of management of illness, Doug. Beezer says everything you have done has been just perfect and that he understands you're trying as best you can to support him without doing anything he doesn't want. Both dogs are very appreciative that you respect their feelings and desires on treatment. They say that many humans don't understand that."

"Really? What would be some things that people do that a dog wouldn't want?"

"Oh, Beezer and Boomer both say the first thing is that people worry too much about everything. And a dog would rather not have the worry, no matter what. Because no matter what's going on in your life, there's always something to have fun about or to enjoy, and so the biggest thing would be not to worry."

"I think they do know how hard I'm trying to overcome the worry."

"Both of them feel that people worry too much about dying, that they think of it as something scary and it really isn't and the dogs know that it isn't really scary. They know it's just going back to the place that you came from. It is simply another beautiful place that's non-physical and that the part of us that's important goes there. People get too caught up in the physical part and that's what makes them worry and be scared of dying.

"They love that you give them a lot of freedom. They both understand that many dogs suffer because they're really not given much freedom because people are afraid and they try to overprotect them. Beezer and Boomer say that there's a real nice way that you balance taking care of them but also giving them freedom. And they both love that you're not afraid to take a chance. In fact, they would put that really high on the list of your fine qualities—that you're sensitive and brave. That the most important thing is allowing yourself to be scared. They say being scared is okay. But just be scared and do what you need to do anyway.

"Both dogs also say they want you to help other people understand that being scared is okay and it's just part of life. You can be afraid and do things anyway—and that's what makes life a great adventure."

"Does Beezer have any unfinished business in the body?"

"Beezer is glad you asked that. He thinks it is important for you to know. He says 'no,' he feels complete. He does add that he just wants to squeeze every bit of happiness and love that he can out of the time he has left. He wants every last drop with you and Boomer."

"Good. That's the way I feel."

"Beezer says this is the most important question you have asked. He says it's important to finish things up—it helps us to stay present."

"Then let's talk a bit about unfinished business. I will wait for a sign from Beezer, if we're in agreement, but if it looks like his body's just about had it, I'd like to have a doctor come over and assist with the transition," I said.

"Beezer says he already made a deal with you that if something is hurting him too much or life isn't good that he will tell you and you will help him. He says there really isn't a straight answer to this; you have to trust each other. He also says you shouldn't act out of fear. He will tell you if he needs help. He says he has a way of telling you that would be really direct, that he would do it with the way that he looks at you.

"Beezer says that the biggest lesson is to absolutely trust that you'll know what to do in the moment. He understands that most people aren't in the present moment; that with their minds, they're either somewhere in the past or worried about something that hasn't come yet.

"If you trust that, and you practice staying in the moment, the right thing to do will always happen. You'll always be able to rise to the occasion and you'll always be able to communicate clearly with the beings that you love. When you asked if Beezer had any unfinished business, he says there's no unfinished business at all, but the beauty is that there are still new lessons."

"I feel like the new kid in school," I said.

"You know, Doug, the past is clear. There's nothing unfinished from the past, so that every moment moving forward is free to bring its own new lesson. And that's a beautiful thing. Beezer is indicating that he's still learning new things and you're still learning new things and if the day comes that you need to help him, that'll be an incredible learning, too."

"Well, we're certainly in new territory. I'll agree with him on that. I've spent all of 2005 in new territory."

"Beezer says he likes new territory. He says it's one of a dog's favorite places."

"Tell him I've spent the entire year walking around, sniffing new places."

"Beezer says, 'Good. Most people are afraid of sniffing new places.'"

~

AFTER TALKING TO SHARON, WE WENT OUT TO CHATFIELD RESERVOIR to start our birthday celebration. That trip is etched into my brain.

Dear Beezer,

The anticipation on your face and Boomer's was priceless as we drove toward the reservoir. You could see the water from the long highway approach, and the familiar pacing in the back of the SUV began. Smiles and an occasional yip out the window suggested you were more than happy with the day's agenda.

We made several turns and soon arrived at the front gate. Our annual park pass allowed the ranger to wave us through quickly, which was fine with you two. The whimpering intensified once we got inside the park. You could see the water on your right; it was so close. I knew you were frustrated by the slow speed of the vehicle, but I hadn't the foggiest idea of how to explain a twenty-five mile per hour speed limit to you. We're close, I assured you, very, very close.

I parked the car, opened the door, and you both exploded out. Boomer was off like a missile. Smells and tinkles were what he'd be about for several minutes. You, by contrast, stayed close to me, spinning and jumping, doing your bunny hop. You aren't sick, I thought. Not right now. You are happy and healthy. I decided to let you lead the expedition.

It was about a quarter mile walk to your favorite pond. You strutted right next to me, smiling, laughing, alive in the moment. You stopped to say hello to some passing dogs, but it was brief; you and Boomer wanted to get to the water.

Boomer was well ahead. He ran up to the edge of the pond, looked across, then sprinted back to us. "What the heck is taking you two so long?" he implored.

"My brother is too impatient sometimes," you said.

Arriving at the water's edge, I reached into my pocket and pulled out a couple of tennis balls. Boomer sounded general quarters upon sighting the ball. I reached back and threw it as far as I could. Boomer took one bound and was off swimming. I chuckled. Never, ever, had I thrown a ball that went too far for Boomer.

But you, Mister, you were a different story. I learned my lesson about long throws. You'd look back at me with a puzzled expression on your face if I really heaved one out there. "That's too far!" you'd say. "You're not doing it right!" We'd have to wait while Boomer fetched your long ball along with his and then start over.

We happily fell into the method of one long one for Boomer, one short one for you. When other dogs would swim into our area, you'd survey the scene and then begin to paddle away from me toward an open spot. I hadn't even thrown the ball yet, but off you'd go. So I'd lob a little throw over your head and it would plop down in front of you. I felt like a quarterback throwing a fade to an NFL receiver. We both got a big kick out of that.

We walked around the ponds for a couple of hours that glorious day, taking breaks for more tennis ball swims at each of our favorite spots and savoring each other's company at every moment. Finally, it was time to go home.

I opened the SUV tailgate and helped two wet, happy Labs into the back. It would have been impossible to detect which of you had a fatal illness if an observer had just witnessed the last two hours.

I was thinking about that as I finished loading you both. You and Boomer turned around and began kissing me on the face. "Thank you, thank you, thank you," you both said over and over. But you, Beezer, were kissing me with such emotion and ferocity that it was almost gentle biting. I was moved at how very special this day had been for you. All I could say was, "You're welcome."

All the way home I thought about you, dear Beezer. What a great lesson about presence and making the most of today. It filled my heart with hope that there might be a cure. Not for your kidney disease, but perhaps for my disease of the soul.

AFTER OUR OUTING THAT DAY, I KICKED BACK ON THE COUCH AND WATCHED a college hockey game. Beezer came over, jumped up and put his head on my lap. I kind of slouched down a little bit to cuddle with him and put one arm around his body and the other underneath his head, cradling it. He moved slightly, cuddled up very close to me and took a nice nap. That was the highlight of my day, or maybe of my year—just two contented creatures sharing a special moment. It lasted about a half hour, and it was the best, just feeling him breathe. His head was resting close to my heart and for that short period of time we really were joined as one. Every once in a while he would wake up and lift his head, and we would look deeply into each other's eyes without even saying a word. Neither of us had to.

Realistically, this would be the last birthday the three of us would share together. I knew that. But that day I felt at peace. The old Doug would have tried to micromanage the day and would have been tense and upset if our last special occasion didn't go as planned. Something had changed.

Boomer immediately took to his pool.

Boomer had his own ideas for the "perfect portrait."

Two bodies, one purpose.

CHAPTER SEVENTEEN

The Gift of Today

THE FOOD ISSUES JUST WOULD NOT GO AWAY. EARLIER I HAD SAID to Beezer, "Look, we have got to trust each other and if you want to go for dog walks in the park and have some more fun, we've got to get some food in you. So you have to make that choice and let me know." We got through a couple of syringe sessions and then went back to the hand feeding and it was much easier.

Those syringe sessions had been particularly difficult and sad. I'd create a slurry of food and fill a large syringe with the tip cut off. I'd then try to fill Beezer's mouth with some of the contents and coax him to swallow. The results were predictably chaotic, with some nourishment, some covering of Doug, some chasing him around the kitchen with a mess everywhere. Conflicted over the wisdom of these syringe sessions, I gave them up after a week or two. Looking back, I think my decisions about force-feeding had been correct— at the time—because they had been driven by my need to extend Beezer's life. I release myself now for this human frailty.

The next Sunday we drove to Cherry Creek and had a nice walk. I could see a touch of diarrhea from time to time and Beezer's appetite was way off. I thought maybe he was just having a bad day, but then again, trying to keep his body healthy felt like trying to hold the ocean back with a spoon. I kept telling myself to relax. The larger lessons were not in the body but in the mind and the soul— and we did continue working on that. Here was another lesson from Boomer. Boomer was all about fun. He was really pretty silly, and that was a grounding, positive message from him. Life truly should be about fun and enjoying every day and being silly and laughing.

I wasn't overly upset about Beezer's waning appetite. I knew, even if it got better for a few days, it was going to get worse. Beezer continued to follow me around wherever I went in the house and stayed so close to me. It was such a tender, loving feeling. What a marvelous gift. What a new affirmation of our lives together that, rather than be by himself or sulk, he was cheerful.

The next day, as we were getting ready for breakfast, I had the feeling it was going to be a big mess. He didn't want to eat but he tried his best. Just a week before, I'd had to chase him around the house to get his pills down him, but that day he resigned himself that we needed to do this and took a mouthful of pills. I found tremendous nobility in that.

Then I tried to give him some food—raw hamburger—but he refused it. Finally he ate a couple cookies. I got almost two hundred calories in him with no phosphorus, and that wasn't too bad. Yes, I was still counting phosphorus amounts. It was nice to see him eat even a little bit on his own. Eating ought to be fun and it just wasn't. I was cognizant that he could change, not only day by day, but meal by meal, minute by minute.

It couldn't be much fun to have food jammed in your mouth when you don't want it. We got in a little more than half of what my goal for the meal was. At the end, he started gagging as if he was going to throw up and I stopped. I didn't want to force more in him than his system could hold. With the medications and vitamins that I was giving him, I didn't want him to lose whatever little bit of nutrition that we'd gained that morning.

On other days we could find the humor in all this. I'd put a pill in with a little tapioca to try and make it appealing, and out it would fly like a shot from a cannon. At these times, I'd look at Boomer and say, "Attention, wet cleanup on Aisle 4," and Boomer would come over and mop up. No matter what type of mess we created, Boomer would be operating right behind us and he'd clean up as we went.

I recalled how I'd been caught off guard by a comment my ex made during the boys' birthday party. She had come over to help celebrate and had brought a very nice birthday cake for them. I have a snapshot of their first birthday cake, and I remarked that I felt a certain synergy in having a cake for their last birthday together. Carolina said I was being negative and was wishing death upon Beezer. That comment bothered me.

First of all, if I could somehow have wished this disease away, I would have used up all the wishes for the rest of my life and done just that. If I could have changed the course of his illness by just being positive and upbeat, I would have done that. But I knew I was not going to find a magic bullet out there. I knew it, Boomer knew it, Beezer knew it. In order to make my life manageable and enjoy the time left, I had to hit this thing head-on, whether I wanted to or not. And believe me, I did not want to. I would have much preferred that the day be carefree. But that was not the way the universe had unfolded. And I knew it would not be helpful for me to live in denial.

I was particularly concerned that I would be ready—when the really bad days came—to have all my questions answered about how the Beez was feeling. I wanted to have searched my heart for all of the things that I wanted to say and do and have confidence that we had explored all the issues that we needed to. So, I had to approach each day as if it was Beezer's last day alive. I had to enjoy everything that that day had to offer and be thankful for the gifts of *today* and not be fearful of what tomorrow might or might not bring. I wish my ex would have understood.

In one of my hospice care books I read that dying people sometimes complain that their families refuse to talk about impending death. They don't realize how natural, helpful and healthy it can be for the terminally ill person to discuss dying with family. Helpful to the patient and also the family. The family is missing an opportunity to have this kind of frank discussion, however uncomfortable. To me, to discuss another person's impending death is to acknowledge our own mortality. We are made uncomfortable not by the other person's death but by having to admit someday it will be us.

We should not be surprised when friends, loved ones and family are resistant to a frank discussion about dying. Such a dialogue raises issues that in our society are taboo. We are not supposed to talk about death or what happens when you die. We are not supposed to talk about if you have a spirit or a soul or where it goes or what happens.

I had yellow highlighted some particularly insightful passages from some of the hospice books for humans that seemed to be talking about my dogs and me. This certainly fit us:

> *We live in a fix-it society with the technology at our fingertips to repair many broken things. We forget that we've all been deliberately designed to "end" one day. When that ending happens, there's nothing to fix. Optimism and a fighting spirit are good things, but at a certain point optimism becomes denial. It's important that patients be willing to fight when fighting is appropriate, but we will all face that moment in life when it is time to stop fighting, to stop treating death as the enemy. This is not giving up. It's accepting what is happening, riding the horse in the direction it's going.*

From *The Needs of the Dying*, David Kessler, Quill-Harper Collins, 1997, 2000

⌒

TO BE FAIR, BEFORE BEEZER'S ILLNESS, IF SOMEBODY HAD WANTED TO talk to me about death, I would have just waved off him or her, the same way Carolina waved me off. And I also would have said to someone behaving like I was: You are being negative, you are quitting on your dog, you are quitting on your family member—they do not need this negative energy.

Well, I did not quit. And, the only time I *would have* quit is if Beezer had told me he'd had enough. It is okay to talk about death of the body. That's not being negative, it's being realistic. Such a discussion does not mean you are quitting on your loved one. Neither are you quitting on your pet. Death is a natural part of life.

If you live, you die. It's our contract from birth. If we are going to go down this road, then let us do it without blinders. And to the extent that we can, we should receive information happily and worry about putting it all into perspective at some later point. It is important to talk with and listen to our pets. Perhaps we cannot prove that our pets hear or understand anything we are saying, but we cannot disprove it either. As for Beezer and me, I have no doubt that our communication was a two-way deal.

This newfound willingness to face the fragility of physical life would serve me in good stead in the coming days.

"Big Duck" was a favorite friend of Boomer.

I'll always treasure having my beloved Beezer close by during the workday.

Two-ball retrieval was a source of particular pride for Boomer.

CHAPTER EIGHTEEN

The Circle of Life

BEEZER'S APPETITE PLUMMETED. WERE WE ENTERING THE NEXT AND final phase? I crossed my fingers, hoping that he was just overly tired and would eat better in the morning, but I was kidding myself. At that next meal and others to follow, he started gagging at the beginning of the meal instead of the end. So was I now to let my dog starve? That would be a really rotten way for somebody's life to end and was just not going to work for me. Not by a long shot. So, I told myself, let's see what today brings. Let's not look any further than that.

I thought about how this story would have made sense if, at the ending, Beezer was merely supposed to fight hard and make it to his birthday. And he had. And I saw I could handle that. I did handle that. And I could handle *more* days and *more* upsets. And I saw I was not nearly as frantic as I thought I would be, facing this final event. I *was* perturbed. As perturbed as I was ever going to be. But I had taken on a solemn duty with Mr. Beezer and I would see it through. What type of person would I be if I had given him very aggressive treatments in the earlier stages, called in doctors from across the country, spent hours on the phone with animal communicators, and then thrown in the towel at this point? If I wanted to just kick back and let nature take its course, it was a little late in the ballgame for that.

More to the point, my intervention had already extended Beezer's life beyond what nature and Darwin would allot in the wild. I felt I had to respect the treatment duty I'd voluntarily taken on and discharge my responsibilities with love and compassion.

The next day was a surprise. Again Beezer would not eat breakfast and I started thinking that I would need to make the decision about euthanasia. But I gave him half a bag of sub-Q that morning and he came around. He even ate some dog biscuits and had a little bit of food that he allowed me to hand feed and it stayed down. The fact that he had eaten even a little and had not vomited was critical. I was relieved that I had a little more time with him. I heard him say, "No, I'm not ready to go yet."

I respected Beezer for working so hard. Knowing I was concerned about his appetite, he continued to try and eat something. He also made the effort to come downstairs to be with me while I worked in the office. Was that for me...or for him? As long as I got that tail wag and he was a happy dog, we were okay.

I called Terri again that day. By this point, we had talked by phone numerous times and she was always able to key right in on how Beezer was feeling. In this somber session she wanted to start by having a conversation with Boomer, to "give him a chance to have the shining light," she said.

"So the first thing Boomer says is that we aren't quite as worried about Beezer as we were. We're a little more grounded," Terri began. "We're going with the flow a little bit better. You know, nobody's in denial or anything, but he says we're all doing better.

"And Boomer says that he's very proud of you. He says that you have been very open. You've really been listening," she added.

"Is he worried at all about Beezer? Does Beezer tell him anything?" I asked.

"Beezer tells him that he's uncomfortable. That his body is, oh, what word would I use for that feeling he's telling me? Diminishing. 'My body is fading away,' he says. Boomer says that scares him when Beezer tells him that kind of stuff.

"...Ah, I love animals. Boomer got real serious and quiet for a minute...and I was trying to keep myself blank, you know. And I said, 'Where do you think he goes? What do you think happens?'

And he said something interesting. He said, 'Look, we all know what happens. We know the body dies. We know the spirit rises. We know the spirit lives on. We know Beezer will be okay.'

"Boomer just sent an image—a magnificent image. Almost like a sunrise. It was like a beautiful bright light getting brighter and brighter. He said, 'Brother, this is about your awakening,' meaning you, Doug. Clear and simple. He said Beezer's got a challenging illness for a reason. He's not meant to die of old age where Doug just says, 'I'm gonna miss you and it's okay, you can go now.' This challenge is here for a reason because it's gripped you to the core."

"Boomer really does understand. Is there anything else he wants to tell me tonight?" I asked.

"Yes, Boomer just said, 'And tell him it's going exactly as it should so don't worry about if it's going too slow, should we speed things up, is it right, is it wrong?' He says it's exactly as it should be. 'There's no perfect timing and there's nothing our brother can do to change the timing or the journey.'"

Then Terri asked Beezer how he was feeling. "He says 'I'm kind of medium. I'm a little bit weak. I have some stronger days and some weaker days. I'm still enjoying life, but I'm very tired.'"

Later in her conversation with him, Terri said, "Ah, here is something else, Doug. He would like you to know that you are not alone. He knows there are helpers—some call them angels, but it doesn't matter what name you use—and he is saying they're there and they're trying to help you...and there's one in particular, which is a male energy...is your father passed away, Doug?"

"Yeah."

"Were you close with him?"

"Yeah."

"Because it feels like your father is really helping you. I feel a real safe, loving, nurturing male energy that is saying, come along, come along, you're gonna do this. I'm walking with you, hand in hand. I'm gonna guide you, like a father does with a little boy."

"My father?" I asked.

"So go ahead and talk to him and call upon him. He's very much there."

"It's funny," I said. "Right when Beezer got real sick, around December 23 when this whole thing started, I called on my dad and I told him, 'You need to get off your butt and help me out on this one.'"

"Well, he came to the calling, Doug," she said. "You needed him, you called on him and he's here. And keep calling on him. He is available.

"Beezer acknowledges you're making the effort to find a balance between utter panic and 'I'm making the best of it.' You are making a conscious effort, he realizes, and he needs you to continue that because a part of what he's trying to teach you is the balancing act between having something really heavy like a dog that might die any day *and* also enjoying the sunshine and the fresh air and the love of your pals. You can have both within you. And so he's really teaching you about the balance—or the yin and yang—of life."

After we hung up, I felt an overwhelming feeling of gratitude for Terri and for the boys. They were helping me sort through my feelings. I thought about what Terri had said about my dad and began to think she may be right.

It lifted my spirits that day to consider the possibility that a spirit of someone I hadn't seen in physical form in twenty-five years might still be looking after me. I felt safer somehow and even chuckled a bit at his earthly memory. My old man had been a real piece of work. I could see him sending me coaching signals from heaven.

CHAPTER NINETEEN

A New Version of Normal

TO SAY THAT MY FATHER WAS HARD-NOSED AND UNBENDING WOULD be an understatement. Summer vacations come to mind. I could write a great screenplay about our dysfunctional trips during my youth—rather like a black comedy version of Chevy Chase's *Vacation*. Each trip was full of unmitigated disasters. We'd usually borrow a pop-up camper and explore the national parks. And even though we did have fun and saw a lot of sights, our family just didn't have the necessary degree of internal harmony needed to optimize the vacation experience. We'd start out tense and the close confines would slowly, but surely, expose our collective weaknesses.

I was in charge of getting our gear ready for each excursion. By the time I got the car and the camper packed, Dad would arrive home from the office, give my work an inspection like a drill sergeant, and off we'd go. "Gotta make time!" he'd bellow. There'd be no stopping. We had an itinerary and, by golly, we'd stick to it. The plan was sacrosanct.

But there were too many of us in the car for too long—my dad, mom, kid sister and me. We had any number of rules, all of which were designed to reduce my father's aggravation, keep harmony and move us as quickly as possible between scenic point A and scenic point B. We kids were scolded often, particularly for failure to observe the wildlife.

Not too long into one trip—I was about ten—I was already teetering on the brink of getting into big-time trouble, having been charged with map-reading duty after Mom directed us fifty miles off course. I was even moved to the front seat for this particular task. The zenith of that trip occurred when a fly flew into the car and started buzzing around Dad's head. The three of us were ordered to rid the car of the pest. We flailed away unsuccessfully as Dad's annoyance at the fly quickly turned into exasperation with us for failing to remedy the situation. Then a hard right jerk on the wheel indicated plan B was being activated. Dad rammed the car into park on the shoulder of the highway, glared at us, and rolled down his window. That little bastard of a fly then flew straight out.

"You people deserve each other," Dad said with disgust as he pulled back onto the road. I immersed myself in the map and prayed I'd get the course correct. The silence was palpable for the remainder of the day.

As far back as I can remember, my mother, sister and I always put up with his short temper. We wouldn't dare talk back. Dad didn't run a democracy. As a defense mechanism, perhaps, we never showed our emotions. Instead, we learned to protect them at all costs. All four of us were closed off from each other, and, to some extent, to others around us. As a '50s family, I believe my parents stayed together for the good of the kids. I grew up thinking this whole way of being was normal.

No matter what a hothead he was, though, Dad had always been there for me—to take me to hockey games and Boy Scouts' meetings. He had been the scoutmaster for my troop for several years. We also took many camping trips, even some memorable winter excursions deep into the Rockies. I look back at those times with much fondness; even the tough times weren't so bad. In fact, I love and respect both my parents very much. They did the best they could. But Dad *was* a hothead. There was no other word for it.

I started playing ice hockey at age five. As a kid, it wasn't a sport; it was a duty to my father. At age ten, every Sunday morning, if it was cold (and it was cold a lot), we'd play hockey on an outdoor rink near my home in Minneapolis, and later in Denver. Of course, we little kids got the worst ice times for games, that is, 6:00 and 7:00 in the morning. Dad would wake me up, get me into my uniform and get out on the road. There was no complaining allowed. But I would always nod off in the car. Dad would divert off the main road and stop the car, then make me get out and jog alongside in the cold air to wake up. I learned very quickly to stay alert on the ride to the rink. When we'd get there, he would glare at me with his game face on and instruct me to "Go get your nose wet." After the game, we'd return home and I'd be handed off to my mom, who would clean me up, get me dressed and cart me off to church and Sunday school.

My mother felt almost as strongly about church going as my father did about hockey. The confirmation process in the Lutheran Church begins around age twelve. This involves a series of classroom lessons on the religion and hands-on training to become an acolyte during morning services. At our church, we boys would take turns assisting the minister during the service. An acolyte is similar to an altar boy in the Catholic Church. As the occasional acolyte, I wore a black robe over my dress pants and what I recall was a brilliant white top. It was so white it intimidated me. I could do absolutely nothing that might soil or dirty this garment.

The acolyte is supposed to come into the church, light candles on the altar, and be seated in front of the congregation. He also assists the minister during communion, again up in front of the entire congregation. Of course, very precise movements and turns apply to these tasks with a degree of reverence and solemnity beyond my tender age. In other words, I better not screw it up.

Since church always fell a couple of hours after the hockey games, more often than not I'd have an eye swelling shut or a knot on my face growing exponentially. Nosebleeds that continued in church were common. I couldn't make any sudden movements, which would draw attention to myself, but had to somehow intercept the blood drops before they'd land on my white top and become a growing crimson testament to my "sins" earlier that morning. With my one working eye, I'd occasionally catch the sharp daggers being sent to me from the pulpit as the minister continued his sermon. It became one of my first forays into the world of paradoxes as I'd discharge my filial duties on the ice only to ponder about my other duties, which apparently required salvation during church. I often wondered how I could get into so much trouble by 11 a.m. on a Sunday when all I had done all morning was mind my mom and dad.

I continued playing hockey through high school. I loved it. But those four years were like leading a secret life. No one knew I played, and I didn't go around bragging about it. It wasn't exactly a popular sport at the time. There was no Colorado Avalanche, only the Denver Spurs, a little known minor league team. So I was under the radar. Even my friends knew nothing about hockey. To them I was just "The Hockey Guy." Funny, a few years ago, after the Av's won the Stanley Cup here in Denver, a friend from back in high school said to me, "I thought of you. It must have been really hard on you during high school. It's such a time for fitting in." He was right.

Only after I began writing this book, at the point when Beezer was so sick, did I begin to unravel this mess of emotions and realize that what happened in the past doesn't have to dictate today. What happens early in life does not cast in stone what is going to happen later on. I wish I could say these revelations came easy. They didn't. I learned that fear kept me from embracing change. Change is both constant and healthy. My resistance to change over the years came from my inner self, my ego, clinging to what was insulated and "normal." The paradox came with the realization that "normal" was unhealthy, but God forbid I should change anything. We can't have that.

"Just an FYI…Labs tend to have it rough with chronic renal failure (CRF)…It hits them hard and fast." This comment was buried at the end of a lengthy reply from Lisa, one of the tireless moderators on the kidney group list. I'd recently posted a cyber 9-1-1 message reporting Beezer's latest vomiting episode and described how even his poor eating habits had grown worse. The dreaded two-headed enemy of creatinine and phosphorus was continuing its attack despite all my efforts. It was a couple of days after the dogs' birthday. Lisa had methodically gone through my post point by point, recommending certain actions, and the FYI comment was clearly an afterthought. It wasn't just any afterthought to me. Lisa's words in passing may have been the single most helpful comment I'd ever received on-list.

When I'd sent the 9-1-1 post, I had still been struggling with what I knew was possible versus what I wanted for my dog. And I wanted so badly to become a wizard on the list. I wanted to post progress reports thanking the group and canonizing the benefits of egg whites and glutinous rice. Mostly I wanted to upload inspirational success stories of how Beezer's illness had receded into the shadows as he and I went about our life. I wanted to be Lance Armstrong. I just couldn't get rid of the feeling that I'd let my teammate down. That he needed me to be my very best and I couldn't do it. I couldn't believe I still carried guilt like an anchor around my neck. Lisa's simple comment helped change that.

Labs tend to have it rough with CRF. It was like biking up a hill, pausing, taking the anchor off, leaving the anchor behind, and resuming the climb. Maybe this *isn't* my fault, I thought. Maybe I'm not supposed to be a wizard. Maybe I'm doing everything I can and in the end it just doesn't matter. Perhaps my ego has tricked me into believing it's my fault that a fatal disease is taking its logical course.

That's the insidious nature of kidney disease. It is sneaky beyond belief. The roller coaster ride of this disease is worthy of all your coupons at the amusement park. The dog feels no pain, but the human twists like a victim in a fantasyland medieval dungeon. The dog eats one day, then fails to eat the next, then eats the day after. The human blames himself. What am I doing wrong? I'd overlain reason and control onto a disease that tactically destroys logic and planning.

Work harder, Mister, my ego would whisper in my ear. You have power over this disease. Of course, the opposite then holds true. My failure to exercise this power properly had caused Beezer's condition to worsen. That's how this surreptitious disease operates.

I talked to Beezer about Lisa's post during our evening sub-Q session. I told him a story about a great clipper ship sailing on the ocean a long time ago. The ship had developed a problem and it was obvious that the proud vessel would sink before it could make port. Aboard the ship were two mates who grew up together and took to the sea for a great adventure. Rather than talk of their impending demise, the friends noted what a beautiful day for sailing it was, the spray at their face and the wind at their backs. It was a grand day to be at sea.

Beezer was snoozing as I finished the story. I sat in silence and listened to my dear friend breathe. I closed my eyes and then looked at him through my fingertips and froze the moment in my mind. I then did something I had never done in my life. I said to myself, "Doug, you did the best you could, and you are continuing to do the best you can. That is good enough."

I then said, "I forgive myself for any mistakes I've made with your treatment; I forgive myself for not having a cure for your disease." I took the intermittent snoring to mean, "No worries, mate!"

Grudgingly, I was becoming less resistant to the change occurring in our lives. Acceptance then was beginning to fill the void as resistance was discarded. My own pain remained as real and intense as ever, but my suffering was beginning to subside. I moved into April just as scared, but far less guilty.

CHAPTER TWENTY

Honoring the Bonds
with Caregivers

A FEW DAYS LATER, I LOOKED AT THE CALENDAR AND REALIZED I HAD a vet checkup for that day. I mulled over the thought of canceling. Beezer had been having more bad days than good. The IV treatments hadn't worked. The endless pill, supplement and diet regimen hadn't worked. The disease struck me as a runaway train headed down a mountain pass without brakes. There was nothing new to try. I had no questions for Dr. Silver. It seemed a bit of a waste of time to go all the way to Boulder, over an hour away.

I'm not sure why I didn't cancel that appointment. Dr. Silver expressed concern at Beezer's appearance. Kidney disease causes weight loss and muscular deterioration in particular. The body continues to require protein even though the kidneys cannot process most edible forms. The body's solution is to consume its own muscle mass. It is gradual, though, and I had not fully grasped the changes taking place in Beezer until the doc pointed them out. My mouth dropped.

We talked candidly in the room that day. I explained that I believed the disease was taking its final toll and the end was approaching. I also reiterated that my plan was to make sure Beezer did not suffer or linger past his time. The Beez and I didn't have to ride the train all the way down. Rob listened intently and said, "I don't disagree with anything you've said."

The visit completed, we went to the front desk to pay our bill and check out. I'd grown very close to the staff over the past few months. I know the feeling was mutual. We all had tears in our eyes as I fumbled through the finances. I wasn't asked when my next appointment was.

Suddenly, and purposefully, the staff emptied out into the waiting room. Jill, Kasia, Allyson and Jon, just to name a few, created a small semicircle around their favorite patient and best friend Beezer. I stepped back, out of the way, and allowed the scene to unfold without me. All the techs were down on one knee, ready to embrace him. Beezer slowly surveyed the room and made eye contact with each of them. Then, one after the other, each person stepped forward and spent a moment with this wonderful creature. A few words whispered, a hug and a kiss, and then retreat back to the circle and let the next person step forward. I just stood back silently as I did not want to interrupt such a spontaneous show of compassion and humanity.

I realized at that very moment the reason for keeping that last appointment. It wasn't about me. It was all about them. It was about Beezer and his caregivers expressing their mutual love and saying goodbye. I was moved beyond words and so deeply appreciative that I hadn't canceled the appointment. Facilitating this moment for the group made me realize how special it can be to help out others who are in pain. I'll remember those moments for the rest of my life.

CHAPTER TWENTY-ONE

Death, Dying and Living with Balance

I WAS GETTING SPACEY. ONE DAY I WENT TO THE GROCERY STORE TWICE for some food for the boys. On the first trip, I got chicken for Beezer and some other groceries, and then decided to pick up a nice beef filet to treat myself and even give a taste to the Beez. But when I got home, I couldn't locate the meat anywhere. I had no idea where I'd put it! I could have left it in the checkout line or in a basket in the parking lot; who knew? Maybe something would start smelling in my house in a week and I would find the meat in the closet. That was definitely out of character for me. I was never absentminded and I usually got furious with myself when I pulled a maneuver like that one.

Then I told myself, don't waste your time! This is all irrelevant and certainly understandable. You have a lot of plates up in the air and a few of them are going to fall and if the most important one that falls is losing part of an order from the grocery store, then I am in very good shape.

We had gone to the Denver internist that day. Beezer's protein loss was increasing, so much so that the doctor now felt something else was a factor in Beezer's decline. He said he believed Beezer also had inflammatory bowel disease (IBD), a condition that allows protein—albumin—to be lost through the intestine in addition to through the kidneys. Albumin's function is to retain fluid in the blood, acting like a sponge to soak up fluid from body tissues. The IBD was probably related to an immune system dysfunction. His immune system had gone haywire and was sending signals to his body to destroy his kidneys. Beezer's own body was attacking itself. He was dying of friendly fire.

I found that news very sad. It's one thing to have an outside agent come into your life and attack the body. Perhaps even the axiom of "it's just old age" could apply. But it just struck me as so patently unfair for the body to elect to terminate itself.

The internist recommended a drug called cyclosporine to treat the IBD. It is used for human transplant patients to prevent rejection of the new organ. The drug suppresses the immune system so the body doesn't send signals to attack what it perceives to be an invader. But the only study done on dogs, ten years ago, had not been promising. Cyclosporine was risky for the kidneys, the internist said. As I listened, I had this distinct image of me painting a floor while moving backwards into the corner. Now my fanny was beginning to touch the wall behind me.

Beez and I talked a bit about the vanishing chess pieces of life as we did sub-Q that night.

"Ah, Beez, I am going to be relieved when this is over. It is really difficult to watch you be this sick. One of the gifts you still give me, even as you grow increasingly frail, is to let me know today is a good day to be alive. I thank you, my friend, and I'm trying hard to listen and be in your moment, not mine." I was surprised to realize I felt no guilt at all in having taken so long to acknowledge this.

My mind wandered. I thought about how the hours spent in animal communication sessions and also my time spent with Beezer during sub-Q had become life-changing experiences. The exercises were a good regulator on the constant chatter of my mind. But more importantly, the old Doug had tried to conform the universe to his expectations and desires. I was now finding peace in doing exactly the opposite—conforming my life to the balance of the universe and trusting its collective wisdom. Heady stuff for a hockey player.

The communication sessions *were* introducing a balancing concept where I held actual conversations with my dogs. I took the concept and experimented with it during sub-Q with Beezer. I would pose a question to him, release any judgment or expectation, and wait for his answer to be heard in my heart. I didn't know how this worked, or even *if* it worked, but I was experiencing something new and profound when I tried. What if I released the need to understand or judge how it worked and just appreciated the benefits?

Places inside me, locked shut long ago, seemed now set free and increasingly were bubbling to the surface. The rough times of the past, in my youth, my marriage, my early career were diminishing as I looked them squarely in the eye. Maybe the communication was less with the dogs and more just me conversing with a very old and special part of my own being.

I still struggled in my mind with the concept of dying. Not death—I was pretty clear about that. But up to now my experience had been limited to dealing with the fact of *death*. My father's sudden death in 1980 had been especially traumatic, but it was also very present. Unlike the act of dying—which is sometimes a long, slow process—the suddenness and the black and white aspect of my dad's death forced me to deal with its finality and the aftermath. Even then, at twenty-two, I'd had the ability to focus my attention and make difficult decisions under stress. Unlike now, dealing with Beezer's *dying*, then I had remained in control.

Pondering this, I recalled something that had happened the year before my dad passed…

IT HAD STARTED AS A MUNDANE MONDAY MORNING IN MARCH 1979. I was an undergraduate at the University of Denver. Before class started, I was reading the newspaper when I spotted an article about an airplane that was missing after a snowstorm. I learned that it was my good friend Dutch in that plane. Making some phone calls, I was told that a search team was out looking for Dutch. I immediately left school and drove to the airport.

I offered to help in the search effort and was assigned as a spotter—an extra set of eyes—in a small plane. Two Colorado Civil Aviation volunteers were also along.

As we scanned the mountainous terrain, we learned that the downed aircraft had been spotted in the grid next to ours. We decided to land our plane, get a vehicle and drive to the snowed-in site. We headed toward a lone mountain with a large mesa at the top and pulled up to the access road just as a sheriff's vehicle arrived. The sheriff declared us the rescue party and sealed the road behind us.

Then we drove to the base of the mountain where we stopped and gathered our gear. Everyone had boots, parkas, ropes and so forth, but me. I made sure to bury my tennis shoe-clad feet in snow to hide them during the briefing. Under no circumstances was I going to be kicked off this team.

The plane was upside down at the top of the mountain when I saw it. It looked like it had smacked the cliff head on. This can't be good, I thought. I alerted the others and quickened my pace to the top. I reached the plane and immediately looked inside. There would be no rescue. It was now around noon. Somehow, I had gone from attending school that morning to recovering a dear friend's body in a plane crash, all in the space of about three hours. I moved away from the plane and sat down on a rock to wait for the others.

The plane was sitting precariously on the steep mountain. The group expressed concern about the aircraft sliding down the mountain if we began working in it. Someone suggested that we secure the site and come back tomorrow. Tomorrow?

It suddenly occurred to me why I was there. I could do nothing for my friend, but I could do something very important for his body and that of the other guy in the plane. "No," I said emphatically, "these people are my friends and we are getting them off the mountain *today*."

Somewhat surprisingly, the group agreed and our first task was to take rope and secure the aircraft to trees and large rocks as best we could.

The recovery proved complex. Since the plane was upside down, both boys also were hanging upside down, still strapped in. Their hands were in front of their faces as if to shield them from an incoming object. Both were frozen. The cabin area was compressed and it was clear they had died on impact.

It was decided to tunnel through the snow under the front end of the aircraft. One of us would have to slide through the opening, then through the windshield (now on the bottom) and enter the cabin. I insisted that I be allowed to perform this task.

I shinnied in on my back and entered the cabin directly underneath Dutch. I began to speak very quietly to my friend. "Dutch, I'm here to take care of you, buddy," I said. "I promise to get you off this mountain today."

The frozen bodies made movement impossible. I was instructed to pull down hard on each of Dutch's forearms, thus breaking the shoulder joint and making the arms move. Then I was instructed to wriggle directly beneath his body and push up on the shoulders, creating slack. The rescuers would then cut the belts and straps. An eerie sense of calm was about me as Dutch's head and face were mere inches from my own. I continued talking to him in a soft whisper that only the two of us could hear. I kept telling him that he could count on me today. I pushed up and heard the cutting sounds. Dutch's frozen body was then lowered on top of my own. From there, I pushed while the rescuers pulled and his body was removed out the door. The task was repeated for the pilot.

By then, an army helicopter had landed on the butte. The bodies were placed in bags and secured with rope. We then moved them up the cliff to the waiting helicopter.

Throughout the day I was able to keep my head. I had kept saying to myself, "This is the last thing you can ever do for your friend. You can't help him tomorrow or the next day. Just today."

BEEZER WAS SNORING AWAY AS I SNAPPED OUT OF MY MENTAL WANDER-
ings. "You see, Beez, this is all so new to me," I whispered. "I
understand the presence of death, but I'm just now learning how to
become present during *dying*. For me, the admission that you are
dying is an invitation to speed into the future. Let's hurry and get the
dying over and deal with the death. That's what I'm good at.

"But you are teaching me to be good at dying as well. You are
teaching me that I don't need to climb a mountain to try and save
you. I just need to be with you. That is enough for you. If so, then
how could it not be enough for me?"

Things were beginning to clarify and I was becoming more at
peace. Beezer ate and did a decent job but then went outside and
vomited it all up and had severe diarrhea. The signals I had been told
to look for were starting to happen. We were getting close to the end.
I had a talk with Dr. Christensen and she agreed. It was a touching
phone call. She and I both started crying and she assured me that if
need be she would come over to assist Beezer's transition.

She agreed that Beezer's high blood pressure could cause an attack
and he could go in his sleep anytime. She offered to increase his blood
pressure medication, but I declined. This had to stop. It was important
that I be absolutely clear now that I was serving Beezer's needs, not
my own. Medicating Beez so I had him for a few more days was pop-
pycock and I wasn't going to do it. Somehow I was finding peace as
the hour grew near, and maybe a little bit of excitement in the event
because very soon Beezer was going to be free of his sick body. I also,
quite frankly, was looking forward to taking the pain of his death inside
my heart so he could be free of it. I would be honored to do it.

Later in the day we went to the doggie bakery. I got him some of
his favorite dry food that he liked and the heck with phosphorus. I
was going to let him eat some of the stuff that he used to enjoy and
give him that pleasure. We were going to lose the battle of kidney
disease, but we would win the battle of fear. At least that was my plan.

CHAPTER TWENTY-TWO

The Gift of Being Wrong

BUT MONDAY ROLLED AROUND AND FEAR WAS BACK, TAKING A FRONT row seat. I looked at my buddy and couldn't imagine him getting any better at all. That was it. I decided I would let Beezer go on Friday. I called Dr. Christensen and scheduled a time with her.

Midweek we went to see the internist one more time. Beezer's diarrhea was horrific and I wanted to get him some relief, if possible. The doctor did a swab, left the room, and came back with some surprising news. He'd now found something new, clostridium, which is a bacteria commonly found in soil. Clostridium has spores that release toxins, which can cause diarrhea and vomiting. The vet felt Beezer's increasing intestinal upsets were related to the clostridium—and treatable! He prescribed an antibiotic and said the Beezer should be improved in several days.

Then he handed me the urine test results, which showed the protein loss had actually slowed. Not much, but the first drop in five months. I was dumbfounded. I allowed myself a ray of hope. I wasn't clear on what I was hoping for—maybe just a few more good days.

We then talked about drugs. The internist suggested a drug for nausea called anzemet. It is used in humans taking chemotherapy. I readily agreed to that idea. We discussed a steroid called budesonide next. I was a bit apprehensive about that but liked the idea that it was less systemic than other steroids, such as prednisone, which can be very hard on dogs with kidney ailments. I decided to give the budesonide a try. I hadn't done much research into the inflammatory bowel disease but wanted to try something to head it off. We went home and called Dr. Christensen to cancel the Friday appointment.

After a day or two of decompression, the Beezer and I had a long talk during the evening's sub-Q session.

"This is a real special night, Beez. You wouldn't be here if things had gone as planned. You know, I was scared the past few days. It's easy to see now. Making a plan even just a few days in advance is projecting out into the future. My fear also encouraged my ego to take control of the situation. Imagine that, trying to project when your death would occur. It seems silly now. I haven't controlled much since you got sick. I didn't control the process at the beginning and I don't control it now. I wonder why I thought I could. I suspect it's my human ego encouraging me to place vast importance on my abilities. Oops. I'm so glad I was wrong. I am so thankful to be sitting on the couch with you this quiet evening, stroking your beautiful black fur, breathing you in as you snooze beside me.

"I also want to talk about suffering, Beez. Your vomiting and diarrhea were the reasons I had set this plan in motion. I had told you I didn't want you to suffer. It seemed you must be suffering if you were sick like that. In truth, the only suffering going on was my own. I'm even happier to be wrong on this point.

"You see, my dear brother, we humans are a strange lot. Even though we say we won't, very often we either end up in the past or the future, both of which come at a high cost because we miss *today*. Had you and I said goodbye yesterday, sometime down the road I'd reflect back and realize I let you go because *I* was the one who was scared, not you. I didn't acknowledge this truth as the reason for your scheduled departure, however. No, my rationale for my decision was to end your suffering—a suffering that did not exist. I'd have carried the guilt of this lie for all my remaining days.

"Ah, you're awake now. So you'd forgive me? But only if I forgive myself? Okay, O wise Labrador, look into my eyes and tell me. The greatest lessons you will teach me don't involve winning; they involve losing. Some of these lessons involve showing me my own fear and shortcomings and giving me the opportunity to work through them and grow.

"I promise you, my dear friend, from here on I will try really hard not to look back and question my decisions with the belittling sarcasm that I heap upon myself. I will take this lesson from you and hold it close for all my days to come. Thank you, Beezer."

I vowed to carry forward this week's practice sessions. I knew saying goodbye to my friend, whenever that occurred, would be difficult, but I wanted to live with the truth. I wouldn't euthanize my dog before his time and then rationalize the decision was made to end my dog's suffering when in fact it was my own. Besides, what if a bit more fun and adventure remained just around the next bend?

Carolina sharing a moment with Beezer after a dog park excursion.

Boomer, age 5.

Beezer, age 5.

CHAPTER TWENTY-THREE

The Paintbrush Incident

Now Beezer's inflammatory bowel disease was getting worse. He also was becoming a bit rickety on his feet and spending more time upstairs rather than in the office. I was relieved that he wasn't trying to negotiate the stairs on his own and seemed content to hang out in his dog bed with his brother. But we had one particularly difficult afternoon, which I later described in detail in a post to the kidney group. It had been a tough week for the group. I had read their posts mentioning that several of their dogs had passed.

This board is in need of comic relief, I wrote. *So the boys in Denver want to share a story from last week...*

I work at home, which has been a blessing during the past few months. In fact, the Labs and I have enjoyed all nine years of their lives together 24/7. My 78-year-old mom was "pup sitting" last week while I worked in my basement office. I went upstairs for something and noticed both dogs asleep. Beezer was curled up on the bare floor sawing wood.

"All is well," Mom proudly proclaimed.

I walked past Beez and into the kitchen, awakening my trusty Lab as I went by. Beez lumbered up to his feet and set off to follow me. I turned, saw him, and noticed strange brown water flying off his body. I quickly dropped to my knees to look under him—nothing. I could now clearly see brackish liquid disbursing in an almost 180-degree arc behind him. My God, I thought, now he's crapping sideways!

Somehow, my light maple kitchen cabinets had come under an artillery barrage worthy of the opening scene from *Saving Pvt. Ryan*. How on earth could he do this? My initial thought was that somehow Beezer had contracted the Ebola virus. Of course! I thought, a rogue infected African chimpanzee had taken up residence in my Colorado back yard. Somehow, through the increasing anger directed at this illusory chimp, one last living brain cell capable of cognitive function screamed, "Idiot! There is no monkey!"

In a nanosecond, my mind then imagined the upcoming telephone call with the vet, who would explain: "Beezer is suffering from Horizontal Bowel Disease. It affects one percent of kidney patients and is always fatal. We treat HBD by high phosphorus enemas, which bring it under control. Unfortunately, a green slime will come out his ears. The dog will feel no pain, so it's really a quality of life issue."

Great, I thought. That's just !@#$-ing great.

The still unfolding event then snapped me back to my senses. Beezer was now sitting on the kitchen floor, intermittently wagging his tail and addressing an itch somewhere near his right ear. He got up, leaving behind a picture out of a crime scene investigation. Somehow, his tail gave the effect of a windshield wiper in need of replacement.

Beezer was still walking around the kitchen as one cabinet after another came under merciless aerial bombardment. They fell like dominos, one by one. I circled the still firing four-pawed cannon, looking for some clue.

Meanwhile, Boomer had retreated to the safe haven of his dog bed and a favorite toy duck. He squeezed out a mocking quack.

"I'll deal with you later," I mumbled at the smart aleck.

My mother made vague reference to "an appointment" as she headed for the door.

"Chickens," I said to both of them.

I then noticed the spot where Beezer had been sleeping. It resembled a pudding experiment gone horribly wrong. My Clouseau-like investigative skills quickly assembled the clues.

While sleeping, Beezer had suffered a lower intestinal seismic event of brief, yet violent, duration. Happily, he slept throughout the tectonic shift. However, his tail, much like a sponge, had absorbed the bulk of the regrettable malfunction. Now awake, the happy Lab was walking around wagging his happy tail. A final Three Stooges show! I could see Curley, with a loaded paintbrush, waving it around and, with each pass, landing a blast on poor Moe.

I was able to coax Mr. Happy Tail through the kitchen and out the doggie door. Now giggling hysterically, I told Beezer, "Quit wagging your tail." Of course, that worked well with a Lab. He then sat down on the porch. I decided I'd deal with Mr. Beezer later. I then turned to survey the damage.

My kitchen now resembled something out of a third world country. A declining third world country. The little fella had managed to deliver his deadly payload almost two feet high. An impressive performance on the one hand. And it did contrast well with the wood and yesterday's aluminum hydroxide spots that he had sprayed all over the place from the other end.

The smaller drops appeared to be hardening, while the larger drops were becoming victims of gravity. The rivulets converged and sped up on their logical journey to the tile floor. "Take me now, Lord, I'm ready," I said to nobody in particular.

I decided the pooch came first. I grabbed my baby wipes and headed outside. Almost immediately, I realized Custer had a better chance at the Little Big Horn than me and my baby wipes. I retreated and authorized use of nuclear weapons. The emergency bucket was filled with warm soapy water and the losers in the "towel derby" decided it was time to volunteer for the mission.

We then commenced EPA Haz Mat clean-up butt operations. SuperFund status has been requested. I explained to
Beezer that everything was okay and that guys do this for guys
all the time. I then volunteered several stories from my college
fraternity days in the hope that he would feel less conspicuous.

With Beez cleaned up, the Haz Mat team enlisted the aid of
Mr. PineSol and tackled the latrine, er, I mean, the kitchen.
Somewhere in the mix, my secretary yelled, "Mr. So and So is
on the phone."

"Tell him I'm in a meeting!" I yelled back.

THE DAYS STARTED BLURRING TOGETHER. THE DREAD I'D BEEN FEELING
was slowly being replaced by acceptance and even an inelegant and
surprising beauty. Yes, Beezer's body was increasingly faulty and failing. The outward episodes were merely evidence of the increasing
internal shutdown. It was sad to watch, but it certainly was life.

Pulling back from the future had opened up my eyes to some
other unexpected discoveries. I called them hidden treasures, something you aren't expecting to find but when you do, they are like a
welcome lode of gold waiting at your feet. The problem was, they
would only reveal themselves if you relaxed. Relaxing and finding
peace itself is a hidden treasure. I had to smile at this paradox: the
harder I tried to find peace, the more elusive it became. Beez and I
talked about that during the evening's sub-Q.

"You are so weak and fragile today, my dear buddy. Thank you
for letting me clean you up. Thank you for letting me take care of
you. I'm finding a new level of trust and love between us as your
body increasingly falters. I don't feel you apologizing about today.
I'm glad you didn't. You haven't done anything wrong. The disease
is just being the disease. I'd rather have a day like this than not have
you here with Brother and me. And thank you for those dog kisses.
I can never have enough of them.

"I feel very special to be the one to help you at this stage of your life. I know now that this is the best job I've ever had, caring for another being as earthly life slips away. What greater duty can one discharge than the honor of attending to your final chapter? I'm moved beyond words, my friend."

~

I'D LIKE TO SAY THOSE LAST DAYS WERE FINALLY TRANQUIL. THEY weren't. I'd like to say I never got exasperated or frustrated. I did. The negative emotions almost always centered around eating, or lack thereof. I never got it through my head that a Lab wouldn't *want* to eat.

But the worst of the days sometimes brought the most wonderful gifts.

One morning, I woke up about 4:00. Beezer was standing beside the bed staring at me. He hadn't wanted to sleep in my bed for weeks. I got up and lifted him into bed at his familiar spot near my pillow. He curled up next to me and I could tell he was at peace. I rolled over and hugged him, placed my hand on his abdomen and gently rubbed. In minutes we were both asleep. I'd get these little snippets of life every now and then, the things that are important and the things I want to remember always.

Having Beezer still in our lives reminded me of the hockey playoff coverage on TV. The scheduled game would end and the network would jump over to an unscheduled game still in progress. They called it Bonus Coverage. I was always deeply appreciative of the network executive with the foresight to deliver one more fix to a hockey junkie. I realized Beezer and I were now in Bonus Coverage for his life. I'm sure glad I didn't shut off the tube and miss the second game.

I knew the coming days would include my dear friend's departure. What I had feared so much so far in the future was coming closer like a ship on the horizon.

A classic
Boomer
moment.

A visibly
ill Beezer on
his last trip
to the park.

The Beezer
Bunny Hop.

CHAPTER TWENTY-FOUR

Whose Master Am I Serving?

THE HARDWOOD FLOORS HAD BECOME AN ICE RINK FOR THE BEEZ. Unfortunately, his skates didn't work. So I pulled out every old blanket, bedspread and moving pad in the house and covered the floors. I wanted his nails to be able to dig into something if he began to teeter.

His instability was due to the increasing drop in his albumin. The IBD was now acting in concert with the kidney disease and was pulling protein out of his body like crazy. The most obvious effect was anemia. And losing the ability to stand.

During our last trip to the reservoir, a foolproof barometer on how he's feeling, I also noted changes. Beezer was very careful in his steps, he avoided the water, and he seemed strangely distant to the entire operation. It was the first time I had noticed a faraway stare in his eyes.

The internist, to his credit, was still continuing to suggest last-ditch measures, including the cyclosporine and an anemia drug called epoetin alfa or EPO. The drug treats anemia by stimulating bone marrow to produce red blood cells. It's the same class of drugs that many endurance athletes have taken to gain unfair advantage. It would have taken the pharmacy a day or two to get the drug and then perhaps seven to ten days before any effect was possible. Some dogs respond well, while others do not. In all cases, the dogs eventually reject the EPO, although *when* rejection might occur was variable.

Here I was, still trying to control things. My immediate concern was timing. Beezer's weekly albumin levels in April were 2.1, 2.1, 1.9 and 1.7. The doctors told me he might become gravely ill around 1.5. It didn't take a mathematician to extrapolate when 1.5 might occur. I doubted whether we had the necessary seven- to ten-day window for the EPO to show any improvement.

I still did not want the cyclosporine. Along with the potential damage to his kidneys (admittedly this didn't seem too relevant any longer), the drug did have an increased risk of vomiting. I thought that was truly nuts! My dear friend was nearing the end of his earthly life and I was considering intentional introduction of a substance that increased his risk of regurgitation? Throwing up is like an act of violence on the body. Beezer and I ought to know that; we'd spent months doing our own "research." This medical strategy and the ethics involved were very troubling to me. Again I wondered whose interests would I be serving, mine or Beezer's? I decided to post my concerns to the kidney group list and see what developed there.

The responses came in almost immediately, as I knew they would. All supportive, all sending much compassion and love. I had shared many Beezer moments over the past few months and the dear people of our cyber community had grown to know the little black dog and our pothole-lined journey. I was moved by the amount and sincerity of their responses that day.

Two lengthy posts, essays really, from different members popped up one after the other. The first essay took the position that we had nothing to lose and an EPO/cyclosporine combo would not place us in any worse position than we were in today. Guilt would be avoided under the doctrine of "We fired bullets till we ran out of ammo." The second essay took the opposite position and pointed out the beauty of my connection to the dogs. I was the best steward for Beezer and I would simply know when the time was right. The essay went on to explain that setting certain limits early on as to prolonging life, before emotion begins to cloud thinking, was helpful.

Both essays were well reasoned and, unfortunately, both correct. They canceled each other out.

Well, what was I expecting? I'd been trying to compute a mathematical formula approach for resolution of this problem for weeks. What I really wanted to do was outsource the problem to someone else who would compute the variables and give me a simple thumbs up or thumbs down. Come on, Doug, life doesn't work like that. I looked at the two essays, sighed, and looked at Beezer. "I'm not going to get off the hook, am I?" Beezer silently stared into my eyes and told me to trust him and trust myself.

I briefly pondered a "letting nature take its course" approach again. This seemed most unfair. I'd seen enough PBS wildlife shows to understand what happens to the sick animal in a group. It struck me as selfish to work the problem as long as I was winning, only to wash my hands of the situation when times grew tough. And as bad as I wanted someone else to make these critical decisions, I equally *didn't* want anyone else making these decisions.

The last piece of the puzzle involved the portion of the blood tests showing kidney disease. Earlier in the month, the urine tests had showed less protein loss. Now, the hated foe creatinine had dropped a bit. I wondered how the heck this could happen, and, more importantly, what the heck did it mean for us? I thought about it and decided it was a gift from the Kidney God. A type of Lifetime Achievement Award. It was an acknowledgement from the universe of a job well done. Beezer's body was simply shutting down and multiple problems were beginning. A brief respite on the creatinine test was meant to allow me to focus on the new and more immediate problem—the IBD/albumin issue. The scoundrel had simply changed uniforms with the guy next to him.

I spoke with my friend Leslie, who had been helping me so tirelessly on the kidney group list with suggestions and comforting words. Leslie told me the word *juxtaposition* kept popping into her head when she thought about me and the Beez. I too thought about that word, which means a side-by-side position, and, again, I considered that all was unfolding as intended. Beezer and I were side by side, and on that final day I'd feel the sun on my face and step forward with confidence that my shadow was behind me, locked in step for step. I wouldn't need to look behind to know my shadow was there. The sun on my face would tell me everything I needed to know.

I called Terri that night. She had been a constant in our lives lately. I had her communicate first with Boomer. He and I had to discuss decisions. Boomer agreed that Beezer was going to need some help with the final step and gave his permission to my plan.

I then tearfully told Beezer that a new fork in the road had arrived, one that he needed to take on his own. Terri said the Beez was proud of how long his body had held up so he and I could experience this incredible journey together. She added that he now saw it as inhabiting a body that would not continue to function much longer. This was the first consult where she had a feeling that Beezer was close to death. I hung up and lay down in the dog bed with my buddy. I wrapped my arms around him, thanked him for nine wonderful years and listened to the stillness of the night, second by second.

The Big Dog

CHAPTER TWENTY-FIVE

Boomer's Salute

O N SUNDAY, MAY 1, 2005, WE SAID GOODBYE TO BEEZER. I CAN'T say I remember much about that evening after returning from the funeral home. Boomer and I both were exhausted and crashed early. Waking the next morning, my immediate reaction was: the Beez is gone. I rolled over onto my back and lay there listening to the stillness. Boomer was down the hall, still asleep; he had chosen to spend the night in his brother's bed. I was really proud of him.

Later I walked around the house aimlessly, knowing I should try and get back to my normal life, but what was that anyway? When Beezer first had gotten sick, I'd care for him in the morning and evening, and try to work in between. *Normal* became caring for him around the clock. Overnight, I was unemployed. I felt like a lifetime worker who had suddenly been laid off from a long-term job.

As I walked through the house, every room screamed "kidney disease." The old hockey stick contraption I'd used for sub-Q was still balanced on a rafter in the living room; my countless three-ring binders, newspaper clippings and assorted papers were strewn around the dining room table; the unopened boxes of IV fluids and supplies were piled haphazardly in a closet like jetsam after a shipwreck; and…my God, the kitchen!

A combined ICU and hospice! One counter was lined with unopened baby food jars; another with bottles of medicine and vitamins, aluminum hydroxide, the pill cutter, and those monster syringes. I had to get all those horrible things out of the house, right then. Not because they reminded me of Beezer; they reminded me of daily pain that I had no control over. Those devices were in control.

But let's not confuse two issues. I wasn't trying to "erase" our experience. I was just very tired of kidney disease dictating what I thought and when I thought it. So I picked up my sword for one last battle.

I started with the prescription dog food—dry, canned, all types and varieties—and the unused IV fluid, lines and needles. Boomer and I loaded them all in the car and we delivered the pile to the animal shelter. Perhaps we could help other animals that were sick.

The baby food was boxed up and given to a friend who had a baby. The loose papers were gathered together, organized and inserted into three-ring binders. I thought they might come in handy at some point. I would even cherish them, but I would look at them only when I decided to.

I took an almost wicked glee with my last task. I got out a large garbage bag and made the rounds. I felt like a vengeful liberating army entering a city held by the cruelest occupier imaginable. My voice was raised and angry as I chastised the perpetrators while making my rounds. The feeding syringes, aluminum hydroxide, IV station, and assorted medications were all discarded with enthusiasm. I even went outside and mocked them in the trash barrel several times as I heard the garbage truck approaching. Good riddance!

I surveyed the house with astonishment. I didn't recognize my kitchen. The crowded counters were suddenly bare. I hadn't seen the tile in months. It was like I had moved into a new home. Next the refrigerator. Out came the tapioca, wet food, cream, butter, glutinous rice, half eaten baby food. Once they were removed and loaded into bags, to my amazement, all that was left was a jug of water and condiments.

My heart felt like my refrigerator, full just a few days ago, but empty today. I stared at that bare, cold box, sat down and cried for a long time.

The following day, a workday, something extraordinary happened. I had been a bit cautious in our approach to "what comes next." My office had always been Beezer's domain. The Beez had a deep sense of purpose in spreading his positive energy in the workplace and had taken his responsibilities very seriously. I knew Beezer's biggest worry had been about his job "opening up." I also had a feeling that Boomer might be a bit worried about having to fill his brother's paw prints in the office.

For his sake, I'd left the blankets used to transport Beezer's body on his dog bed near the living room. I thought the smells might comfort Boomer and didn't want the Big Dog to think I was rushing to get rid of Beezer's presence. I also had placed Beezer's collar and tags on an elevated cushioned portion in the corner of the dog bed. Perhaps Beezer's spirit was even able to linger downstairs a little longer—just to get the workweek started off in the right direction. Maybe Boomer knew that. I don't know these kinds of things to be facts, but with my new philosophy I took much comfort in asking myself, "What if this were true?" That simple question opened the door to endless possibilities that would otherwise be out of reach.

Before I headed down to my office, I watched Boomer lying in his bed and pondered what must be on his mind. I walked over and sat down beside him.

"I'm scared too," I confessed, "but we are really lucky to have each other." I began to pet the Big Dog softly. "Both of us just have to get used to this new version of normal. How about coming downstairs and working with me for a while?" Then it happened.

Boomer stood up, smiled, and began to wag his tail. I said, "C'mon, let's get a little work done," and began to walk toward the stairs. Boomer looked at me, still wagging his tail, and then turned and walked in the opposite direction. I paused on the landing to watch, my elbow on the staircase, my chin resting in my palm. Boomer walked over to his brother's bed and approached the collar. He softly began to sniff it and then, ever so gently, licked it once.

He then turned, walked past me and headed downstairs, leaving me behind, mouth agape.

My brain and eyes conferred and verified the scene, and my heart chimed in that this was one of the coolest things I had ever seen. I was amazed at the continuing bond between these two brothers. And it dawned on me how far I had traveled over the past few months. I had finally learned how to slow down to observe the Labs and allow myself to view this miracle of life from the most unlikely of sources.

I caught up with Boomer downstairs and got down on the floor. We spent a few minutes rolling around, hugging. Boomer was kissing me as I told him over and over that I didn't want him to try and be Beezer. I wanted him to be himself and that he was welcome in the office any time. I told him to make the job his and to do it any way he felt best.

I had scheduled a call with Terri for the evening and solemnly brought out the box containing Beezer's ashes and placed it on a dog bed. Throughout the day my mood grew more somber as I planned my speech to Boomer during the call about the significance of this little wooden box. That evening, I asked Terri to explain reverently to Boomer that Beezer was now "inside the box."

Suddenly, the telephone erupted in laughter. "What's so funny?" I snapped at her, in no mood for frivolity.

"Well," she said, "I sent your message to Boomer exactly as you framed it. Boomer said, 'How'd he fit?'"

So much for my solemn Arlington National Cemetery moment.

OVER THE WEEK AFTER BEEZER PASSED, BOOMER WAS ALWAYS THERE TO console me and he even smiled at times. We went for walks often and I was happy to have him along but felt out of sorts. In all our previous walks, the two Labs would bounce off each other and pull in different directions. It used to get exasperating; now I missed it. When I thought about what really was bothering me, though, I realized that only part of my pain was about *missing Beez* and part was about not wanting *change*. They both hurt but in very different ways.

Talk about change—the first time I went to the grocery store after Beezer passed, I stood in the entryway and froze. I had no idea what to do. For months I had gone to the store almost daily with the sole purpose of finding something Beezer would enjoy eating. Now I was shopping for myself. The stacks of cans and boxes on the shelves were strange-looking objects. The fresh vegetables in bins were a foreign concept. I hadn't been in that section for months. I stood there with tears streaming down my face as customers stepped around me.

It got worse. Cooking on the grill later that day, I actually felt guilt as I flipped the chicken and looked forward to my first real dinner in ages. I said out loud, "I'm so sorry, Beezer." I think he was actually listening, because inside my heart I heard him say, "Huh? What are you talking about?"

Beezer was right. Why was I feeling guilty? Guilt is something we humans do to punish ourselves for not being perfect. I had nothing to feel guilty about, and, quite the contrary, I have everything to be proud of and maybe even happy about. That last one was a new concept I began trying on that week after Beezer passed. I decided to write a letter to him:

Dear Beezer,

My dear friend, you taught me to not feel guilty and also to not be afraid. Thank you so much for these priceless gifts. I've tried them several times and they work! And when I release my fear, I can immediately feel your love fill the void.

You gave me so many gifts every day and especially after you got sick. The humanity, compassion and spirituality you helped me find are so far beyond my ability to write. I just close my eyes and thank you, silently, from my heart.

Lately I've been crying a lot. I don't get it. Before you got sick, I never used to cry at all. But now, it seems a life-time of pent up emotions is cascading out in a stream I cannot control. I'm not trying to hold back the tears or deny their existence. I just let them do what they want to do.

On the other hand, Beez, you remember how much I liked to laugh. I was always the guy who got told to "Wipe that smile off your face." I never would. So I'm not wiping the tears off my face, either. You see, you can't be in bal-ance without both the tears and the giggles. They go together like mustard and relish on the dogs at the ballpark.

Your brother surprised me the day you left. I was expecting him to examine your body carefully afterwards. It didn't happen that way. He never approached your body. No licks, no sniffs, nothing. He just stayed close by. Boomer later told me he didn't because he didn't need to. He said he saw your spirit beginning to leave your body after the first shot from the vet. He said you were ready and almost didn't need the second shot. So there was no reason to attend to your body.

I'm still out of sorts and having trouble sleeping. I'll just keep working on it, Beez. It's been a week since you passed, I took Brother to the reservoir. He was happy swimming and chasing tennis balls in the water. This was our first trip to the reservoir since the three of us went that last Saturday. I'd throw a ball and Boomer would swim out and grab it. Swimming back, he'd look from side to side as if searching for something. I told him, "I under-stand, Boomer—I miss him, too."

…We're back from Chatfield Reservoir, Beez. Brother and I put together a nice ceremony in your honor.

I cut a few holes in a tennis ball and filled it with rocks so it would sink. Kind of like a "Missing Man Formation" for

Labs. I then took a bit of your cremains, mixed them with soil and added them to the tennis ball. The dirt was from directly outside the window in my basement office. You know the spot, where Boomer would spy on me hard at work. The ball, filled with cremains, sinking in the lake was ceremonial for you and Boomer. It signified earth, fire and water. I left open space in the ball to be filled by air. In fact, it was Boomer's idea. Your brother sure is a smart dog, huh?

We also celebrated your life by walking around our favorite spot on earth. At 2:11 p.m., exactly the time you passed, I called Brother to my side. I said, "Thank you for being here with me today. I love you so much and together we will honor your brother, who is now formless but in all form. Then we will move forward." I then threw the tennis ball I had prepared. Not too far, as you never did like long throws. We watched as the ball bobbed for a moment, filled with water, and disappeared from view. Earth, fire, water and air were one.

Beezer, I know your spirit remains in spite of the absence of body. I shall think today about earthly emotions, such as fear and ego. These emotions are human based and limited to this earth. I'll also think about the universal emotions, love and trust. I have faith that these emotions survive and choose to believe that. Proof no longer matters.

Thank you for a remarkable journey on this earth. I look forward to our spirits intertwined throughout the ages.

We'll always be together, my brother. We'll always be together.

~

It wasn't until after Beezer left that I realized how tired I had been during his illness. I took to coming upstairs after work, flipping on the TV, and collapsing deep into the couch. The first night after

Beezer left, Boomer sauntered over, ever so slowly wagging his tail, and looked me in the eye. I looked back, said, "Sure," and scooched over a bit. The Big Dog leaped up and curled next to me, all in one motion. My mind disappeared into some TV program and my left hand moved over to pet him. Our cuddle reminded me of sub-Q sessions with his brother only days before as we were now in the exact same position.

My hand absentmindedly moved over Boomer and I felt his ample back muscles and the powerful fore and aft musculature in his legs. Suddenly, my mind snapped away from the television and I looked down at him. As the alpha dog, Boomer had always been a bit stronger than Beezer, but I hadn't realized the difference until now.

My dear Beezer had become a walking skeleton before he died. Kidney disease had ravaged his body so badly that his own muscles were being devoured to meet his nutritional requirements. I'd understood this but hadn't realized how significantly things had deteriorated until I ran the same test with Boomer. What a valiant effort little Mr. Potato Head had put up to stay with me as long as he could. I thanked Beezer for taking such good care of me over the past few months, reached down, hugged the Big Dog, and thanked him for taking care of me in the days ahead.

THE LETHARGY WE WERE FEELING DRAGGED INTO MONTHS. NEITHER Boomer nor I felt like doing much except hanging out at home. I rarely went to the gym. I hardly talked to friends or family. We both slept a lot. But we did still go for walks and, of course, to the reservoir. It was important for Boomer and me to continue to have fun. I didn't want him to think my happiness died with his brother's body.

In December Boomer had root canal surgery to correct a persistent sore on his cheek that had opened up and begun to drain. He recovered quite well and I followed up with a urine test in January. I had decided to run quarterly urine tests and semiannual blood tests for the remainder of Boomer's life. I was not going to be surprised again, knowing that kidney disease ran in the family.

When in January his urine test showed above-average urine to protein/creatinine or UPC ratio, I braced myself. This could be explained by one of two things. The most likely and best-case scenario was a urinary tract infection, which would account for the increased protein in the urine, or it even could be a post surgical reaction. In the back of my mind I couldn't help but recall that the sad fact with kidney disease is that no definitive test for it exists. It is a process of eliminating everything else it could be, leaving kidney disease as the only answer.

So I asked the internist to run a number of different cultures on the urine, all of which were designed to look for a urinary tract infection. I had several samples sent to different laboratories for analysis because I'd learned that UTI's can be easy to miss. I also insisted that the normal culture time be doubled because some persistent UTI's can take a bit longer to culture than a normal laboratory might allow. My vet team was great about accommodating my wishes and made certain the culture times were extended. I tried this over a several-month period, but we did not find a UTI. I also had them do the normal associated tests for tick-borne diseases (although they are rare in Colorado), added an abdominal ultrasound and even did a test for Addison's and Cushing's diseases, which can sometimes mimic kidney disease. Everything came back negative.

Meanwhile, I immediately placed Boomer on a medium-low phosphorus diet and instituted all of Beezer's kidney disease supplement protocol. It couldn't hurt. It seemed like only yesterday that I had done chef duty for Beezer in the kitchen. My dietary notebooks were coming in handy after all. I switched Boomer to a complete fresh food diet I cooked for him. Brittany and Ashley, my nieces, came over and steamed and pureed fresh broccoli, asparagus and green beans, which I froze in weekly-sized Tupperware containers. I'd alternate between barley, white rice and sweet potatoes for carbohydrates, and use egg whites and fresh meat for protein. The fellas in the meat department at Whole Foods, glad to see me back, always enjoyed getting progress reports on their favorite customer as I'd rotate through beef, buffalo, chicken and turkey purchases. The Big Dog enjoyed his fresh diet immensely, wolfing down everything I gave him. The months dragged on. Kidney disease seemed a distant threat. But, if it came to pass, this time we were ready for it.

Later that winter, I decided to find a companion for Boomer. Checking on the Internet, I found a website for Labs and a breeder located north of Denver. My requirements, I told the breeder, were for an adult retriever, not a pup; I wanted Boomer to finish out his years as master of the house. He didn't need any youngster challenging him on how to run things.

The breeder said she had just the dog. So we drove up there and met Coral, a yellow Lab who was a bit sweet and silly when we first saw her. (She still is.) She'd had many litters over her lifetime and looked frazzled. She was also about forty pounds overweight; and, I discovered, she was one of the most shy, skittish and fearful animals I'd ever seen—like the anti-Labrador. Boomer was very cordial. We brought her home on Valentine's Day and eventually the Big Dog and I grew very fond of her. I think Coral was a lost soul looking for a family dog experience. Boomer and I took it upon ourselves to make her feel at home.

When the weather warmed, I planted nine new roses in my yard. Each one of the prepared holes included a spoonful of Beezer's cremains. Every spring now, I look forward to the new blooms and a reminder that the Little Dog remains close by.

Helping Others Helps Me

A S WINTER GAVE WAY TO SPRING, I FOUND MYSELF DRAWN ONCE again to the kidney group list on Yahoo.com. Many people drop out after their dog passes as the list can be a very sad place at times. It was the subject matter we dealt with; there was no cure, everybody knew that going in, so we all did the best we could for as long as we could. Ours was a remarkably symbiotic relationship and deeply personal, especially when considering the impersonal nature of the Internet. In any event, I felt the need to give back and offer support to those who had been there for the Beez and me.

So most days I would spend time watching the posts to see which members I could help. The list has layers of simultaneous conversations. Some are complex and well above my knowledge and expertise. Things really get complicated when diseases overlap, such as kidney disease together with heart or pancreas problems. I thought I lived on a small piece of real estate with the Beezer. Our problems seemed miniscule compared to the multi-disease issues some people faced. I wisely steered clear of those discussions.

Reading through the posts, it was easy to spot those where I could offer my perspective. People seemed lost. Sometimes, it was guilt over a past decision or indecision. I'd read these messages and realized I had felt exactly the same way months before. So I began to talk with these people. I especially remember a dialogue with a very kind woman named Onalee. She had a black Labrador named Dutch. The post started with Onalee remarking, "I see my old dog fading before my very eyes…"

Dutch had been having a tough go and Onalee had been advised not to take the dog to the lake or the stream by their home. It was thought that Dutch could pick up something from standing water, which could make him worse. Fair comment on one hand, I thought; however, the body of water in question was Lake Huron in upstate Michigan. I pondered Dutch's dilemma all day before writing her back. I also thought about what I had wanted most for Beezer when he was sick, and shared it with her:

> Hi Onalee, your message sure pulls at my heart. Your shoes are my shoes. Continue to do your best and release the result. I'm not going to tell you what to do about the lake, but I'll tell you what I did with Beezer.
>
> We have a reservoir close to home with ponds and an off-leash area. Beez was worse than Dutch about not drinking water at home, but he was always happy to drink pond water. I was pleased to see him get liquid. I felt we were getting cornered. Beezer wasn't a healthy dog anymore, and his favorite place on earth was the reservoir. I couldn't take that away from him just because I was scared.
>
> This is your journey with Dutch. Not mine, not the kidney group's. Follow your intuition and heart. Consider letting your buddy enjoy the lake and go for a swim. If he wants a drink then let him fill up. That's just my opinion. I did that with Beezer and I'm glad I did.

DUTCH'S BODY FAILED TO MAKE IT THROUGH ONE MORE SUMMER IN the upper Midwest, but before he died Onalee made several more trips to the lake and streams that she and Dutch so dearly loved. For me, by helping Onalee work through her fear and find what was important to share with Dutch during those last few weeks, I found a sense of purpose in life that I'd never experienced. I was truly honored to have been able to help.

Onalee and I became good friends and months later she e-mailed me pictures of her Dutchy-Dog. I sat back in wide-eyed amazement. Dutch was a short, muscular black Lab with a wide head. He could have been a third B Brother. It would have been hard to tell them apart.

Sometime later I got an e-mail from a person wracked with guilt because she had accidentally struck her dog with her car and the pet had died. I mulled that one over and suggested an approach, a role reversal, that I believed could help. Under my hypothetical, the *human* had run across the street chasing her dog who was chasing a squirrel. Unfortunately, the human was struck by a car and killed. The dog witnessed the imaginary event and was devastated. The family reported that this happy, energetic dog had become lethargic, wouldn't eat, and kept to himself. The universe had allowed the human spirit one minute to converse with the dog before she moved on. Whether this dog recovered or failed was now up to the spirit. What would she say in this one minute? I suggested that my Yahoo correspondent take a piece of paper and write down this story to the dog. Share it with no one. Then take the paper to a place of significance to her and the dog and read it to him. I also urged her to search her life for something that would make this experience meaningful. Perhaps this event was the impetus for great healing. I shared that my experience with Beezer taught me to forgive myself for my shortcomings. I never would have learned this lesson unless the Beezer story had unfolded exactly as it did. I hoped my lesson might be applicable in some fashion to her story. My friend later reported that she was able to work through her guilt and actually adopted a new dog.

That summer, I was drawn to a series of posts from Jody, owner of a Chesapeake Bay retriever named Ichabod, who was suffering from kidney disease. Jody's posts revealed that she had a problem-solving approach where she plotted out every conceivable variation of cause and effect in a matrix of possibilities. It was like she was inside my head when Beezer first got sick. I visualized a set of complex three-ring notebooks spread out on her desk as Jody wrestled with this late into the night. Of course, this kindred spirit and I began to talk. Her focus on outworking and battling kidney disease reminded me so much of my own system—a system that had been in place since I was a kid.

My system came primarily from my dad and was based on hockey. What else? Dad had played for years, first youth hockey, then high school and college. He also was on a professional hockey team for a while. Hockey was what you did if you were a Minnesota kid.

On and off the ice, Jack Koktavy was one tough SOB. He was 5 feet 10 inches, about two hundred pounds and had no neck—one of those guys who has to rotate their shoulders to look sideways. But he knew the game inside out and insisted on a 100 percent in-your-face effort from everyone he coached. Dad was forgiving of athletic miscues, but his disgust would be palpable at any sub-par effort or lack of aggression by any player. If *I* didn't give 110 percent, he'd chew my ass.

Dad taught me early that the game was a microcosm of life. One day, while still a young man, he was playing semi-pro hockey and had a game on an outdoor rink. He wasn't known for playing a finesse game and years later went to great lengths to impress that fact on me. In his day, spectators would stand behind three-foot-tall boards on the side of the rink (outdoor rinks were seldom totally enclosed back then). They could literally reach out and touch the players. That day, my father had been attending to his duties with his normal gusto, committing some on-ice transgression invoking the wrath of spectators; and, in all probability, the opposing team. Pop wore number 6. At one point during the game, he skated down the ice in close proximity to the sideline boards. As he skated by, a woman spectator screamed, "Take that, you dirty number six!" and swung her purse with particular force, knocking the miscreant to the ice. I feel confident that incidents such as this were not isolated, but I never did find out what specific conduct justified this bit of frozen frontier justice.

⁓

IT FOLLOWED THAT JACK KOKTAVY'S SON WOULD PLAY HOCKEY. I WAS always the most physical (albeit the smallest) player on my team. Dad would not hear of any other way to play. He attended every practice and indoctrinated me into the Koktavy way to play the game.

His ways of reprimanding me after I'd played an uninspired game particularly left a big impression. Do you remember a child's doll popular in the fifties and sixties named *Thumbelina*? When Dad was mad at me for lack of effort, he'd bark, "We'll just sell all your hockey gear and buy you a Thumbelina!" Other times, to get my attention, he'd call me *Gwendolyn*. I never got up the courage to ask where that came from.

I began my first team play when I was about eight. This would have been around 1966. Throughout my hockey years, facemasks were nonexistent. Of course, they are mandatory now, but back then kids wore only hard plastic helmets. That is, every kid in North America except *me*.

I got Dad's hand-me-down leather helmet. It looked like something out of a football museum. I was horrified when he handed it to me and told me to put it on. There was no crime worse for a young boy than voluntary and conspicuous indifference to the "system." I might as well have worn knickers to grade school and carried a briefcase. Not fitting in was simply an unpardonable sin.

"Can't I get a regular helmet?"

"There's nothing wrong with this helmet."

Dad consistently opined that the Bronko Nagurski Special was a "perfectly fine" hockey helmet and served *him* well over the years. The fact that the helmet was manufactured in the 1920s was irrelevant and the discussion was closed.

Fortunately, along with being the most physical player, I also was one of the best. So the in-house abuse was minimal. The other teams? Now that was another story. By the time I was twelve, the helmet was good for starting at least one fight per game. Nowadays, you get kicked out and suspended for fighting. Back then, you got five minutes in the penalty box.

Dad would observe and analyze every nanosecond I was on the ice. He knew what the opposing kid was *thinking*. I knew that even the slightest wise-ass comment from the opposing kid would require a prompt and substantial response on my part. And I certainly learned how to deliver appropriately. If during a game I heard my father's trademark single blast high-pitched whistle, it was meant for me immediately to look into the stands where I'd see this middle aged guy, hands on hips, glaring at me. I swear I could hear his whistle two seconds before it went off. One look said it all. To this day a similar sound will cause me to stop dead in my tracks.

After several years in the rink, I was developing into a hard-nosed power forward. My favorite spots on the ice were the areas with the most collisions. I wasn't particularly gifted athletically; I excelled because of my desire and hard-earned skills. I excelled because my dad taught me that a bloody nose, while looking bad, doesn't really hurt. And I came to view that fact as a metaphor for life. I learned that hard work overcomes fear. If you didn't want to play hard, you had no business being on the ice.

I still have that old helmet. It is perhaps my single most prized possession. Over the years I've often thought about what topic I would discuss with Dad if I were granted a short celestial meeting. You know: you have a brief chance to visit with your dead dad, but can only talk about one thing. What would be your choice? It's easy. All the lessons were in the helmet. That's what I'd want to talk to Jack about. If I could talk to him just for a minute, I'd ask him about that helmet, and then I'd thank him.

IT WAS NOW BECOMING EASIER WHEN I'D READ POSTS ON THE KIDNEY group list to recognize those who had their own "helmet story."

Of the many topics my alter ego Jody, the Chesapeake Bay retriever's owner, and I covered, our most memorable discussions centered around my suggestion to "do your best, but *release the outcome*." We spent many an evening e-mailing and talking on the phone about that one sentence.

At first, we went round and round. She thought that "release the outcome" meant her efforts were meaningless as the outcome was predetermined. I assured her that was not the case. Her efforts were keeping Icky alive. Many exchanges later, Jody sent me an e-mail titled, "I Think I've Got It!" It read: "Release the Outcome: Don't concentrate on how you think or fear it may turn out because your focus will be on that fear or outcome. This will blind you to opportunities to enjoy NOW and to possibly enjoy another outcome entirely." I was really proud of my friend for working through her fear to solve her problems herself. She helped me, too. I finally understood the paradox involving fear and guilt layered upon a fatal illness. The real disease is fear. That condition is curable.

I continued to pop into the kidney group list occasionally and send comments where I could. Helping people as broken hearted as I once was filled the enormous empty reservoir in my heart. I felt closer to Beezer when I helped another person become less fearful and closer to his or her dog.

I also began to notice a change in my office. Boomer had now adjusted his schedule and was spending significantly more time dozing at my feet while I worked. Even my staff noticed the change. It made all of us feel very good indeed as that first summer passed. I'd frequently work online as my big Lab sawed wood next to me. My life was getting easier as I embraced change rather than resisting it.

Much like a dog circling the floor, I'd found my spot and plopped down. I still hadn't become a wizard, though, but that fact was becoming increasingly insignificant. In fact, I chuckled about the irony as I compiled a list on guilt for the kidney group...

Beezer's Top Ten Reasons Not to Feel Guilty
(COMPILED BY BEEZER THE BLACK LAB FROM THE BRIDGE AND SENT BACK TO EARTH)

10. Jeez! If you're born, you die. Think about it!

9. Fear is the real enemy, not kidney disease. Fear is curable. I'm with you right now, just invisible. I'll be waiting at the Bridge when you arrive. Don't be afraid. Trust me.

8. Live with balance. The list of what went "right" with my life is so much bigger than the list of what went "wrong." My body died from kidney disease, but my spirit always soared because of you.

7. What you focus on expands. Honor my earthly life and memory. Does feeling guilty help you remember all our good times, adventures and mutual love? Of course not.

6. Live with presence! Don't despair about yesterday. Don't fear tomorrow. Otherwise, you'll miss out on the Gift of Today.

5. Thank you for taking my pain into your heart on that last day. I'm so proud of you for that selfless act.

4. Didn't you always forgive me when I made a mistake? I forgive you for any mistakes you made during my illness. You made the best decisions possible with the information available at that time. All I took with me on my final earthly journey was our love. Please accept my forgiveness and release the guilt.

3. Pat yourself on the back in between crying. Your effort to treat me was a supreme act of humanity, love and compassion. Our

relationship was never more meaningful than during my illness. Please recognize your character and commitment. I do.

2. Guilt is what you humans do to punish yourselves for not being perfect.

1. You didn't have a cure for a fatal disease. My body stopped working because of this fatal disease, not because of something you did or did not do.

©2005 B Brothers Press

The list must have struck a chord. I got a number of responses and kudos for it.

CHAPTER TWENTY-SEVEN

Melancholy Fall

F LIP A COIN. TWO FEET OF SNOW OR 70 DEGREES? IT WAS ONE OF
those late fall Colorado days when anything can happen. Fortunately, for us, it was the latter. We were well into October 2006
and the trees were transforming their glorious colors. The aspens
had already turned golden higher up in the mountains and the gilded
hues were sliding down the slopes toward Chatfield Reservoir.
Boomer just couldn't get enough swimming in. When we went to
the reservoir and I tossed tennis balls, he had the steely focus of a

professional golfer lining up a money putt. Both eyes were trained on me to the exclusion of all else, even other dogs.

Boomer did, however, enjoy every opportunity to show off. Occasionally, a dog would leave a tennis ball out in the water and return to shore empty mouthed, much to the chagrin of the owner. Boomer would smile and I'd throw a ball close to the now abandoned and stranded floater. Boomer would swim out and pick up both balls. Swimming back, I think Boomer could hear the other dog owner's words of astonishment and admonitions to her dog to take a lesson from a *real* retriever. He would exit the water, stare at the owner, pause, shake the water off, prance over, drop both tennis balls, smile, pause a second time, and trot back to me—ready for the next round. Boomer was a real showboat and his productions reeked of theater.

Wouldn't you know it, Boomer would always execute his Tennis Ball Rescue operation for attractive young women. He was quite a lady's man. In fact, once, when I was walking toward my car in the grocery store parking lot, a pretty girl remarked with a smile, "Your dog is flirting with me." Sure enough, Boomer was leaning out the window striking up a conversation.

On this day at Chatfield, we worked our way around the first pond. Not being a big-time water dog, Coral was happy to tag along. The beach was only fifty feet wide, so all the dogs and their people jostled for position. We'd always try to get one of the corners and throw away from traffic. Things could get a bit testy in the water, and tennis ball theft was commonplace. Assuming these inherent risks, we'd spend a great deal of time at the first beach blowing off steam. Slowly, we'd move on and walk along a path, greeting other dogs and owners as we moved around the lake. Boomer would insist on periodic tosses during the walk.

Directly across from the first beach was a small area where we'd had the tennis ball ceremony. A hole in the vegetation led to a small beachfront. There was only enough room for one group of dogs and people at a time and we prized our turn in this special location where we had the place to ourselves. I called it Beezer's Spot.

I was thinking a lot about time that day—Boomer's kidney problem, if there was one, seemed under control since he was on his new diet. Or perhaps a better way of looking at it was the disease simply hadn't shown itself yet. It certainly hadn't yet sent out any alarms. My mind drifted back to the first time I found out that his brother was losing protein in his urine. It had been December 2004. The Beez was then diagnosed with glomerulonephritis in August 2005, about eight months between protein loss and really getting sick. If I added eight months to May 2006, when Boomer was found to have the protein deficiency, I could project major problems surfacing in January 2007, using the Beezer model. I knew I was living in the future again, but I just couldn't shake the willies.

My 2006 hope for Boomer had been that kidney disease had picked off the weaker dogs of the litter and would leave the stronger ones alone. I hoped for their sakes that diet and supplements could ward off deterioration and they could live a normal lifespan. This theory went poof that spring: the boys' sister, Nellie, was also a patient of Dr. Silver. Rob called me one day and told me Nellie was now seriously ill with kidney disease. I knew then that kidney disease was after the entire litter. Shortly after, sister Nell joined Beezer and several brothers. The litter was down to three: Vinnie, Shadow and Boomer.

I had been greatly puzzled by Boomer's responses during animal communication sessions earlier this year. I'd lay out conclusive evidence of kidney disease to Boomer and make inquiry. To my spectacular frustration, Boomer would consistently and cryptically remark, "My kidneys aren't the problem," or "My kidneys aren't a problem." However, Boomer never once said, "My kidneys are fine."

Lawyer Doug would pounce on these ambiguities during animal communications and cross-examine the Labrador at length. Boomer never wavered and insisted that his kidneys weren't a problem. I'd hang up with Terri, who'd passed along Boomer's comments, questioning both her abilities and the entire nebulous world of animal communications. Maybe I just had rocks in my head to think a human could communicate with a dog.

Okay, to be fair, communications with *any* animal can get garbled. After all, ordering a cheeseburger with mustard from the drive-through results in a statistically probable event of coming home and unwrapping a fish taco. But the Big Dog never backed off his position and I was left to ponder what appeared to be a mysterious riddle.

So there we were at Chatfield, feeling way too melancholy for such a beautiful day. I was thinking a lot about the approaching winter. The first extended bitter cold spell could happen at any time. This would cause the pond to ice over. We always switched to another dog park when the pond froze. I don't trust Denver ice. Every winter I would read about someone and his dog venturing onto ice and getting into trouble. It wasn't going to be us. No, for us, winter meant the end of the Chatfield dog park until the next spring.

We continued to work ourselves around the first pond. The next stretch had a high wall of trees and solid vegetation lining the shore. Only a dog could maneuver through and make it to the water. I'd show Boomer the ball and then arc the throw up and over the row of trees. Neither of us ever saw where it landed. We'd just hear the "plop." Off he'd go, crashing through the underbrush and down into the water. I'd look for holes in the foliage and peek through. Boomer would get in the water and then begin a methodical search for the ball. Swim and search. Clear one area and then move to the next. He'd show up a minute or two later holding the ball in his mouth, dripping, wagging his tail and happy with life. We called this game "mystery throws."

The outing moved on to the second pond and another favorite area. A small peninsula in a marshy area jutted out from a low spot on the pond. This point was as treasured as Beezer's Spot because only one human-animal team could occupy the peninsula at any one time. So we'd watch and time our walk as somebody was leaving this prime location. The peninsula was about fifty feet long and had a three- to four-foot-wide shelf about six inches below the surface of the water. I'd aim my throws to land just off the point of the peninsula. Boomer would sprint down the shelf and dive into the water at the point.

What I really enjoyed was watching him come back, retracing his steps and running down the shelf to return to me. Picture this. Open water on one side, reeds and cattails on the other, spray flying up on all sides. The shallow water of the shelf gave Boomer the appearance of running on the top of the water. I never got tired of looking at his face, and especially his eyes, as he'd run down the shelf directly toward me.

I looked deep into Boomer's eyes as we played this game. He was so present, so in the moment, so joyful. This was as good as it gets. Then I looked at the leaves falling off the trees and wondered if we were spending our last few minutes together at our special place. I wondered if we'd make it to spring 2007. Boomer ran down the shelf, happily dropped the ball at my feet and looked at me quizzically. My face was wet with tears. The Big Dog must have thought I was nuts.

DR. NEELY WAS A VETERINARY SURGEON AND A FOUNDER OF THE VET specialty and emergency hospital in Denver where I occasionally took the dogs. I'd made an appointment with him for December 15 and was now explaining that Boomer had been limping a bit on a hind leg intermittently for several weeks. I had first noticed it while we were at the park and had not given it a second thought at the time. Now I was concerned that we blew an ACL. I wanted to have Boomer seen by a specialist before the holiday season started. The limp was minor, but I didn't want the condition to progress into something that could cause Boomer distress with winter upon us.

Dr. Neely listened to my description, reached over and felt Boomer's leg. Then he silently looked up at me with wide eyes and stared at me for a few seconds. "I think we need to get an X-ray of this," he said. I explained that we hadn't done any blood work since August so perhaps we might get that added to the procedure.

"Let's take this one step at a time and the first thing we want to do is get an X-ray," he said. I said okay and Boomer disappeared with the doctor into the back, leaving me alone with my thoughts in the small examination room.

I sat behind the closed door and thought, this sounds rather odd. Dr. Neely seemed very concerned. I was also surprised at the refusal to take a blood draw. Why on earth could that be a bad idea?

They came back a few minutes later with the X-ray, which Dr. Neely popped into the wall viewer. He took out his pen, pointed to a shadow on the film and explained that Boomer had a tumor on his leg. It was highly likely that the mass was bone cancer, a form called osteosarcoma. Then it was my turn to stare with wide eyes at the doctor. "What are the options?" I asked. Dr. Neely explained that a staff oncologist, Dr. Glawe, would meet with me for a few minutes. I thanked Dr. Neely for his time, took Boomer by the leash and wobbled over to Dr. Glawe's office.

Once inside the office, the doctor expressed how sorry she was for the news. She only had fifteen minutes but wanted to give a quick overview for me to consider over the weekend. I explained Boomer's history, the early stage kidney disease and the family history with Beezer and the other brothers. Then I sat back and listened.

Dr. Glawe said that if I did nothing Boomer might live for up to four months. The tumor would continue to grow, as she knew it was a rapidly growing type, and would cause increasing pain and could metastasize quickly. As the tumor grew, strong and healthy bone in the leg would be eaten up and replaced by weaker tumorous tissue. This deterioration would place the bone at increasing risk of breaking. Such a break was called "pathologic fracture." The four-month window would likely be unchanged if I amputated Boomer's leg, since cancer cells would probably have spread to other areas, but at least the pain issue would be resolved. Furthermore, the risk of pathologic fracture would be eliminated. If I amputated the leg and did chemotherapy, then the life expectancy could be as long as one year. However, the chemo drugs were toxic to Boomer's kidneys, which would rule out that option. Radiation might be an option for pain, but that also would not affect the four-month window. It was a straightforward conversation. Boomer was fine this morning and by lunch time had four months to live.

I paid the bill and Boomer and I got into the car for the drive home. I began to think about Beezer and threw out questions to the universe. What possible lesson had I not learned the first time around that now made a second journey necessary? Why bone cancer? I had used that cancer versus kidney disease analogy over and over when Beezer was sick. Kidney disease was so hard to cope with because of its sneaky and unpredictable behavior. Kidney disease was also relatively painless. Conversely, I would say the biggest pain monster around was the bully known as bone cancer.

Had I unconsciously wished that upon my Boomer? Naturally, my ego was front and center to help out. For God's sake, I yelled as we drove home, you idiot, you don't have the power to give Boomer, or anyone else, bone cancer! But why was I being singled out for yet another tryst with the devil? I drove home in a daze.

Coral, the lady
of the manor.

Sure, I've
got room for
another friend!

New roses,
Beezer's
ashes, one
watchful
manager.

CHAPTER TWENTY-EIGHT

A Dog's Life

THE NEXT TWENTY-FOUR HOURS I WOULDN'T WISH ON ANYONE. I was sitting in the living room shaking my head over the latest development. Another terminal illness…another long, sad journey. Did I have the strength for this? And was I now going to have to expand the book I was writing? I'd thought my story about learning dog lessons was done, but apparently I was only halfway through. I contemplated *this* paradox.

Some critical decisions on Boomer were squarely in front of me. I knew chemo wouldn't be one of them—Boomer's kidneys couldn't handle it. No, the vortex of this dilemma revolved around amputation. Should I or shouldn't I? Boomer had significant arthritis in his hips, as many big dogs do, and I was concerned about his ability to navigate in his world on three legs. I was also concerned about turning my alpha dog into a freak. Would Boomer want that? I pondered whether this apprehension was mine, not his. Could I handle seeing the Big Dog on three legs? I recalled my treatment limits when Beezer was sick. Was I to go through that again? I had left no stone unturned during the course of Beezer's kidney disease treatment. Didn't Boomer deserve the same focused, dedicated game plan? Could I really consider doing less for him? That seemed like a sure-fire recipe for guilt. At this point I wasn't so sure I really had mastered guilt.

And what about my life minus both boys? Could I go through losing another good friend?

After pondering these questions for hours, it began to dawn on me what *was* going on here. I told Boomer we were going to have a talk. It was a quiet Saturday afternoon. No television, no radio. I sat on the hardwood floor stroking the Big Dog. He had chosen the spot where we were going to have the talk—the exact spot where Beezer passed a year ago May.

"Boom, when I first saw you, I knew you were the alpha male in the litter. You let all the other pups know who the boss was. You caught my eye. Our bond grew. We became friends, and you, your brother and I formed bonds of love and caring. I want to thank you for coming into my life. I never had anything as enriching as you two. Your brother taught me to think deeply and spiritually. You taught me to have fun again.

"I believe that our spirits *were* together before I came to earth and that the three of us coming together on earth was something meant to be. It wasn't random. I just want to tell you how much you have meant to me, tell you how lucky I am. You have been my best friend, my confidant, my playing partner, and occasionally, you played very good jokes on me. I know you laugh when you swim in the water because you are so happy.

"I pledge that whatever journey lies in front of us, the final part, I'll continue to act in accordance with the love and respect that we have for each other and that you deserve. This illness will be all about you and I'll do everything I can to respect your wishes. Once your earthly life is over, I'll take the lessons and move forward.

"I'll watch for the sign from you—you tell me, 'I'm not having fun today,' and I will take action. I love you, my magnificent friend, and I look forward to whatever time we have left on this earth. Part of me does look forward to you and your brother being united because I know you'll be waiting for me when it's my turn and it'll be three old friends together again."

AND, WHAT EXACTLY WAS BOOMER FEELING ABOUT ALL THIS? IT WAS time to go back for an assisted talk with my dog. Although Terri usually provided her services by phone, she lived nearby at the time and came over for a visit later that day. She and I had developed a great friendship over the past few years. I think she took particular delight in perhaps the oddest client in her stable, the male hockey player-creditor's attorney. We'd laugh from time to time as I'd remark, "How'd I get in the middle of this?" Our running joke involved the fictional university, Spook U, where the lessons were taught, and the very strange student in the power suit sitting quietly in the back, taking reams of notes.

That day we sat in my living room and had a talk with the Big Dog. He lay between us on the couch, drowsy but attentive.

"There is no turning back now," Terri said. "Now we have to put all the cards on the table because there is no turning back. He has been feeling his body changing and shifting, he says, but he has not really given it much thought because he has been busy living his life being Boomer. He feels like it has crumbled down all at once. He agrees with you that fear and pain are issues."

"My Big Dog? What is *he* afraid of?"

"He does not want to walk on the tile. He is afraid of slipping."

"Would he like it if I could put some runners down?"

"Yes, that would help him."

"How is the pain in his leg?"

"His leg feels, on a scale from 1 to 10 with 10 being excruciating pain, right now he says it is about a 6 and when the new pain medication you're giving him is wearing off it gets up to about a 9.

"When I ask him how long has this been hurting, he says, 'Well, I just do not really think about my body like that. I am just busy being Boomer, hanging out, having fun, doing my thing,' and he says he feels like it had to get to a certain point, a pretty extreme point where he finally said, 'All right already, I am noticing it,' and that is when he started limping and showed you.

"I feel like he is kind of matching you, actually. He is not freaked out. He is disappointed, he is sad, a little worried, but he also knows that whatever is going to happen is going to happen. I also sense that he is worried about leaving you.

"He says, 'It is my job to take care of Doug. I won't be here anymore and it's my job.'"

"He does a great job," I said.

"But I just get a lot of disappointment. He is disappointed and he does not want to go. He is disappointed in his body. He says, 'I have been so happy,' and you know he got through the grief of Beezer being gone and recalibrating and kind of getting to know Doug on a different level. It was the two of you for a while and then welcoming in the new friend and it has all been going really well. It has all been flowing nicely and feeling comfortable. So, if he could, he would say this is really crappy."

"He gets up a lot and changes position," I said. "I am trying to lower the pain medication so he will get a little less sluggish. This kind of stuff just breaks my heart, getting up and taking a few steps, then lying down."

"That is definitely an 'I do not feel good, I do not feel good' sort of movement."

"Yeah, I know what you mean. Is Beezer around?" I asked.

"He says that Beezer has come to take care of him and to talk to him and to soothe him and, yes, he has been coming around and Boomer says that he has actually told him to scram because he does not want Beezer coming in and saying, 'You know, this might not be good news and maybe we need to look at you joining me.' So Boomer says, 'Would you scram? I do not want to think like that yet.'"

"What does he think about amputating the cancerous leg?"

"He says he cannot function without it. Boomer says he does not have the strength in the other leg to move around. He sends me a feeling of despair. 'If I do not have my leg, I may just lie around in despair.' I sense he says this because the rest of him does not feel real hearty. He says his fatigue level is rapidly increasing. 'I am getting more and more depleted.' I interpret that to mean whatever is happening is a combination of things and is happening very fast. He is not sure he could even survive the surgery."

"Oh? Does he then understand that, soon, he is going to be invisible?"

"I do not think he is quite facing it completely yet, Doug. My sense is that he is upset, he is disappointed in his body, and he is just now processing what the heck that means. I do not think that he has quite grasped the full picture of what that means."

"Tell him that his situation seems to be the opposite of Beezer. With Beezer, we had a long, aggressive treatment and Beezer never really experienced any pain. With him, this could be short because we may not have the ability to treat the cancer. The pain in his leg is going to get worse and I won't be able to do anything about it. I want him to be aware of that and that I am going to do everything I can, but it is going to beat me the way Beezer's illness beat me. We are not going to have the kind of time that Beezer had because of the pain and the cancer. We are not going to have that much time and I am not going to let him go through pain."

"Boomer says he is hurting more. He is irritated and not able to lie comfortably. One of his biggest fears is that he does not want to die behind a closed door or without you being there."

"Tell him I won't let the pain get that bad. Tell him I will do everything I can so he transitions here at home, just like Beezer, and in peace. We saw Dr. Christensen this morning and I'm sure she would come over and help if he needed it."

"Boomer says he wants Dr. Christensen by his side when it is time. He says she is very sweet and he trusts her and loves her."

"Good. Is there a reason this journey appears to be so different from Beezer's?" I asked, looking for wisdom.

"'Yes,' Boomer says. 'We have always had fun, like running and swimming, but we have also learned many lessons. You learned how to let go with Beezer. You fought as hard as you could, but you had to surrender when Beezer's body could not receive any more help. No matter how much love, caring and nurturing, you come to a point where you have to let go.' Boomer says this is different because he does not have the courage Beezer had. Boomer has much admiration for Beezer but cannot do a long, drawn-out fight. He would rather go to the universe. Boomer also says he has a lot of pride and doesn't want to hop around on three legs. He shows me feeling pathetic. It's not me, he says. If I can't be Boomer then I need to move on."

"I want Boomer to know that I'm not giving up on him or that I love him less than Beezer."

"He knows. He wants you to know he is not a coward or afraid, but he feels that if this is what is going to happen, then bring it on.

"He also says to take your love and pour it into Coral. He says she has never had a life like this and your love will help her."

"What does he want to do with the time left?"

"He says that he wants to try and not think about what is going on. He does not like thinking about his legs, he does not like thinking about the pain, and he definitely does not want to think about a whole bunch of people coming to say good-bye to him. This is not okay. If people want to come over and play with him and give him kisses, that would be fine."

"Tell him congratulations…his blood test came back today and everything was still normal for kidney disease."

"He *did* tell us that, didn't he?" Terri said. "He told us that was going to be the case. You are something, Boomer, absolutely something! You told us that those kidneys were not an issue and that they are taking care of themselves.

"So, depending on how things unfold over the next few days, I mean if he continues to…if it is just so dramatic then the writing is on the wall of when he is not eating and he barely gets up and moves…he is telling you to have Dr. Christensen come over."

"Is that how he is going to tell me?"

"Yes. That is how it feels. He is just going to surrender to it, is what I get. When it is too hard to move his body around, he is going to be done and he will just lie there."

The day ended on that somber note. I was going through such contradictory emotions. Part of me still wanted to amputate the leg and buy us some more time together. But I also wanted to trust the sessions with Terri where Boomer had said no to the procedure. Certainly both positions were defendable and made sense. I don't think I ever saw a movie where the hero said, "Just go ahead and take off the leg." Quite the contrary.

I had faith in Terri, and her help with the frustrating issues I faced was much appreciated. But on this one issue, amputating Boomer's leg, I still had the human mind that couldn't help questioning. And bottom line was that I would be the one responsible for all decisions on Boomer's behalf.

I approached Christmas with a conviction to move treatment decisions in a manner that honored my dog's wishes. I wondered if there was a way to amputate the leg and still have the "Big Dog" afterwards.

CHAPTER TWENTY-NINE

A Christmas
of Hidden Treasures

DENVER EXPERIENCED A BLIZZARD THE WEEK BEFORE CHRISTMAS and we got about thirty inches of snow, creating significant practical problems for both Boomer and Coral. They'd go out the doggie door only to be greeted by a wall of the white stuff. During the storm, I shoveled out the porch and an adjacent area to give them a relief station. When it continued to snow, I shoveled out a series of interconnected trails and loops throughout the backyard. The trails followed along the fence and around trees and then crisscrossed. The design reminded me of a series of cross-country ski trails. The dogs were able to patrol this Labrador Nordic Center to their heart's content. Coral stayed pretty close to the house but Boomer was smiling as he scampered about. That was the best Christmas present I could have received.

I thought long and hard that Christmas morning about the journey the B Brothers had taken me on over the past two years. In 2004, two days before Christmas, I had shut the drapes, turned off the lights, closed out the world and cried. Two years later, I was looking outside at a postcard straight from the North Pole. In the shining eyes of my best friends I felt such a sense of appreciation at our being together this Christmas morning. Cancer was meaningless today because it had no effect on how we would spend our day. I sat down and began to write.

Dear Boomer,

It's Christmas morning. My gift to myself is to write a letter to you. We are so lucky to have each other today. The winter morning in Colorado is cold, crisp and a trackless expanse of white. Everyone else is busy inside with presents, so we will have the whole neighborhood to ourselves. I like that. I will read this letter to you as we walk.

I'm not going to wish for a Christmas present of cancer remission, a cure or even a miracle. Those would be future events and you know how I try to stay out of there. I've learned that these things are out of my hands, and, in fact, never were in my hands. I'll try my absolute best to give you quality care but will release the outcome. It's not for me to decide or control.

In this way, I can live with balance. I will embrace your illness in order to fight it on my terms, not the disease's terms. I will invite it into my heart and soul. Only there can I defeat its progeny: fear. All outcomes are good when I walk without fear.

I will wish for one special moment each and every day, a moment so seemingly innocuous that only you and I recognize that brief second. A moment where we both look at each other and say, "This is why I love you today; this moment makes today special." You see, my dear friend, I know that I might easily miss these treasures if I'm not looking for each one. The snapshots simply pass too quickly in the movie we call life.

I also wish for a Christmas present of continuing to place your best interests first. It's not about the quantity of life, it's about the quality. You are so much about fun and lightheartedness, my Big Dog. You are about the silly things that make me laugh and enjoy your company. I wish for a few more of those moments and the objective eye to see when they slow down and cease altogether.

I wish for you to have control and participation in the daily events in your life. It's not about me, it's about you. I will speak to you in frank terms about your condition and request your counsel and instruction. I pledge to respect your Christmas wishes as well.

Also on the list is a guilt-free journey. I know this is your wish for me as well. I remind myself that I don't have a crystal ball and there isn't going to be any way to pick the exact 100 percent correct solution to take care of you. What I can do is weigh each option that is available, discuss it with you, and make the best combined election. What matters is that the decision comes from a place of love and compassion. Under these circumstances, the outcome is irrelevant.

Most of all, my dear brother, I wish for a happy day. We are intertwined in each other's lives today and nothing else matters. I am grateful for the gift of today and all the magnificent times we have had and the adventures to come, both here and beyond. You and your brother and now Coral are the best things ever to come into my life and I'm so very, very lucky to have you in my life this day.

Thank you, my best friend, and Merry Christmas!

With much love, your brother, Doug

WHAT A DIFFERENT CHRISTMAS THAT ONE HAD BEEN! I WAS DETERmined we would celebrate with gusto and squeeze out every last drop of the holiday season. Playing Santa, I had gone to a Boomer favorite place—the doggie bakery—and bought him a bag of biscuits, several canine confectioneries and a few good-old-fashioned chewing things. Coral also got some goodies and I got a huge tail wag as my gift from her.

Of course, I still remained sad and a bit melancholy, but I was able to recognize the healthy humanity in these emotions. Being sad and being scared are two distinct emotions. I was sad about Boomer's illness, but the sadness was healthy and an understandably human reaction to the situation. It was an interesting paradox and this discovery was a hidden treasure to me. So I chose to embrace it and work through it. I would include sadness as part of today but remind myself to isolate and ignore fear.

A friend once said to me, "You're always finding paradoxes in things." She couldn't understand why I found a paradox so beguiling and worthy of contemplation. They are everywhere, if you look, and I now looked for them like a curious detective. Finding a paradox is like having a mystery to solve. And if you are open to them, you can find some good paradoxes in the most unlikely places. In Boomer's case, is the situation unspeakably hopeless or is it perhaps an opportunity to grow and evolve in one's personal human experience? That is for the individual to decide.

The first step in this process, which I call paradox resolution, is recognizing the potential for something other than the obvious outcome. We have all been taught and socialized to react to situations in specific ways. I've found that certain societal imprints no longer serve my needs. So I discard them. They aren't necessarily bad, as who am I to judge? They just don't serve my needs.

It's this judgmentally neutral position that allows me to pick and choose specific events, outcomes, and most importantly, decisions, and leave the rest behind. For example, I now avoid the judgment of "right" or "wrong" when analyzing a decision. Sometimes things work, sometimes they don't. Yesterday's decisions are over. Tomorrow's decisions won't arrive for twenty-four hours. Being judgmental about my decision only freezes me in the present.

Equally true is simply allowing myself the freedom to change my mind if the circumstances warrant. How sad that our political leaders are vilified as being "flip-floppers" when prudence dictates a change of course as the ship bottom of life scrapes on the rocks. I'm finding newfound freedom by putting away the cracked crystal ball, which never worked anyway, and am now starting to enjoy the adventure that each new day provides.

I also find that paradox resolution is a key to new purpose in my world. I believe that many problems are based on ego. For example, the human race is destroying the planet due to the vain thinking that we have a right to do so and we believe that our technology is so superior that we will somehow save ourselves later on.

The day that I first realized that Beezer was teaching *me* things was a hidden treasure. Dressing my ego down was the lever that allowed me to follow my curiosity (my desperation?) several years ago and ponder what if everything was unfolding as intended? What if the animals really "got it" even as I walked past the very answers I claimed to be looking for?

Paradoxes are all around us. It's like living inside a puzzle that each person has the option to solve. Failure to recognize these paradoxes means a person is relying on science and control to solve the problems in life rather than on intuition and acceptance. Of course, when relying on science and control proves inadequate, the ego is empowered to higher levels in response. The more fuel the ego gets, the greater the trouble it causes.

I had recently joined another listserv on Yahoo that dealt with canine bone cancer. This group focused exclusively on the disease and was just as helpful to its members as the kidney group. The comments were often very thought provoking. Of course, I was quick to get into the mix with my two cents. I got an e-mail from a woman from this bone cancer group expressing guilt over her dog's death two weeks prior. I asked her to consider whether her guilt derived from her ego urging her to believe that she'd had the ability to control bone cancer. Since she had failed to exercise that inherent control, she must feel guilt. In short, she had concluded that it was her fault her dog died of bone cancer.

Naturally, we had a big laugh about that. Working in reverse, we discussed her feelings about her complete lack of ability to control this fatal disease. Once divested of inherent control, the ego is forced to withdraw, along with its battle lieutenant, guilt.

It follows that a major paradox is misplaced reliance on ego. The critical element is to identify and differentiate those situations where we do have control from those where we don't.

With my dogs' illnesses, it was never really about the body; it was more about the soul. Our journey was never about fatal disease; it was about my growth. Therefore, since the journey was about the soul, then the fatal illnesses were actually positive events. How fortunate I am for not listening to ego chastise me for my alleged underwhelming treatment of Beezer's disease.

From the earliest time when Beezer got sick, I was focused on curing him. Get better doctors, more doctors, more treatment, work harder. I thought, initially, that loss of the body simply meant loss. Conversely, I had an opportunity for Beezer to teach me spiritual growth. I had a choice. I could remain focused on the body, and Beezer's life would be defined by normal dog stuff: walks, cuddles, swims. Looking for the hidden treasure and taking the right fork in the road led me to the possibility that Beezer was sent into my life for more than purely canine adventures. I had an opportunity to learn from an animal—a seemingly illogical, and thus paradoxical, proposition. It was a great leap of faith to recognize the paradox and take the chance of stepping into the unknown.

Another step in paradox resolution is taking the opportunity to explore it. Sometimes the resolution easily reveals itself, sometimes not. I certainly don't understand why human beings behave so abominably to each other. However, I believe that growth and opportunity involves taking a life situation, especially one that seems hopeless, turning it inside out, and seeing what you get. The most hopeless situation was actually the key moment of growth in my life.

I would even go out on a limb and say that paradox recognition is the key to a happy life. Something bad happens and I now look for the paradox. It is the hidden treasure that awaits me. I envision it being like a pair of magic glasses. You put them on and you see things that were invisible moments before. The treasure was always there, you just couldn't see it without the magic glasses.

When Boomer was diagnosed with bone cancer, I was struck by the irony. All the time his brother was sick, I'd comment to myself and others that kidney disease is so much harder than having cancer. If it had been bone cancer, the increasing pain would have made final decisions easier. Again and again I'd compare Beezer's disease to the other beast, cancer. With cancer there is pain. I'd even gone so far as to remark, "Well, it isn't like he has *bone cancer*." And this was a year and a half before Boomer was diagnosed. Paradox? You bet.

WE HAD A VERY DIFFICULT NIGHT ON CHRISTMAS INTO THE MORNING of the 26th. Boomer and I spent most of the night awake. The Big Dog was moaning, constantly getting up and changing position and was just a very unhappy camper. About 3:00 a.m., I got up and gave him some extra pain medication to try and bomb him into sleep. I took my pillow and blanket and curled up in his dog bed with him.

The next morning Boomer ate a little. After finishing his breakfast, his ears went to alert and his head tilted up, and he looked at me quizzically as if to say, "Okay, time for a walk." I told him, "Are you kidding me? You can't go for a walk." He most assuredly told me, "Not only can I go for a walk, but I want to go for a walk." So, we went out and he was his old self, smiling ear to ear.

But two days after Christmas, seeing that Boomer was in increasing pain, I called Colorado State University Veterinary Teaching Hospital in Fort Collins and spoke to an oncologist, Dr. Langova. I told her Boomer had had a really bad week. When she said, "Just bring him on up and we will make time," I liked her immediately. I knew Boomer would get excellent care at CSU. She asked me a lot of questions and spent time listening to my answers. The doctor was thoroughly amused by my elaborately detailed three-ring notebooks containing all the dogs' medical records.

Dr. Langova went through our options. She confirmed that traditional chemotherapy was out because of probable kidney disease. A biopsy was briefly discussed and eliminated. Bone cancer has a high probability of diagnosis from competent examination of X-rays, so a painful biopsy would have added little. Then we discussed amputation, but I said no, largely to honor Boomer's wishes as Terri had conveyed. That left radiation.

Radiation would include four sessions. Boomer would have his first session that very day and a second the next day. The remaining sessions would be done back in Denver with the local oncologist,

Dr. Glawe. Our hope was to relieve the pain and allow Boomer to live out his life as normally as possible.

Dr. Langova also suggested two additional tests. The first was a glomerular filtration test (GFT). This would reveal kidney function on a percentage basis and confirm kidney disease. I knew that the traditional blood tests, while very useful, do not indicate the presence of kidney disease until overall function has dropped below 25 percent. Stated otherwise, a dog could lose 70 percent or a bit more of kidney function and still show "normal" on a blood test. Dr. Langova had hoped that enough kidney function remained to permit the vet school's internal medicine and oncology departments together to develop a modified chemotherapy protocol to treat Boomer's cancer. I agreed to the GFT, as a diagnostic tool.

The second test she suggested was a bone scan. Boomer would be injected with a type of dye, and X-rays would reveal the presence of any bone cancer other than in his hind leg. Once again, a sensible means of assembling useful information in order to make decisions.

Actually, my biggest decision of the day didn't involve Boomer, it was about me. Radiation and testing would begin first thing in the morning. My choices were to either return to Denver that day and turn around very early to go back to Ft. Collins sixty-five miles north, or I could leave him overnight at the vet school and come up later in the day.

It did bother me a bit to leave him overnight. Boomer had never been away from home. A year ago, I would have rebelled at the idea—I had said no emphatically during Beezer's illness. That was the old Doug. I also recognized that the crown jewel for animal care in this region, maybe in the country, was the CSU vet school. There was something the matter with me if I couldn't release enough control to allow these wonderful people to help my dog. So I took it as a step in my growth that I opted to leave Boomer for the night and take care of my obligations at home.

My law practice was busier than it had ever been in the twelve years I'd been practicing on my own. If everything happens for a reason, then Boomer's illness during this peak time in my office must mean something. Perhaps it might have been time for me to let go of some of the treatment practices that I had done exclusively on my own and learn to be comfortable and guilt-free about having qualified, caring people help me. I am the guy who always provides help to others but seldom asks for or allows anyone to help me.

But still, it was strange not having Boomer around that evening. I reminded myself that what I was feeling was that old pain of change and was temporary as I'd be headed back to Ft. Collins the next afternoon. But I spoke to Dr. Langova the following morning and learned the GFT had been scrubbed. The machine had failed just before Boomer's test and we'd have to reschedule. And the doctor decided not to do the bone scan either as she didn't want to introduce dye into the bloodstream when the exact status of the kidneys was unknown. I appreciated this cautious approach. So Boomer had had his first radiation therapy and was now undergoing the second. I could still pick up the Big Dog that afternoon.

I chuckled as I drove back to CSU later in the day. The GFT malfunction was but the latest collision between proof and belief in my life. I had wanted the GFT done to prove the very thing that my heart told me was unnecessary—that Boomer had progressive early stage kidney disease, which would mean no aggressive chemo.

As I drove I felt at peace with what had happened, regardless of the outcome. Focusing on outcome was where guilt comes in. I didn't have any assurance how things were going to turn out, but I was proceeding from love and compassion for my best friend and I was making decisions that were outside of fear and guilt. There was no such thing as an incorrect decision. No matter what happened, I would not feel guilty afterwards.

Boomer seemed to be his chipper self when I arrived at the hospital. The vet student taking care of him shook her head and said,

"He's been flirting with every female student who walks past his cage." Several of them had even purchased a rotisserie chicken for him, preparing a plateful without the bones. I rolled my eyes and looked at the smiling black dog. His tail was wagging like a propeller on an airplane and he had an ear-to-ear smile on his face. "I want to be Boomer for as long as I can be Boomer," he seemed to say.

Later in the week I followed up with Boomer's third radiation treatment in Denver. About then, Dr. Langova called to reschedule the GFT since the machine was fixed. I thought about it and said I'd have to call back. I really *had* the test result already. It was simply stored in my heart, not my brain. I never did reschedule the test. To this day, I'm glad I trusted my feelings and instincts. I'm glad I trusted my dog.

Boomer did a nice job as successor "shop dog."

Boomer, the alpha dog, could spend all day in the water.

Boom and his buddy catching forty winks.

Fiduciary Duty

Fiduciary Duty: The highest legal duty of one person to another. It exists where there is special confidence entrusted in one who is bound to act in good faith and with due regard to the interests of the one giving the confidence. The person owing the duty may not exert pressure or influence on the other, take selfish advantage, or deal with the situation in such a way as to benefit himself or prejudice the other. – Black's Law Dictionary

I HAD BEEN MULLING OVER THE DECISIONS OF THE PAST FEW DAYS. Boomer now had received three of the four necessary radiation treatments, but one glaring problem persisted.

As I continued my Internet research on bone cancer I was becoming increasingly concerned about the possibility of pathologic fracture. The tumor was in an area of Boomer's hind leg roughly equivalent to a human knee. The cancer had started deep within the bone and was destroying the joint from the inside out. The swelling of Boomer's knee illustrated how healthy bone was being destroyed and replaced by tumor-ridden bone. This diseased bone was substantially weaker than healthy bone. Therefore, as the disease progressed, I could anticipate a day when my best friend might get up for a drink and fracture his leg on the walk over to his water bowl.

The pain from such an event would be horrific. I visualized my dog in agony as I frantically tried to get him into the car for an emergency dash to the hospital for the final time, perhaps on a cold concrete floor, new and unfamiliar faces and no chance for any sem-blance of a calm and reflective goodbye. And what if the leg broke when I wasn't home?

I thought long and hard about the fiduciary relationship the B Brothers and I had forged early on and carried forward over all these years. These dogs always placed my needs first. All I ever tried to do, beginning with Beezer, was meet the high standard of care they established. It was a butler door and it swung both ways.

Was I placing Boomer's needs first if I allowed a situation to develop where pathologic fracture could occur? What, if any, were my alternatives? *Who* was I serving by my decision? What if my deci-sion was not to make a decision? The current plan appeared to be that "we will get radiation for the pain and *hope* a pathologic fracture doesn't occur." This sit-back-and-wait plan had to be one of the more ridiculous ideas I had come up with in some time.

The counter argument to the do-nothing doctrine would be to amputate his leg. Although not statistically extending his time, an amputation would alleviate both the pain and risk of pathologic frac-ture. I still had some misgivings about this plan of action. Boomer was an alpha dog and indicated that he disapproved of this measure. Terri had said as much. He also had normal, big-dog degeneration in his hips and a stocky build. I was concerned about doing more harm than good by removing a leg. As usual, no clear options pre-sented themselves. I did, however, see precious sand filtering through the hourglass with each passing moment. I was convinced that something very bad would happen when I ran out of sand.

Boomer had a Fentanyl patch on his leg, which needed to be changed every few days. A strong opiate, the patch was designed to relieve pain and make Boomer comfortable. As 2006 drew to a close, it became clear that bone cancer pain was getting the upper hand. I tried to supplement the patch with pills, but Boomer never really liked being "out of it" from drugs. His whimpering and anxiousness clearly indicated how disaffected the medication caused him to be.

I carried the weight of indecision around like a sack of bricks. How could I possibly look my best friend in the eyes and tell him my "plan" is to hope nothing dreadful happens? My dilemma took me back to my childhood lessons from the rink. "Always protect your teammates," my dad instructed. It wasn't mere advice; it was a crackling indoctrination punctuated by a forefinger jabbed one-two-three to the chest that slowly rocked me backwards. Now, I was standing around watching this disease take advantage of my beloved furry teammate, my line mate in life. Inside my head, I could hear the shriek of gears grinding as wisps of smoke filtered out my ears. "Go get your nose wet," I heard a mystical figure from my past bellow, hands on hips, glaring down at me from the bleachers.

I spoke to Dr. Christensen about my concerns and she gave me a prescription for several days' worth of methadone for Boomer if the pain got severe. It was one of the saddest moments of my life to fill *that* prescription. My plan was to hold the methadone as the very last line of defense. Once Boomer started on it, I would call the doctor and arrange for her to come over, then I'd call Beezer to come and get his brother. There would be no turning back. Some plan.

The next day, Boomer wasn't in agony, not yet, but the pain situation had worsened slightly, I could tell. I grabbed the methadone, stared at it for what seemed like hours, and then walked over to his pet bed for a conference. We were now down to two choices and only two choices. I had a long talk with my best friend that day in early 2007. I knew he would understand me.

"Boomer, I need your help and your support. Thanks for the kisses. I take that as a yes.

"All right, here's what happened today. We changed out your pain patch and I didn't realize it but the new patch took a number of hours to activate. When I took the old patch off, it kind of left you in limbo, so I knew you were in a lot of pain. You didn't want to move, you whimpered, and you wouldn't even eat a hamburger. All signs that the pain in your leg is winning.

"We've got to do something about that. Really. I think what we ought to do is to take that leg off. You need to realize the pain is just going to get worse. I know you don't want that, and I know I don't want that.

"The scariest thing is there is a bad disease in that leg, and it's eating away at the bone. That's why you are hurting. So, I would like your permission, I'd sure like your permission, to take this leg off. We will get rid of the pain and we can get rid of the risk of this bone breaking.

"Here's my problem, Big Dog. You told me you didn't want the leg to come off. You said you didn't want to lie around in despair and if you couldn't be Boomer then it was time to move on. I'm trying so hard to listen to you and honor your wishes. But what if you are wrong? What if you *could* live with hope and confidence on three legs? I don't think being the Big Dog means you need all four legs. I think you are the Big Dog because that is what your heart tells you, not because of what your paws do. No matter what, you are always going to be the dog on duty in this house. I just don't think it's time for you to move on because I believe you can still be Boomer and will always be Boomer. I bet dogs can change their minds, just like people can. Maybe we were both in shock a few days ago and needed some time to think.

"Would you think about that? Thanks for the kisses. Is this a good idea? Are you with me on this? Do you trust me? Huh? Do you trust me? Yeah.

"By making this decision, Boom, we are fighting for a little bit more time together, a little bit more fun time. It's going to be hard. You and I are going to have to work together on this. But I am going to be able to help *you* for a change. Just the way you helped me after Brother left; in the way you have been helping me your whole life. I will help you through this and we'll enjoy whatever time we have left together. I think it's going to make for a more special relationship between you and me because best friends help each other.

"Keep in mind that you've always got my permission, if during the surgery you don't like what's going on, to leave your body if you'd like. I understand, but I just can't take the risk of this leg breaking. And if the situation were reversed, I know you wouldn't let me take that kind of risk because you love me that much.

"You and Beezer helped me through my fear before. Maybe the circle is intended for me to help you through your fear, the fear of losing your leg and being something less than an alpha dog. Maybe a part of our journeys is for all of us to overcome our fear."

I GAVE MY DEAR FRIEND A LONG HUG AND ASKED HIS FORGIVENESS IF I was proceeding against his wishes. I guess I just wasn't ready to say goodbye quite yet. I put the methadone back on the shelf and called Dr. Silver. I'd bring Boomer in on January 4 and we'd take the leg off. No matter what, Boomer and I would end up in less of a jam than we were in today. And I damn sure was going to step in and protect my teammate.

Looking back on those days now, I still don't know whether I honored Boomer or disobeyed a direct order. In spite of all the preparation, soul searching and experience, I remained confused but I think I did the best I could.

CHAPTER THIRTY-ONE

Three-Legged Dog

MY DAD HAD AN ODD WAY OF EVALUATING MY YOUTH HOCKEY games. Wins and losses, important to other parents, were less consequential to Jack Koktavy. My athletic ability was more often a topic of humor. Failing to complete an athletic maneuver would draw a wry smile from the big defenseman. "Don't worry," he'd say, "your job isn't to score pretty goals." No, my dad was most proud of me when I left the ice looking like the last car running in the demolition derby, helmet turned sideways, too exhausted to talk, and some sort of growing lump on my face in need of ice. Jack would put a hand on my shoulder and tell me how proud of me he was. He'd say, "You'll remember days like this later in life when the times get tough."

How many times during my life have I followed a course of action just because it was the direct line I had planned from the outset? Life just isn't that way. It involves zigzags, turnarounds and even mistakes. I might have made a mistake with my earlier plan for Boomer. Then again, perhaps judgment wasn't necessary. Circumstances had changed and yesterday's plan no longer served Boomer's and my interests. But that wasn't a problem today because I was simply making a minor correction and getting back on course. Today, the action that supported me was getting the nasty leg off my pal.

Boomer and I had a very touching moment the night before. I slept out in one of the pet beds so he wouldn't get up and move around. These beds are large so I wasn't uncomfortable, but I was a bit restless. Boomer was wrapped up in a couple of blankets and I could easily reach over and stroke him a bit as we dozed. About 1:30 he woke me up. He started walking around and around and I figured that he wanted me to follow him. He went back to my bedroom and I watched as he stared at the bed and then at me. Back and forth he went, bed, then me, then bed. I guessed that he wanted to sleep in the bed. I lifted him in and he immediately got out. Strike one.

So I stood next to him for a few minutes and he kept up the revolving glances between me and the bed. "I don't know what the heck you want," I told him. Strike two.

I finally got into bed myself. Once I pulled up the covers, Boomer turned around and went back to his pet bed. Then it hit me. My buddy put me to bed! All Boomer wanted was for me to get a good night's sleep. It was almost 2:00 a.m. and I was stunned by the compassion in my buddy. The Big Dog knew I was exhausted and that tomorrow would be a long day. So, he put me in bed. I was very touched by him taking care of me even when he was in so much pain.

NEXT MORNING, I HAD ONE MORE QUICK HEART-TO-HEART TALK WITH him before we left for Boulder. I sat down with him and looked into his eyes.

"Buddy, I think you can and will be the Big Dog tomorrow and in the days ahead. You have never had a day of despair in your life and I promise you won't start now. And you know what? I think you have some good days ahead of you, Mister. You've proven that. Even though your body is sick…your spirit is strong."

Boomer had given me several additional face washes after that, as if to punctuate his approval of the new plan. I thought about the decision as we drove. Life and death choices in the palm of my hand involving a living entity that I loved deeply—to use the word difficult is an understatement.

I thought about the *process* of arriving at these monumental decisions and realized how little judgment of the result mattered. To layer judgment onto the decision is to Monday-morning quarter-back. It would be easy to look back from some point down the road and judge the results of today's decisions. However, that perspective was irrelevant to the process of making a decision today. I just didn't have a crystal ball.

What if I could remove all judgment from the process? It actually was easier than I thought. Without the surgery, Boomer was down to hours of life. Today or tomorrow would be it, after being drugged up on methadone. Alternatively, with surgery, I was giving Boomer a chance at some additional quality of life without the hideous pain wracking his body. Boomer didn't think he could remain the vital alpha dog. Perhaps animals fear unknowns just as people do. Perhaps this was an opportunity for an animal that had every physical gift during his life to overcome a new physical limitation? I don't know these to be facts, but they raise endless possibilities when I ask myself *what if?*

There weren't any guarantees, but there was a chance of something good happening. To me, this decision was one of promoting health and life. Therefore, I thought, there isn't a right or wrong decision looming—a results-driven decision. There is only a decision that I can live with later on—a process-driven decision. I also realized a process-driven decision would insulate me from heebie-jeebies of guilt later on if things didn't work out.

I gave this concept a bit more thought and realized how these distinctly different analyses needed to be recognized and appreciated. Perhaps early in a treatment plan Boomer and I might be better served by considering a results-driven decision. Which option, of several presented, provided the best chance of a quality life moving forward? Of course, finances, time commitment and the myriad of other intangibles would factor into a results-driven decision. Opinions from friends, family and medical providers might factor into a results-driven decision. But we were beyond that now. It occurred to me that my overall treatment plan, from this day forward, would acknowledge the differences between these two ways of resolving conflict within me.

I also filed away the concept of process-driven decisions for a potentially difficult day down the road. The result of such decisions would become irrelevant as long as I could focus on the process. Having this concept at the ready might serve me very well both today and when circumstances changed and seemed to paint me into a corner.

AT THE TOP OF THE FINAL HILL ON THE ROAD TO BOULDER IS A SCENIC spot overlooking the entire valley. As I crested the hill and saw the city below me, a powerful rush of love came into my heart. I began to cry, for reasons I could not fathom. But I believe Beezer had brought on the feeling, showing up to keep an eye on me, and, more importantly, to keep an eye on his brother. It felt so good to feel his presence.

Arriving at the vet's, I set up my mobile law practice once again, this time in Dr. Silver's office. He continued to be incredibly accommodating to my needs. I felt like I'd gotten a promotion, as I could sit and use a desk as opposed to sitting in the dog run leaning on my briefcase. I connected my laptop to the Internet and logged back into my practice.

Spotting a large dry-erase board in the exam room, I wrote: DNR—IT'S STILL A GOOD DAY IF BOOMER JOINS BEEZER. I then helped lift up Boomer to the prep table where he would be shaved and readied for surgery. Rob briefed me on the procedure and invited me to gown up and observe. I was happy to be invited, but respectfully declined. I was able to peek in a window from time to time and check on progress. Giving Boomer one more hug, I told him how much I loved him and retired back to the office.

My day's work agenda was formidable. The large legal case I had been working on involved several hundred financial institutions and numerous attorneys. The last month had seen marathon conference calls between everyone to the extent and degree I had never seen before in my twenty-three years of practicing law. A morning conference call was scheduled that was expected to take three-plus hours. It was technical in nature and involved highest levels of management from the client perspective. The only mistake I made that day was forgetting about the office clock.

Dr. Silver has a cuckoo clock, except the cuckoo is a dog. Every hour, on the hour, this dog would announce the time in a series of loud throaty woofs. The conference call started about 9:30 a.m. and I was all set up with note pads and my discussion points. We were well into things as the clock moved forward, 9:57... 9:58 ... 9:59. I levitated straight up out of my chair as the dog proudly began to alert everyone listening that it was now 10:00 a.m. In yet another admission of technology gone past me, I began frantically pushing buttons on my cell phone looking for the mute button. I think I hit speaker first, "WOOF, WOOF, WOOF," as I could sense a general disquietude in the conference call participants. I quickly hung up and let 10:00 a.m. formally arrive, then dialed back into the call. I was very careful to be on a break at 10:58 a.m.

Meanwhile, things were proceeding in a decidedly more organized manner in the operating theater. I'd poke my head in from time to time and get progress reports. All was going as anticipated. Rob took a sample from the diseased leg and sent it to CSU for analysis. It *was* confirmed to be bone cancer. After the leg was removed, Boomer was returned to our now familiar dog run.

Late in the day, Rob and I loaded Boomer, still on his stretcher, into my car and transported him to a twenty-four-hour facility several miles away. This way, Boomer would have vet techs and a doctor caring for him round the clock. Rob invited me in as he spent a good thirty minutes discussing Boomer's case with the staff and going over instructions. Boomer was the second dog in the facility, which was staffed by three vet techs and a doctor. I very much liked those ratios. They invited me to spend the night in the facility with Boomer. I thanked everyone and then did something unheard of when Beezer was sick. I said no.

I didn't need to stay; I had a new agenda. I was convinced that part of the lessons of this journey involved me trusting others, asking for help, receiving help, and just letting go. Coral was at home and needed me and I needed to ready the house for Boomer's return as a three-legged dog. Sleeping in my own bed also might be a good idea, and Boomer had people literally watching his every move. Rob assured me that he would pick up Boomer first thing in the morning and transport him back to his clinic. I could then come up for the day and we'd evaluate Boomer's progress.

I ARRIVED AT ROB'S THE NEXT MORNING AND SET UP SHOP IN THE DOG run. Boomer was in and out of sleep and whimpering a bit. The gentle whining instantly subsided as I sat down and began to stroke his head and talk with him. With me nearby, he drifted back to sleep. Occasionally I would glance over at my gauze-wrapped, now three-legged buddy and send a silent prayer that he'd be okay. I didn't care that he was missing a leg and I hoped he didn't either.

He spent one more night in the aftercare facility before coming home. We drove back to Denver in a blinding snowstorm where the roads were littered with wrecks. The highway system literally closed behind me as we slowly made our way home.

Dave and Boomer haggle over yet another doughnut.

Boomer remained full of life even after his surgery.

Lunch break during work became special time in the front yard.

CHAPTER THIRTY-TWO

The Hang with Boomer Club

W E DIDN'T MAKE IT BACK UNTIL AFTER 8:00 THAT EVENING. IN the car Boomer had been smiling and his eyes held their old sparkle. As soon as I got him home we went into the kitchen for a long drink of water. I devised a sling to slide under him to help him move about. It was cumbersome and we had to work together, but we managed. He was still groggy from the drugs in his system, which challenged his brave three-legged efforts. We then went outside and he took a very lengthy tinkle and we walked through the Nordic Center for the remainder of bodily function activities. The going really wasn't that difficult with a bit of teamwork.

Although Carolina and I were divorced, we had remained friends and she always enjoyed visiting the dogs on occasion. Both Beezer and Boomer had cared deeply for her. She had two mischievous dogs of her own and loved dogs as much as I did. So I was pleased to discover that while I was in Boulder she had outfitted the house for Boomer. She came over and set down a trail of non-slip runners on the hardwood floors and an old carpet on the kitchen floor. Boomer now had a series of paths with steady rubber backing for traction. He would seldom venture off these tracks as he moved about the house. I was grateful for the idea and the help.

In keeping with my new resolve, I then called a couple of the neighbors who I thought might want some part-time work as pet sitters and also arranged to have one of the vet techs come over every day. Even Coral offered her version of support, amounting to some extra tail wagging.

Then I looked at my work schedule for the following week—full of court appearances and meetings that required my personal attention. Since offers from other neighbors and friends were coming in, I decided to take everyone's help. I had finally made peace with the fact that I didn't have to do every single thing myself. Other people were offering, they cared, and I needed to let them help. I created a three-column sheet where each column had a designation "morning," "afternoon" or "evening." The horizontal rows were then labeled with days of the week. The time slots where I had a meeting or other commitment were given asterisks to indicate importance. The top of the page read:

HANG WITH BOOMER CLUB!

Not surprisingly, everyone I called was eager to help and sign up for a block or two. Before long, my entire week was covered and the Hang with Boomer Club was full.

THREE DAYS AFTER SURGERY, I WAS SPENT. BOOMER HAD BEEN UP ALL night. A little bit of whimpering, a lot of panting. I could not tell if it was pain or anxiety, so I just lay in his pet bed with him all night. It is sleepless nights like that that test your fear factor, and your resolve about not having guilt goes right out the window. You start wondering at 3:00 or 4:00 in the morning if you made the right decision. Of course, there are no do-overs. So, I kept telling myself that it was just one day, one night. No matter what, I'd made the best decisions with the information I had available. But I was so very tired.

At about 9:00 that morning, surprise! Boomer got up and followed me into the kitchen. I was beyond belief happy and lavished praise on him. Ten small doggie steps, one giant leap for Labrador retrievers.

When Carolina came over again, she took one look at me and flashed her disapproval. I had set up a lawn chair and was sitting right next to Boomer, who was lying in his dog bed.

We stared at each other.

"What the heck are you doing?" Carolina said. "How would you like it if you were sick and somebody was standing over your bed staring at you?"

She said that I was nurturing Boomer to death and actually creating a negative situation. She asked me to go downstairs while she had a talk with Boomer. I think it was kind of a tough love talk—for both of us. Anyway, when I came back, Carolina had removed the lawn chair. I think she made a good point. She said that Boomer was confused because he had no idea why I was sitting and staring at him and what he was supposed to do in response. So, my actions probably made him anxious and the best thing I could do was try and get back into a normal routine. They were wise words. It was time to let Boomer be a dog and work some stuff out on his own.

Later my neighbor Pat came over. Sometimes changing the people changes the dynamic and the energy of the situation. I had been trying to get Boomer to take water all day without success and, when Pat offered him water, he took a lengthy drink out of his bowl. I also had Pat feed him some food that he had refused from me as well. Perhaps he was frustrated, maybe a little bit angry, about his situation. Maybe he was a bit had-it-with-me and wanted to send me a message to back off. And like any of us, we take things out on the ones closest to us. When Pat came over, maybe it was a time for more manners. I don't know, but it was nice to have some people in the house. It not only changed Boomer's energy, it changed mine.

The moderator of the bone cancer group had given me her number, and I called her. Ana, an M.D. , was most gracious with her time and very helpful. She said it is very normal for a dog to be depressed, no doubt like a person in the same situation. Boomer was certainly working through all the physical issues and getting the anesthesia out of his system. She also said it is typical for a dog not to have a tremendous appetite at this time. I appreciated the confirmation.

Sunday night saw some more nice surprises. Boomer followed me to bed and I let him decide where to sleep. He looked at his dog bed and then mine, back and forth, mulling it over. He finally decided on my bed and I lifted him up. To my great surprise, he moved from the foot of the bed up to the top and plopped down with his head on the pillow. He had taken Beezer's spot. A strong effort from a guy who really didn't cuddle too much. I was very proud of the Big Dog.

I woke up around 3:00 a.m. and looked around. Boomer was no longer in bed. I looked further and was astonished for a second time that night. Boomer was now curled up in bed with Coral. This had never happened before either.

Coral had been struggling the past few days. Her routine had been so disrupted that she had refused to eat lately and had generally been nowhere to be found. I could tell this ultra sensitive little soul's world was upside down. Perhaps Boomer was reassuring both of us that everything was back to normal and the Big Dog was on duty. I decided to take the lesson to heart and declare a moratorium on craziness.

But when I awoke that morning Coral was asleep in her bed alone. Now where was he? I walked out to the living room and found Boomer curled up in his own bed. He had taken care of both Coral and me last night and then retired for some uninterrupted snoozing.

Later that day I again talked to Terri. I wanted her to convey to Boomer some messages from me, as only she was able. I thought that maybe one of the best things I could do was keep reassuring him that nothing had changed, that he remained the Big Dog.

"Is he glad to still be here?" I asked her.

"He is definitely glad to be here," she said. "But he is really tired. He wants to just be Boomer and bounce around and also now deal with the fact that he has three legs, but his body is really tired out. I am reminding him that surgery is a big deal. Medications in your system are a big deal and having your body fighting cancer is a big deal. Will you be doing any chemo or radiation treatments?"

"I don't think so. I may do very little else. What we did with the leg wasn't the final resolution to this problem. It was more like we got pushed into a corner. We had to do this. I am going to be sensitive not to go beat him up with chemo and I'll get some opinions and I'll talk to him," I said.

"He is really glad that you are taking some breathing room," Terri added. "You are having a chance to come down from all of this, which neither of you has had since the day you were told the news about the bone cancer. He is really glad that you are not feeling like we have to do something more and he is really glad that you are remaining relaxed about this."

"Me too."

WATCHING BOOMER HOBBLE AROUND, SEEING HIM DIMINISHED, WAS tough. His efforts reminded me of something that I hadn't thought about in a long time. In 1975, my dad had suffered a stroke and as part of the stroke, his voice center was scrambled and he had to learn to talk all over again. I remember watching him read from a little grade school reader—See Spot Run. Run Spot Run—and how shockingly painful that was for me to watch. Shock, pain and fear had been my first reactions back then. Later I also felt embarrassed for him. Why do the negative emotions come forward first? Did I have any ability to empower a more constructive outlook? Perhaps an alternative meaning that might better serve my needs?

I certainly respected my dad for doing the hard work and rehabilitation and was as proud of him battling through his picture book as he was of me on the ice. Dad had been knocked on his keester, but had gotten back on his feet. Boomer was working his butt off to learn how to walk again and get that independence back that was taken from him four days earlier. Rather than be horrified by it, or do what I normally do, which is rush to help, I saw that I had to let him skin his proverbial knee as he learned for himself how to deal with his new situation. I needed to trust Boomer more to work through his challenges on his own. And I needed to dress down my ego a bit. People and animals can solve their own problems and, sometimes, I can have my problems solved with a little help from trusted friends. Sometimes, the best action is the inaction of stepping back and letting things unfold. I thought how much I appreciated those friends—Terri, Pat, my other neighbors, Carolina and all the good people at the vet's.

I WAS SITTING AT THE DINING ROOM TABLE SEVERAL DAYS LATER, WRITING on my laptop. The high temperature was eleven degrees, with light snow. Boomer had cabin fever, but the conditions were so bad outside that I had elected an inside day. The Big Dog had curled up at my feet as I worked. It was a new position for him. He had been cuddlier of late and I was happy to reach down and pet him from time to time. Perhaps he was taking a page out of Beezer's book. Boomer wanted to be near me. What a gift. His body was compromised, but his only thought was to stay next to me. With that, my vision blurred a bit.

I wasn't upset. Quite the contrary, I was moved. Boomer's pure devotion and my belated recognition of how much I was able to see and feel when I slowed down and stayed in the moment had moved me. I felt gratitude. I wanted to write about Boomer snoozing at my feet to etch this memory into my mind forever. It wasn't about cancer. It never was. It was about my best friend wanting to savor every minute of earthly life with me. It was about our special bond. It was about the preciousness of being together today.

I stopped typing, closed my eyes and reached down. My hand found my buddy and received one long, enduring lick. *I can't see you, but I feel your presence.* I was grateful for this moment and, as the days passed, found more of these nuggets right under my nose. Now I looked for them with a peculiar tenacity. The old Doug used to walk blindly through life, missing the nuggets because I was busy. I never even saw them. Now I slow down, look and listen. The treasure is everywhere.

CHAPTER THIRTY-THREE

To Fear Is to Fuel

A FEW DAYS LATER, THE WEATHER HAD IMPROVED BUT THE ROADS were snow packed and congested. Driving to an appointment, I got stuck in traffic on a six-lane highway, literally bumper to bumper. Sitting there, my ears perked up. The man in the car to my right was agitated. He was honking his horn, pounding the steering wheel and mouthing what appeared to be an impossibly long sentence punctuated by a series of single syllable words. Mildly intrigued, I looked around for the object of his outburst. Finding none, I then gazed left. The woman in that car appeared to be singing a song. Not rocking out, mind you, but some slow inspirational song. She appeared relaxed and at ease with her surroundings. Not the slightest hint of stress or discomfort. I chuckled at the dichotomy as traffic eased and began to move, and filed the incident away in my subconscious.

Later that evening the experience popped back into my conscious thought and I began to think about it objectively. Both drivers had the exact same incoming message: the highway is at a standstill. Both drivers processed this same message and came to exact opposite interpretations as to the meaning. The male driver concluded it meant anger, frustration and, perhaps, *this is not fair*. Conversely, the female driver interpreted the message as an opportunity to relax, an oasis and, perhaps, peacefulness. Now I stopped what I was doing to consider this example on a deeper level. What *had* I witnessed?

My next thought made me smile. What if the message—stalled traffic—had no meaning at all? It was simply that cars were stopped.

If there was a meaning, it was supplied by the participant. Now the pieces fit.

Both the man and the woman possessed the power to attach whatever significance they wanted to the message, and both were equally clear. A hypothesis began to form in my mind. *Messages mean nothing until the participant attaches a meaning.* This type of analysis was my forte; I enjoyed these types of puzzles.

I broke the process down from there. Many times in the past I would interpret a message and meaning as one unified step. "You made me mad" is one example. What if the assembly of incoming data was really a two-step process? In other words, the incoming message is step one. The message is neutral on the surface and has no meaning. Step two is my subjective attachment of meaning to the message.

"You made me mad" then becomes step one: "You spoke unkind words," and step two becomes "I then decided to become angry." I then took the example and altered it: "You spoke unkind words" and step two, *"I couldn't care less."* Under the second example, I attached no significance to the incoming message. The message arrived in a neutral state and passed through into the cosmos in the same irrelevant fashion. I immediately saw opportunity. Could this concept be applied to my journey with Boomer?

The Yahoo kidney and bone cancer groups were filled with people in fear. Battling monsters, despairing the cruelty of disease and losing fur-kids were everyday topics. Certainly I had been the poster boy for fear during the early days with Beezer. Could I change the message of fatal disease? What if the sense of victimization resulting from fatal disease was nothing more than a way of interpreting the incoming message? The exciting concept involved potentially applying a two-step process to the same incoming message of cancer and kidney disease.

I'd assume fatal disease, like any other message, was neutral on its surface and meant nothing. This took a bit of faith, but it was my experiment. The more I thought, the more the statement rang true.

After all, if you breathe, you will die. It's our contract at birth. All of us understand that and live our lives with that agreement. Few people are thrown into chaos by this contract. This was step one.

Next was to decide what fatal disease reasonably meant. This would be step two. I use the word "reasonably" because I couldn't fairly equate cancer with winning the lottery. Therefore, the experiment had to contain a degree of self-truth or intellectual honesty. It seemed clear that fatal disease couldn't simply mean death. I'd resolved that issue in step one. The fatal disease had to bring something else to the table besides death.

The obvious notion involved "immediacy." I understood Boomer would die one day. I just didn't want it to be this soon. I thought back to the early days with Beezer. I had been terrified about the immediacy of his death. Kidney disease had meant unavoidable death, a one-step process. The result was the same even with a two-step process. The message was neutral, but I attached a meaning of immediate death. Same result.

The key, it seemed, would be to process the message in such a manner as to attach a meaning other than immediacy of death. Could I do that and remain honest?

I decided to identify the *goal* of the disease. Perhaps I could launch a counteroffensive if I knew what the objective was. Clearly, the objective wasn't the death of my dog. It was the death of today. The goal had a sinister aspect as well. The disease couldn't destroy today *on its own*. To be successful, the disease had to convince *me* to destroy today myself. On a deeper level, the goal of the disease was to brainwash me to voluntarily relinquish today. I'd take a precious day, all the more valuable by the tangible evidence of death courtesy of the disease, and simply forfeit it! Just hand it over and give it away. In effect, I'd be saying, "Here is today. I don't want it. What I do want is to give it away and waste it because my dog is dying."

I started to get angry when I realized the disease was a simple con artist out to embezzle today from me. I was angry at the crook, but even angrier at myself because of my voluntary participation in the scheme—a victim's role I'd executed with lemming-like precision when Beezer first got sick. I took a deep breath, quickly released my anger and returned to the process. I now clearly understood the message. Fatal diseases wanted me to destroy today with Boomer. I now had the power to ascribe whatever meaning I wanted to this message. This power, and thus the meaning, was mine and mine alone. The diseases couldn't alter my interpretation. I realized I now had the power to fight back.

I also finally saw that my fear of the disease was the very fuel that was used against me when Beezer had been sick. Devilishly clever, my enemy was not kidney disease, but me! I was the power source used to generate the negative energy destroying my own being and wasting a special day—many special days—with my beloved dog.

This paradox was glaring. I had thought the growing presence of Beezer's kidney disease was causing my mounting fear. In fact, just the opposite was true. My daily increasing fear was causing kidney disease to grow and become more powerful.

My objective now would be to focus on today to the exclusion of all else. I did have one problem. What would I do with cancer and kidney disease? Boomer's kidney disease had never been either confirmed or ruled out, so in my mind it was also a present bully. I couldn't pretend cancer and kidney disease didn't exist. They did. What about engaging in a daily battle, some sort of epic struggle invoking forces of light and dark? Or on a simpler level, two sworn enemies stuck together in a broken elevator. It seemed exhausting and counterproductive to my strategy of focusing on today with Boomer. Fighting even one minute with cancer was one minute less that I could spend with him. I thought long and hard. I reminded myself that I had the ability to attach whatever meaning I wanted to the message. My journey had taken me to another fork in the road.

The left fork was the traditional route. Cancer and kidney disease were murderous monsters. Engaging these beasts would unleash a barbaric fury in me. I would meet them and fight them on their terms. No surrender, no truce, no peace. It would be a fight to the last man, with the odds in favor of the monster. The imagery reminded me of playoff hockey games from my earlier days.

The right fork was decidedly unconventional and opposite. I would recognize these monsters as the simple con men they were. Embezzlers of life. Nothing more. They had no power, absent my fear. The famous line from the *Wizard of Oz* comes to mind: "Pay no attention to the man behind the curtain." If I could overcome my fear, then I could use that new power against the monsters. To overcome my fear, I had to face it and hold it close. I couldn't do it from afar.

My decision was part logic and part trust. Logically, a terrific amount of energy is expended in a fight. I knew, from my battle with Beezer's illness, that the diseases could simply bide their time and wear me out. In the meantime, I'd be squandering precious time that would never be recouped. Similarly, monsters are scary and difficult to beat. They live in the dark corners of closets and under beds, so they are hard to get at. I saw nothing beneficial in classifying the incoming message as monster generated.

Shannon Parish

Just as with the Beez, I knew that everything happened for a reason. I certainly already knew how to fight. Maybe Boomer's illness was happening *right now for a reason*. I was intrigued by a voyage where the destination was uncertain. The right fork would once again cause my dog to be my teacher. I'd have to trust in his wisdom that something extraordinary might happen. Just as with his brother.

The diseases were already part of our lives. I accepted that. So I made a decision. I invited cancer and kidney disease to stay. But our home was our sanctuary and that would not change. There would be no fight at home. There would be no fear at home.

We would empower doctors and treatment protocols to do any battles. However, the medical steps we would take would not be guilt-based but done to promote life and good health. It was critical to Boomer and my plan that our home and "today" be ours and ours alone. We would take whatever steps necessary to safeguard this territory. Our home was sacrosanct.

Next I had to devise a method to overcome my fear. I'd learned much from Beezer, but my lessons had lacked clarity and focus. I devised a game. It would have a winner and loser, every single day. I called it "The Daily Point." There were two teams. The first was Team Labrador, comprised of Boomer, Coral and me. The other was Team Fear, comprised of cancer and kidney disease. Each day, one point would be up for grabs and that point had to be awarded to one team or the other. There would be no ties and we would never go into overtime. Each day, Boomer and I would awake and look at each other. Our eyes would meet and speak to each other. "Let's make sure we win today's point." Boomer, the all-about-fun dog, was gung ho.

Nothing else mattered but winning the point. Even on the bad days, we'd stubbornly refuse to give in to fear for the simple reason that we didn't want to lose today's point. We became obsessed with enjoying today and never looking further than how to win. We were in our element.

CHAPTER THIRTY-FOUR

Dealing with the Monsters

THE GAME TOOK ON A LIFE OF ITS OWN. SOMETIMES BOOMER WOULD take the lead. One Saturday, he nudged up to me while I worked on my laptop, inching closer and closer until his head lay on my thigh. Then the whimpering began. I'd seen this a million times before. The winter spell in Denver had lifted into a bright, mid-50s day. Boomer knew it was not a regular workday. I looked at him and his ears went to alert.

"Are you sure?" I inquired. A quick bark in response.

"Why...don't....we...go...for…a…?" and never finished the sentence. It was like a bell went off in a firehouse. Peter Rabbit was hopping around the house on three legs. We went for that walk, with every bit of gusto and glee that a man and his beloved dog could muster. That day's point was awarded to Team Lab.

Sometime later, Boomer spied several dog friends in the neighbor's back yard. Before I could open the people door, he had scooted out the doggie door. One point was awarded. Last week, Boomer had started an altercation with the husky dog next door. Fortunately, a chain link fence separated them, but the Lab was his old rambunctious self. I chuckled at his snarl, raised hairline and aggressive stance, all the while balanced precariously on three legs in deep snow. One point. Another day, my coworkers and I were deeply involved in a project when we were interrupted by a series of deep "woofs" from upstairs. I went up to investigate and looking out the window saw a loose yellow Lab making his way down the street. I went out and gathered in the wayward dog. Later on, a frantic human scurried past obviously looking for a lost pet. When I handed over the Lab, she tried to thank me, but I'd have none of it. "You need to thank Boomer," I said. "He's the DOD—the Dog on Duty." Another point.

The pre-amputation Boomer had taken great delight in lying in the yard right outside a window well and watching events transpire in the basement office. He would sit like that for hours, motionless as a zombie. One day, I was standing at my desk talking on the telephone when my gaze passed over to the window. At eye level I noticed a black dog lying on the ground with his muzzle resting on the window well staring at me. Not missing a beat on the call, I smiled at the animal and held up one finger.

We'd have a combined effort to have fun whenever we could. I would make time every day to lie down with him. I created games where he wouldn't have to move around too much. My goal was for both of us to get immersed in the moment so we'd forget about his mobility issues.

One day, he dragged out his old tennis ball. I sighed, thinking about how he couldn't run and fetch like he used to. But he sat down in front of me and had that ball in his mouth and was ever so slowly biting down on it and then easing up, staring at me with that glimmer in his eyes. He was taunting me with the ball! He then dropped the ball between his front paws and looked at me as if to dare me to get it. I slowly extended my hand and marched my fore and middle fingers toward the tennis ball.

As I got closer, he swatted my hand, using his paw like a flyswatter. I retreated and began again. Same result. I started to laugh and saw Boomer doing the same. Every now and then I'd get the tennis ball. Payback is tough, so I'd slowly wave the tennis ball back and forth from my position. I then slowly rolled it toward him. To my great surprise, he lifted the front paw closest to the ball and flicked it back toward me. Three-legged indoor soccer! Boomer had a smug look. Finally, as I marched my hand toward him, he swatted it and gleefully licked my face. I rolled over in laughter as Boomer lay on my chest and pinned me. My legs could feel the rapid wagging of his tail. My arms held my loving friend, my brother, close as he finished off with a solid face washing.

We'd even found enjoyment in plans that didn't quite work out right. Often we'd go for a short walk. I'd use a sling that resembled a soft carrier for firewood. Placing the sling under the rear portion of Boomer's torso, I lifted up on the handles. That helped compensate for the lack of a rear leg. But steering was now problematic. A normal out and back walk, comprised of two straight lines, was replaced by a zigzag course through open space. I pictured the rear driver on a hook and ladder fire truck, steering the vehicle. Just one problem, though—no front end driver.

The hard part wasn't getting the daily point. The hard part was recognizing how easy the point was to obtain. I'd like to take credit for this pearl of wisdom, but the continuing lesson of presence and staying in the moment is brought to you by the B Brothers, my furry teachers of life.

Our first thought every morning now was, "How can we win today's point?" Bad news from the vet? Let's make sure we do something to win today's point. Did Boomer have a bad day? We might have a long talk, or a car ride, or perhaps a snuggle together. We'd laugh at that one. Who knew snuggles with a couple of the fellas could qualify for a point?

———

BUT WHAT TO DO WITH TEAM FEAR? SINCE I'D RESOLVED THAT KIDNEY disease and cancer could stay, I needed to do something with them. I certainly couldn't ignore them. These two were troublemakers. Left to their own devices they would surely present no end of problems. I'd already decided I wasn't going to empower Team Fear by fighting them at home. Still, I had to take the lead. Don't ignore them, don't fight with them. What was left?

I had no clue how to deal with fatal disease, but I had a great many ideas on how to deal with bullies, malcontents and assorted ne'r-do-wells. Either play ball my way or have a seat on the bench. Easy stuff that anybody can understand. Even Team Fear. The actual election between these two choices was easy. I knew Team Fear had no interest or intention in playing ball my way. That left one option—embarrass the bullies and *make* them play according to my rules.

When a neighbor held a yard sale, I dropped in. I walked around trikes, bikes and even a few tykes. Then I saw what I was looking for. Small, multicolored kiddy chairs. I briefly tested one. My fanny was less than a foot above the ground, knees pointing straight up, diaphragm compressed. Perfect! I told my neighbor Carla my plan (she had a yellow Lab herself) and she happily dispatched me with the chairs.

Boomer gave me a quizzical look as I walked in with the kiddy chairs and walked around the house, looking for the perfect spot for them. Then I got busy with a sheet of paper and a marker. That task completed, I walked over to the chairs and taped the signs to the seat backs, then summoned both cancer and kidney disease to come forward and face me. This was easy. Starting with Beezer's illness, the diseases had been hanging around like bad BO. I never had to look too far to find them. Once I felt their presence, I began to speak to the diseases:

"You have chosen to interject yourselves into our lives. You weren't invited. We didn't have it coming. We can't make you leave. You two continually try to bait us into a fight. You want to fight because you both are bullies. You aren't interested in a fair fight. You will cheat, lie, deceive and take any action whatsoever to break our spirit. You will scare us with setbacks only to raise our expectations with periods of blue sky. You will go back and forth and, each time, claim a bit more of our free will and zest for life.

"You will trick us into focusing on the fight because that is where you live and thrive—in the fight. You are nothing more than bloodsuckers on my emotional veins. I know this now.

"When I focus on cancer and kidney disease, I lose focus on Boomer and life. The fight causes me to live in the future and ignore today. You win when I focus on you. Those days are done. I'm done being afraid of you. I'm done worrying about you popping out of the shadows or lurking around the corner. This is Boomer's and my house, not yours.

"Like any guest, there will be rules of the house. You are uninvited guests, so these rules will be followed to the letter. You have no power to contravene the rules.

"Rule #1 is that you will, from this moment forward, be confined to your special chairs. I hope you feel honored because I bought them especially for you. You are free to be as scary as possible, but remember—you cannot leave your chairs. Yes, I understand that monsters don't sit on kiddy chairs. We all have to do our best.

Shannon Parish

"Rule #2 is that you can never, ever speak directly to Boomer or me. You may only speak when spoken to. Being a gracious host, even to uninvited guests, I give you permission to hold up signs whenever you want. "Can we scare you today?" is a fine example of permissible signage.

"Rule #3 is that both of you will wear big pink, fluffy slippers when in your chairs. Yes, I realize your concerns about lack of dignity, but that is your problem, not mine.

"Three rules. That's it. Yes, yes, yes, I understand that these rules are unacceptable to you. But we have been forced to coexist and Boomer and I welcome you both to stay, but you will follow these rules. You play your games; I'll play mine."

⌒

I FINISHED MY REMARKS TO A WONDERFUL SOUND—SILENCE. BOOMER hopped over to me with a big smile on his face. My heart felt Boomer's approval, and, down deep, the approval of something or someone I couldn't quite comprehend. I turned and walked away as Boomer looked at the chairs and paper attachments. The paper read:

TEAM FEAR—PERMANENT TIME-OUT AREA

That night, Boomer and I were both feeling a bit smug that the marauders finally had been dealt with. And, instead of having my stomach in knots, I was relaxed and focused on my connection to Boomer.

The next day's fun outing was more than enough to gather the day's point. About a year or two earlier, Boomer had gotten in the habit of going to the bank with me during my biweekly business deposits. I drive an SUV and the car windows are at the same level as the commercial bank drive-through window. Boomer would be in the back of the vehicle. We would pull up and when the drawer would extend for the checks, Boomer would be hanging out the window looking into the bank. Of course, the bank tellers all saw that and started providing dog biscuits in the drawer. So, Boomer got the idea that it was a magic gift drawer. All we had to do was drive up and this drawer would extend and give him free cookies.

In anticipation of these wonderful treasures, he would hang his head out the open window and drool down the side of the door. A good week of deposits would result in a vertical trail the entire length of the car door. This spectacle prompted the tellers to gather at the window and fawn over the black dog. Naturally, the scenario prompted more cookies from the bank tellers, and the phenomenon took on a life of its own.

One day, Boomer put two and two together and realized that the stamping of the back of the checks in my office was the precursor to going to the bank. I had a number of checks and had taken out the checkbook and started stamping the back of them. I got about three done when Boomer hopped over to where I sat. He put his front paws up on my lap and started kissing me, whining with anticipation and generally being a nuisance during the check deposit calculation.

We got the deposit ready and I got my jacket on; all the while Boomer was whining in delightful anticipation. We drove up to the bank and he made a major withdrawal of cookies.

I often thought that Boomer must marvel at how I take these worthless pieces of paper, clip them together, take them to a special building, put them in a mysterious drawer and, much like a magician, say "Alacazam" and the drawer takes this paper and gives back dog treats. I am sure, in his mind, it is the most no-brainer, easy-deal going, and the real question is, why do we ever go anywhere other than the building with the magic drawer? It sure made me laugh. Even on the tough days, all we had to do was go cash a $20 check and get enough laughs to collect the daily point. The bank became our secret weapon in that regard.

Other unforgettable memories involved Boomer's friends. One night I was trying to work at the computer and he kept coming over, placing his head on my thigh and looking up at me with those wonderful, big Labrador retriever eyes. I would pet him and he would start wagging his tail in his patented, circular motion. I called him "Mr. Propeller Tail." I always told him to be careful because if he got any happier, he was going to take off like a helicopter, fanny first.

I petted him for a few minutes, noting how gorgeous his jet-black fur looked. All the fish oil and fresh food that I had given him were making his fur glisten. His incision was healing nicely and never seemed to bother him. I brought him back to his bed, but he kept getting up and coming to get me. "Okay," I said, "I understand. You want me to come over and give you some undivided attention." So I stopped what I was doing and lay in the oversized dog bed with him. I had to push a pile of stuffed animals aside.

Many dogs take a new stuffed toy and gleefully shred it to pieces. Not Boomer, not the Big Dog. He always was tender with his animals. He would often lie on his stomach and gently take a stuffed animal between his front paws, then suck on the animal like a child would suck on a pacifier. His tongue and lower jaw would be underneath, his upper jaw closed on top, and, ever so gently, he'd rhythmically close and open his mouth.

He'd keep track of all his friends and get very agitated if a human picked up one or had the audacity to play tug-of-war with it. Friends would last for years and years because of his devoted care. New ones would arrive every now and then, but nobody ever left. I think Boomer knew each and every stuffed animal, which numbered a few dozen after a while.

They were kept in a pile by his dog bed and he somehow rotated through his stock whereby everyone got a turn. Big Duck, Tiger, Little Elephant, Gorilla, Scroungy Bear. He also had a security blanket, which we called his "wooby." He'd wad up the wooby to create a ball between his paws and then suck on that. Other days, Boomer would pull the wooby around the premises as he conducted Dog on Duty operations. I'd sometimes mention in passing to him that "Nobody is going to take you seriously if you haul around a blanket." Boomer would somehow manage a single woof in response, all the while chomping on his blanket. I just couldn't *not* laugh.

Over the years, Boomer would be especially concerned on Thursdays when the cleaning lady came. This meant the dogs had to stay downstairs for the duration. Beezer had been content and happy to lie next to me. Coral stayed hidden. Boomer was another story. He would pace by the closed downstairs door and stare. Once I heard the cleaning lady leave, I'd crack the door open and Boomer would bound up the stairs. I'd follow him up and find him at his dog bed, sniffing each and every friend. I think he was taking a head count. Boomer never really did trust the cleaning lady.

Some of his friends looked like they were going to disintegrate. Over time, everybody built up a coarse outer layer of gunk. Occasionally, I'd take them and put them in the downstairs washing machine. Boomer would then sit at the dryer waiting. Once the friends were clean and dry, he'd lean into the dryer and get them and bring them upstairs, one by one. It was his stuff and I was always happy to let him have full control of his friends.

Boomer continued to honor his friends as he convalesced. I'd watch him in his dog bed and remind myself of my pre-surgical promise. I had to continue to devise methods to bring forward the Big Dog's soul. It wasn't difficult. Boomer never seemed to miss his leg and his spirit was unflagging. I was eager to live up to my bargain.

CHAPTER THIRTY-FIVE

Transforming into the Big Kahuna

ONE DAY IN MID-JANUARY I HAD AN EARLY MORNING COURT APPEAR-ance and was up before sunrise to give Boomer his pills with a jar of baby food. I was using the old Beezer slap shot technique into his mouth. After eating, he surprised me by navigating out the door on his own and into the Labrador Nordic Center.

I stood in my bathrobe and watched in the dark as he shifted to a quality spot and steadied himself. I noticed he positioned his right front leg a bit forward, while his left front leg moved a bit back. This allowed him to stretch his right hind leg well back and assume a low center position any football line coach would be proud of.

Boomer slipped and fell the first few times out there. I tried to be supportive, both physically and emotionally, while letting him learn these critical operations on his own. The uneven snow pack in the back yard didn't help, but that wasn't under my control.

Every day I would ask Boomer, "What are you going to teach me today?" Above all, I would keep my radar in constant operation in search of ways to get the day's point. We must win the point!

We were both experiencing change, I knew that. But I also knew it was temporary. Change is like a ripple on the water. It is here one minute, gone the next. That day, I thanked Boomer for the lesson on the temporary nature of change. I then headed downstairs to check my e-mail before going to court.

I spent about fifteen minutes responding to messages. It was still very early and dark outside. The house was quiet and I was engrossed in my business thoughts. Then I stood to go upstairs and get ready for court. As I turned around, I immediately stopped in my tracks and my jaw fell open. Curled up in a ball, behind my chair, was Boomer! He had silently navigated the flight of stairs, taken a position behind me and gone to sleep. It was thirteen days after his leg had been amputated.

I congratulated the Big Dog at length on his conquest of the basement. His tenacity and commitment to today and the moment were truly impressive. His place was in the office, beside me, and it was time to get back to work, he was telling me.

I had pause to think once again about fear—a dog's version of fear. It had to provoke apprehension to point yourself down a flight of stairs if the method of arriving at the bottom was uncertain. Boomer committed, in spite of the most reasonable and understandable anxiety. He realized what I had yet to learn—fear isn't a wall. Fear is a mist—you can go right through it.

At 6:00 a.m. on January 17, I awarded the daily point to Boomer. I was immensely proud of my teammate. I helped him back up the flight of stairs. This was nothing new—I had helped him for months because of his arthritis in his joints. Now, our improvised teamwork was flawless. He hopped over to his upstairs bed and curled up, my proud Big Dog.

As I walked toward my bedroom to grab my jacket and tie, I glanced at the corner where the kiddy chairs were lined up. They were empty. I wasn't surprised.

⁓

LATER THAT WEEK WE WENT TO THE CANINE REHABILITATION CENTER in nearby Englewood. On Wednesdays, you can rent the indoor swimming pool for private time with your dog. We had made this our winter swimming hole after the weather turned, and we both enjoyed it immensely. We opted for only a thirty-minute test swim because Boomer hadn't been in the water since his surgery. I had no idea what to expect, but he had been telling me he was anxious to do more. So I took the Big Kahuna for his first dip.

Boomer was very excited once we got to the facility. A couple of Labs, yellow and chocolate, were finishing up their swims, so we waited patiently. At least I did. The Labs' owner invited us to join them, but I declined. I felt the first time ought to be just Boomer and me. He might be a tad nervous and nobody wants an audience if he is unsure. I told her, "No, we'll wait for the knuckleheads to finish." I immediately wondered if I had just insulted this woman and her enthusiastic dogs. Fortunately, I hadn't. She laughed when I remarked, "You know, it is a term of endearment when you refer to an aqua-Lab as a knucklehead. In fact, Boomer hopes to get off the injured list today and regain active knucklehead status." She got a kick out of that so I knew I was okay.

The Big Dog generated a lot of interest. Everybody came over to greet him and wish him a good swim. One of the therapists, Becky, fitted him with a life jacket and we moved over toward the pool. The pool is an above-ground type with an eight-foot ramp up to a deck and an equal-length ramp down into the water.

Boomer hadn't liked the ramp when we were here in December and he hadn't grown any more comfortable with it. Fortunately, the life jacket allowed Becky and me to lift him a bit and coax him up the ramp. He was equally reluctant to go down the ramp into the water. Of course, this made sense. Boomer realized his new limitations and was understandably hesitant of new situations, especially where they presented potential danger. So, we repeated the lifting and got him down the ramp into the water.

Becky had on a pair of waders and was able to move about with Boomer. Unfortunately, house rules prevented me from joining them. I could only go down the ramp to the water's edge. I'm sure some lawyer somewhere had written an opinion letter on why getting in three feet of water was a bad idea. A question of liability. In any event, this was about Boomer, not me.

The Big Dog's apprehension lessened as he began swimming. Becky used the lifejacket to move him about in the water and she even tossed a couple of tennis balls. Boomer fetched one and, ignoring Becky, swam past her to the ramp where I waited. He came up the ramp, and thus out of the water, just far enough to get his head and neck out. He stopped there, dropped the ball for me and then used his front paws to turn himself around. I was reminded of a seal wriggling about in shallow water. It began to dawn on me that Boomer wasn't a handicapped dog in the water. His swimming steadily improved over the half hour we spent. I'd toss a ball from the ramp and my buddy would happily go get it and return to me.

Boomer had a new gleam in his eyes that day, something that made both of us smile and revel in the moment. I vowed to make each Wednesday, at noon, our time at the pool. We had a standing reservation from that day forward.

RETRIEVERS ARE AMAZING SWIMMERS AND MINE WAS UNPARALLELED, even with three legs. I regretted that one of Boomer's lessons to me couldn't be superior swimming skills. My forays into triathlons over the past couple of years would have gone a lot better. Every pool event I was in during those months of training for a triathlon involved some sort of aquatic fiasco. One time I even got an ovation from the crowd when I finished—and believe me, it wasn't for breaking any records, either. But those hiccups paled in comparison to my first open water competition. I say open water because the one-mile swim that year was in Boulder Reservoir at an event generally known as the Super Bowl of Colorado triathlons.

By the time of the event, I was in good shape, having trained diligently for the summer. My theory on the swimming segment of the competition was somehow to gut it out in the water and compete hard on the bike and subsequent run. I was scarcely parked at the reservoir when I realized I might have jumped up a class too quickly. Warming up on expensive bikes were some very fit, very focused people. Surveying the swim course didn't ease my fears. A one-mile horseshoe was marked by large buoys. The distance was intimidating and seemed roughly equal to an LA-to-Honolulu race. I could feel my heartbeat increasing. I tried not to be afraid, but every logical brain cell was warning of impending disaster.

I decided on a simple strategy: stay out of the way and don't drown. I looked around and found my group. There were ten groups of up to one hundred fifty people. Each "wave" of swimmers was comprised of similarly aged people of the same sex. Two other groups were size-defined: the Clydesdales, a men's group, and a women's group, all rather large people. I made a mental note to stay away from them.

Back to my strategy. The counterclockwise course meant the shortest distance was inside, on the left. Most people would stay in traffic on the left. I decided to swim on the right, or the outside of the horseshoe. Less traffic. I ought to be able to plug away at my own pace. I took a deep breath and entered the water at the back of my wave. My heart was now racing uncontrollably. I felt like MacArthur leaving the Philippines without a boat. "I shall not return."

My problems began immediately. Everyone was swimming in a straight line for the first buoy. Conversely, my course resembled an upwind leg in a sailboat race. I would tack to the left, then tack right; I was all over the place.

While I dawdled, later-starting waves would periodically catch up and pass me. It was more than a little unsettling to have one group pass me on the right and, later on, have another group pass me on the left. This can't be good, I thought. From time to time I would have to stop and survey my situation. At one point, I found myself in the midst of several sailboats, moored in the marina area. Later I looked around and saw nothing. No other swimmers, no buoys, just water. "Maybe I'm in first place," I giggled to myself.

About then I noticed the kayak patrol monitoring my progress. Every time I looked around, one guy in a safety kayak was keeping a close eye on me.

Energy was beginning to be a problem. I couldn't control my heart rate and my inefficient stroke was rapidly depleting my resources. I wasn't even halfway yet.

About then, I heard a strange sound. It was growing louder. Somehow, I had blundered into the middle of the course. Now, the men's Clydesdale wave was bearing down on me en masse. For God's sake, I thought, they're grunting! I was run over moments later, much like the poor coyote poised to catch the roadrunner in the old Saturday morning cartoons.

A race official on a jet ski drove over. He had a radio headset so I figured he must have been a person of some importance. He looked at me and said, "The referee thinks you've had enough." I thought about my day and decided to raise my arm signaling my disqualification. I climbed aboard the jet ski and rode back to the beach. My triathlon day was over.

I continued working on my swim that summer, and the following year I completed several Olympic length triathlons. I'm still not fast, but I can swim in a straight line and am comfortable in open water. I even returned to the Boulder Peak in 2004 and completed the race.

That day in Boulder taught me much about my life. I discovered I really do enjoy the challenges that new athletic adventures bring, even though I am no twenty year old. They keep me in touch with a part of me I really like...the little kid. I always enjoyed watching children snow ski. They fearlessly attack the mountain, crash, get up and try again. They are oblivious to what people think of their efforts. I rediscover that feeling when I go for a triathlon swim. I really ought not be there; I'm not very good and I look ridiculous. But that is exactly why I need to be there. Competing—even poorly—connects me with my innocence and reminds me that I can still learn new things and be anything I want to be.

I'd like to think my Big Dog enjoyed a similar feeling in the rehab pool that day, his reconnection to something old and almost forgotten and a deep sense of appreciation at stepping back in the time machine and enjoying those old simple pleasures one more time. It was my honor to give this gift to my dog and his honor to teach me to recognize it. Point earned.

The kiddy chairs and slippers on prominent display.

The Big Kahuna solos.

Boomer makes a test run at the rehab pool.

CHAPTER THIRTY-SIX

Nooners with Boomer

A NOTHER GLORIOUS EARLY SPRING DAY IN DENVER. NO CLOUDS AND a sky as blue as the ocean. The snow now a memory. I was even able to get the landscaped stream in the front yard running. Only a few weeks ago it had been frozen solid. I was reminded of the passage of time as I sat at my computer and listened to the calming running water.

Boomer was by the front door, half snoozing, half awake, enjoying the day as well. I changed out the glass portion of the door to screen, which allowed him to hear and smell everything going on. He would awaken whenever someone walked by and provide a single, perfunctory woof. That would always make me chuckle. Boomer had to remind all the neighbors that some things hadn't changed. He was still the DOD.

I sensed Boomer was a bit down in the dumps. He was lying in his dog bed staring off into nothing. The good weather would normally allow for long walks on a Sunday. That had been our pattern for years. But his new body made old-style walks impossible. My challenge now was to find outdoor activities that would provide stimulation and fun to a Labrador retriever who was used to running and swimming until his tongue dragged on the ground. I also needed to keep feeding the spirit of this proud alpha male.

Briefly, I felt a fresh wave of guilt over the amputation: I'd turned Boomer into a freak, condemned my best friend to a life he had no interest in leading. Then I realized what was transpiring. Someone had gotten loose from his assigned Time-Out Chair.

I recognized the jailbreak and immediately took the miscreants into custody. "Away, you two," I shouted. "You know the rules; you will abide by the rules." Guilt free, I looked at Boomer and suggested, "Would...you...like...to...go...to...the...park?" The "P" word did it.

Instantly, the dog was transformed. He sat up in bed with his ears alert. The expressionless face of moments ago had been replaced by the familiar giddy-with-excitement eyes of a Lab about to have an adventure.

Today, I decided, the local park would be a destination, not a journey. I opened the garage door, and, as if reading my mind, Mr. Bunny hopped over to the back of the SUV and waited. We weren't going to walk to the park; we were going to drive to the park. I loaded up both Boomer and Coral and we drove around the subdivision to an access road leading to a baseball field inside the park. Once there, I unloaded them and watched as Boomer moved about on his own. He got busy sniffing the grass, which was just beginning to turn green. I found a sunny spot and sat down.

Boomer intently explored his new area, his nose rarely coming up from the ground as he followed one scent to another. My gaze was momentarily distracted by Coral. She had found a pile of fresh poop and proceeded to roll in it. The contrast against her yellow fur was striking. I found this bit of playfulness extremely helpful to the expedition's anticipated success and thanked her for the strong effort.

My attention returned to Boomer as I got up and walked toward him. I looked into his eyes and saw pleasure. Boomer was now sniffing around majestic old pine trees and leaving his own calling card for the next canine visitor to come along. We hadn't walked far, maybe fifty feet or so. In fact, meandering would better describe it.

In years past, we would briskly walk the circumference of the park several times over an hour or so. That day we covered a fraction of that distance. I lay down on my back in the grass, watching Boomer while telegraphing this question: "Does this make today worth living?" Shortly after, perhaps sniffed out and marking completed, the Big Dog ambled over to me and sat down. I was still lying on the ground, now looking up at him in profile. I saw the face of a contented creature. He was watching people and other dogs in the distance, occasionally turning his nose up to get a whiff of something special. I silently repeated my question over and over.

Boomer looked down at me as I rubbed his tummy. He stuck his nose in my face and licked me over and over again until my entire face was wet. I started laughing and then he lifted his head to survey the park, his park. Then he dropped his head and gave me another face wash. We repeated this process again and again for about fifteen minutes. It would have been tough to tell who was having more fun.

Finally he got up and, to my surprise, started moving back toward the car. Park time was over as he'd had enough. It wasn't about the length of the trip; it was about being together for an outing. I appreciated the moment and marveled at the dog's adaptability to his circumstances. Not so much the physical change, which was obvious. I was impressed by the emotional flexibility to find joy in the simplest circumstance. Boomer wasn't upset about not being able to run in the park. Boomer was overjoyed about being *in* the park.

With that outlook in mind, one day I came up with a grand idea. We would have lunchtime breaks together. I called them Nooners with Boomer. Every day at lunch I would go out in the front yard with the two dogs. It occurred to me that, for a dog, the front yard is a bit of a diamond in the rough. The dog constantly gets to see it, but only from behind a glass door. I recalled seeing a vacant lot from my bedroom window as a little boy. I'd go past the lot on foot frequently, but the real fun was just staring at that lot from my window, immersing myself in fantasies. Treasure hunts and cops 'n robbers come to mind.

During my typical work days, the phones would be ringing, there'd be papers to prepare and file in court, and administrative duties to handle. People scurrying about getting things done. But, in less than one minute, I could be sitting in my front yard with a small waterfall behind me, the stream babbling as it tumbled toward a waiting pool. I was fortunate to work at home where this serene scene was no farther than several steps out my front door, with the dogs beside me.

We didn't go anywhere on these adventures. We just were. Coral and Boomer surveyed the perimeter with their noses dutifully recording the passersby on their turf. Of course, being in the front yard allowed unfettered direction of all neighborhood activities. Boomer's favorite was the UPS truck. Mark, the driver, knew Boomer well and would stop to give the pooch a treat. A brief conference would ensue between those two. Good for you, Boomer. Good things happen when you play your position well.

These little outings put a smile on my face. I certainly enjoyed spending time listening to the water, and I was glad to find one more little thing to add to Boomer's list of daily activities. The Big Dog lounged next to me as we both sat studying the kids playing across the street. As he watched, he moved his nose over toward me and nudged my arm. I responded by moving my hand on top of his head and petting him ever so slowly. No eye contact was made and no words were exchanged. The brief interlude was orchestrated entirely by touch. We silently enjoyed the moment as we watched the kids play.

WE WENT TO BOULDER THE NEXT DAY AND VISITED DR. SILVER. WE hadn't been there since his amputation. Rob was excited. He had found out about an experimental treatment using a substance called arteminisin. It is derived from a plant native to Southeast Asia and historically has been used as a malaria treatment for humans. Formal research on it was in the infancy stage, although suggestions indicated "Arty" showed promise also as a cancer treatment. Dosing and frequency were yet unknown. Rob recommended that Boomer try the injectable form along with capsules.

I listened carefully to him and pondered whether Arty was right for us. The drug was expensive as it was shipped from a distributor in Hong Kong, and the injectable version was difficult to administer. However, Rob was aware of no side effects so his conclusion was that it would either help or simply have no effect. I did like the idea of trying something, and the fact that I could treat Boomer entirely from home was an important consideration. The three of us talked it through and decided to give it a try. Boomer seemed stable now, but a reoccurrence of the cancer could be just around the corner.

Rob then demonstrated the injection procedure. I was beginning to get a feeling of déjà vu and shivered. The injectable Arty had to be reconstituted with a liquid and was very light sensitive. So, in his demo, Rob turned out the lights and covered the windows. He cracked open an ampoule, mixed the solution and drew it into a syringe. He then used his fingers to measure a short distance from Boomer's spine and expertly injected the Big Dog with an intramuscular shot. I would have to repeat this process every evening after dark, he told me.

My mind immediately flashed back two years to the horror I felt initially at having to give Beezer sub-Q treatments. That seemed like a cinch compared to this maneuver. I wasn't saying no to the procedure, but I was a bit daunted by its technical nature, especially since I would have to accomplish this task *in the dark*.

"Ah, a moment of your time, *doctor*," I said while holding up a forefinger using the international signal for "wait a frigging minute."

"Just use two fingers to measure the correct distance from the spine," he continued "and insert the needle into the muscle." Boomer and I looked at each other and then at Rob.

"It's only a matter of time before I inject my finger," I said.

"Well," Dr. Silver paused and deadpanned, "at least you won't get malaria."

SUNDAY EVENING ROLLED AROUND AND IT WAS TIME TO SOLO WITH MY new buddy Arty. Boomer was snoozing. We'd had a nice supper with egg whites, vegetables and some canned food he liked. I still was not taking any chances with possible kidney disease problems, so I continued to monitor protein intake.

As it got darker, I sat and thought about the challenges ahead. I made a vow to quit focusing on fighting cancer and instead to focus on life and enjoying every moment with Boomer. To that end, I designated Arty to be our fighter. Arty could do battle with cancer. Boomer and I were just too busy.

I also reminded myself not to attach any medical expectation to my efforts with this new regimen. I didn't control this outcome. Moreover, I expected to have a happy day today with my dog. The separation of these expectations was important. I didn't control tomorrow, but I sure as heck could control today.

My concept of expectation had been jumbled in a blender when Beezer had been sick. I had inserted my ego into an area it didn't belong in. I had attached failure to my efforts when my expectation wasn't met. Not this time! I would do my very best and release the result. The outcome was really never mine to decide.

I looked at my watch; it was 9:00 p.m. Time to get this show on the road. I began turning off lights and moved to the bathroom. Boomer was lying in his dog bed visiting with a fluffy friend. He looked so relaxed and I realized even I was feeling relaxed. Before getting started, I even gave Team Fear a preemptive two-minute penalty for interference and a ten-minute major for misconduct. The ten was a bit of a cheeky call and brought a chorus of chirping from the kiddy chair brigade, but it was my whistle and my game. Those two would be out of my hair in the penalty box.

Earlier in the day, I'd written a protocol for Arty and, before getting started, reviewed the sequence one more time.

1. Flip off top of syringe and tap down to remove top. Tighten needle one-quarter turn and set aside.

2. Remove ampoule from box, tilt to allow liquid in top of ampoule to drop.

3. Crack top off ampoule (this was the most difficult part).

4. Draw liquid out with syringe.

5. Turn out lights.

6. Insert syringe into vial to reconstitute powder with liquid.

7. Shake to mix.

8. Draw reconstituted liquid back up into syringe and bleed out air.

9. Inject into Boomer's muscle.

10. Turn lights back on and thank Boomer for his bravery and help.

This became our nightly ritual. Boomer was always a champ. He'd see the lights dim and sit up in his dog bed awaiting the needle. He never even flinched, despite my clumsy injection procedures. He'd wait for me to get done and then lie back down to cozy with his friends. Brothers to the end, both of the black Labs made my medical chores so much easier with their patience and cooperation.

Three legs or
four, Boomer
was always
very clear
about who was
in charge.

Doug going left,
Boomer going right.

Coral peeks around
the corner while
Boomer gets his
weekly massage.

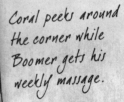

CHAPTER THIRTY-SEVEN

Tightrope or Trailhead?

WITH ARTY PART OF THE MIX, WHAT TO FEED BOOMER NOW? THE dietary contradictions were striking. For example, a kidney disease diet involved less protein and higher carbohydrates, but a cancer diet was just the opposite. Carbs were thought to fuel cancer cells; therefore, you avoided carbs and increased protein. Practical and philosophical resolution of this problem involved much reflection on my part. I could handle the practical. But, assuming everything happens for a reason, what was the reason we were faced with such a conundrum?

Just as curious was the Boomer riddle of his two terminal illnesses, in which kidney disease butted heads with cancer. Boomer's family tree was full of kidney disease. His urine tests suggested early stage kidney disease, and the collateral tests ruled out other explanations. On the other hand, his blood work was normal and Boomer had insisted, through Terri O'Hara last summer, that, "my kidneys aren't a problem." The only way to rule out kidney disease would be a biopsy, which I had no intention of doing.

Now even supplements and vitamins worked against each other. Cancer cells are thought to be iron rich. As a defense, the Arty was attacking the iron through an oxidation process. Conversely, Boomer was on numerous *anti*oxidants, such as omega 3 and vitamin E, to support his kidneys. Would the antioxidants diminish the effectiveness of Arty? It seemed the kidney disease and cancer formed a perfect storm.

Of course, no emotional day involving self-discussion would be complete without a small detour into yesterday's decisions, bringing guilt to the front and center. Boomer's kidney tests were normal. But because I had feared kidney disease, I hadn't opted for chemotherapy, which possibly would have kept the cancer in check and given Boomer a year or more. Therefore, said the rotten little bastard of an attorney inside of me, I doomed Boomer to an early death from cancer because of my poor judgment in selecting his treatment plan. Or better yet, the rat continued, your fear in selecting *any* treatment plan. *You killed your best friend*, he said, smirking.

"Are you finished?" I asked the lawyer. Seeing a seemingly bulletproof cross-examination, the inner attorney nodded approvingly. I walked over to the cancer time-out chair and pointed to the pink fuzzy slippers. I then reached into my wallet, removed a dollar bill, and placed it inside one of the slippers.

"Congratulations, counselor," I remarked. "Have a seat in the penalty box with your friends. I placed an object you treasure in the sin bin, so you'll have no trouble finding your way."

Given my experience over the past few years, I had the ability to hammer Guilt Law, LLC, anytime I wanted, but I decided to have a bit of fun first.

"There are four undisputed facts," I said. "They are:

1. Four of Boomer's littermates died of kidney disease.
2. Kidney disease generally reveals its presence in urine tests before blood tests.
3. Boomer's urine has suggested kidney disease for the past sixteen months.
4. 75 percent of kidney function is gone before blood tests reveal the disease.

I rest my case."

Indeed, as I knew all along, Boomer could have lost 50 to 70 percent of kidney function and still have normal blood tests. I'd exhausted every other possibility to explain the abnormal urine tests, which left kidney disease as the only possible explanation. I saw no benefit in living a lie, giving him chemotherapy and decimating what little remaining kidney function he had left. Such action would have been the height of arrogance and indifference to my best friend. So whatever I did, I couldn't do chemo. That was a fact and counselor was just going to have to deal with it.

Where I really lost the little bastard was over the cost of *proof*. Proof eliminates belief and belief includes the heart. Certainly, proof and science have their place. Unfortunately, these principles placed an over-importance on my ego and led to my spiritual bankruptcy when confronted with the fatal illnesses of my canine brothers. Proof can't get you where you're going and it can actually lead you astray. The little bastard's argument made my point. I'd either kill Boomer with chemo or kill him without. Either way, it was my fault. What a miserable way to live.

No, somewhere along this odyssey I needed to damn well decide what I believed in and what I didn't. I could also give myself permission to change my mind, and I could attach whatever significance I wanted to events and lessons I had learned. My only guides were my conscience and my counsel with my dogs.

Both dogs' illnesses made abundantly clear how self-destructively I'd lived: if something didn't work out in my life, either business or personal, it was my fault. The same kindness and understanding I'd shower on others was inapplicable to me. I'd punish myself unmercifully. I'd taken the doctrine of personal responsibility, which I still believed in, and given it radiation sickness. The doctrine mutated into a formula whereby *every* problem I encountered was mine to solve. My inability to solve every problem subsequently became a linchpin for guilt and unhappiness.

The B Brothers taught me how much guilt I dragged around every single day of my life. I *still* punished myself for things that happened years ago. I *still* punished myself and found fault for things I didn't control; and, in fact, never did control, like my dog having cancer and I couldn't fix it. Apparently, that was my fault too—at least that's what the little bastard in my head was whispering.

Later I discussed the enigma of cancer and kidney disease treatments with one of my vets. She remarked, "It sounds like you're on quite a *tightrope*." I gave the word tightrope much thought for the remainder of that day. Visually, a tightrope at a circus is a narrow-tensioned wire between two points with steep drops on either side. I thought of a circus performer carefully making his way across, using the thin pole for balance. I saw a defined beginning and a defined end. You got to where you were going, as long as you kept balanced. This didn't seem at all the situation with Boomer and me.

There was no clear path, however dangerous. In fact, there wasn't any path at all, I thought. My situation was much more akin to a maze, an intersection of numerous unknown paths. Then it hit me. It wasn't a tightrope, it was a *trailhead*.

My mood immediately improved as I envisioned a trailhead at one of the magnificent hiking locations in our Rocky Mountains. Boomer and I were standing before a large wooden sign etched with the names of mysterious and wondrous destinations: Hidden Lake, Upper Beaver Pond, Ute Meadows. The names went on and on, each conjuring its own enticing, yet different, story and treasures. Boomer and I had the ability to choose any hike we wanted. We could proceed at our own pace. We could stop at a waterfall, meander in a mountain valley and just enjoy the time together.

What if the confluence of kidney disease and cancer in our lives made sense and was the intended purpose of the universe? What if the lesson was to avoid stepping out on a tightrope, especially since the tightrope did not exist, and instead have two dear friends take one more hike together? An outing where we controlled the beginning; we could select any hike from the trailhead, and not worry about the destination? Because to worry about the destination, or what might happen after the hike, was to destroy the whole purpose of the outing.

This realization made my treatment plans for Boomer's remaining days much easier. I decided Boomer was exactly right when he said his kidneys weren't the problem. They really weren't. His cancer superseded the early-stage kidney disease. Interestingly, I'd hoped that Boomer and I would be able to hold his kidney disease at bay through diet and we'd gotten our wish. His blood work never did reveal increasing numbers, which would signify what I was sure lurked right beneath the surface. So going forward we would enjoy our victory over kidney disease and eat protein with a purpose. Chemo remained off the table.

BOOMER CONTINUED TO GET HIS PILLS AND SUPPLEMENTS, HOWEVER. I would make up the week's allotment on Sundays. It was staggering the number of pills I now was giving him daily. A friend, Liz, would come over on Sunday afternoons and while watching television would sit in the living room and painstakingly fill empty capsules with the powder.

One Sunday as I was loading up bags of pills for the week, I heard a familiar Lab whimper behind me. This was followed by a louder whine.

"Hurry up," Boomer implored. It was about seventy degrees and the Big Dog was ready for the park. I had to smile over his impatience. This dog was so much more about fun than his brother had been. Why dwell on disease?

I finished the pills, loaded up the dogs and drove to the park. I lifted Boomer and Coral out of the car and off they went. I took out a shorty lawn chair and walked a few steps into the park and set up shop. I had brought coffee and the Sunday paper and sat down to enjoy the outing. The dogs sniffed about while staying close to me. Boomer had many friends—both human and dog—in the park and, probably noting his new "look," they all came over to say hello and spend a few minutes with him. I patted myself on the back. An earlier version of Doug might have been discouraged about Boomer's inability to run through the park. That version might have attached sadness to the park and avoided the park entirely. Not any more.

Today was what Boomer and I made of it. There were so many adventures the Big Dog and I could still take. It was my responsibility, and delight, to translate old ideas into new concepts. Five years ago, a Sunday morning walk in the park would have had so much less meaning. Today, for Boomer and me to spend an hour together in the park meant everything in the world. I was so grateful for this shared hour. Our bonus time was what made today special.

WE'D BEEN HOME FOR ABOUT AN HOUR WHEN JASON, BOOMER'S MASsage therapist, arrived for his weekly massage. I'd started Boomer on this healing therapy about a year earlier as part of the ongoing management of his hip arthritis. It had helped significantly and both Boomer and Jason had developed a friendship over these visits. The massages had become vital since Boomer's amputation. It was important to keep the existing hip in as good a shape as possible. I'd been pleased with Jason's reports about Boomer's increased tolerance for deeper massage work before his amputation. Today, Boomer lay on his amputated side for the first time, which allowed Jason to work directly on that hip. A good sign, indeed.

I was going about my business when Jason summoned me over. "Feel this," he said. His hands were under Boomer's chin in the throat and neck area. I reached in, found Jason's fingers where they pressed on Boomer and he simultaneously removed his hand. I felt a small lump, perhaps a bit larger than a grape.

We looked at each other and I said, "I wonder if the lymph nodes are there?" I stopped and considered my potential emotional reaction. If you become fearful, you'll be moving into the future, I sternly reminded myself.

"We see Dr. Christensen tomorrow for acupuncture and I'll bring it to her attention," was all I said.

Later, after Jason left, I sat down to think about "the lump." One way or another, it would probably be something like this. Canine bone cancer generally metastasizes to the lungs, its final assault. When that happens, you're done. It was just that simple. I accepted that one of these days I might find something on Boomer that signified cancer's presence. I was just not going to dwell on that now.

The key to my successful journey with Boomer lay in the application of presence. Nothing could ever hurt us if we stayed present. Ever.

We were both alive today and we'd had a grand outing in the park. We'd grilled some chicken outside and I'd had the delightful company of a furry "grill monitor." Several small "mistakes" were dropped over to the monitor for a quality control check. Apparently, I cook chicken rather well. All of these things demonstrated that *today* was a special day for Boomer and me. Cancer, kidney disease and the mysterious lump had zero impact on the success of today. I then walked over to the penalty box and reminded Frick & Frack that I had my eye on them. They had better stay glued to their chairs for the remainder of today or else.

I want to explain my jokes and seemingly flippant attitude toward cancer. Cancer isn't funny. I was not making light of it. What I was doing was breaking the process down into smaller, manageable parts. Perhaps it was simply a survival technique.

Boomer was diagnosed on December 15, 2006. I was surprised, disappointed, upset—all the normal reactions. The monster came out of the closet, just as for anyone else. However, I chose to think back on December 15 like any other date, neither good nor bad. It was a historical fact and nothing more: it was a very sad day, but that day was over. My silly statements about cancer represented reminders that the past was history and I controlled the meaning of today. Heck, I may have cancer or heart disease and not know it. If I dragged December 15 forward, then I was choosing to move through life dragging this anchor. I could also leave the anchor in the past and move forward free of that weight.

The following day the vet aspirated Boomer's lump. It was negative. Just another fatty tumor and absolutely no big deal.

CHAPTER THIRTY-EIGHT

Happy Birthday, Big Dog

I WOKE UP EARLY AND LOOKED AROUND THE ROOM. BOOMER WAS SLEEPing on the bed next to me. I closed my eyes and felt him breathing. "Thank you for being here today," I said, petting him. I'd come within a day or so of saying goodbye in early January. The pain had been so bad. A real close call. It was now March.

"How 'bout we go to the reservoir today?" Thump, thump, thump went the tail. I scooched over, curled up around him and whispered, "Happy birthday, my dear friend. We're so fortunate to be together today."

Boomer was lying on his side with his left eye staring at me. Slowly, very slowly, he lifted his head and stretched around to where my face was. Very gently, he gave me one long, slow lick, then set his head back down and closed his eyes.

Our great cure-all-for-what-ails-ya was still the dog park. This was going to be our first trip to Chatfield Reservoir since Boomer's surgery. What better birthday present could we both have? After I lifted the dogs out of the car, we made a beeline from the parking lot to the water. I helped Boomer by using the sling so he could devote all his energy to swimming. Several people stared at us, unsure whether to rejoice in today with us or give us the privacy reserved for funerals. I simply noted the uneasiness as I was far too involved with our mission—get to the water as soon as possible. There was no zigzagging on this trip.

I carried the life jacket, although our time spent last week at the pool indicated it wasn't necessary. Of course, I had several tennis balls. Coral was along in her capacity as Shore Mom. I couldn't get her in the water for a million bones, but she was happy to tag along and supervise.

We started with a few very short throws, maybe five to six feet out into the water. The water was dreadfully cold and I wanted to make sure I could easily retrieve the Lab if necessary. It wasn't. I watched in awe as something magical transformed my buddy.

Boomer hobbled a foot or so into the water, turned, sat and looked at me. I threw a tennis ball about five feet or so behind him as he lumbered around while still sitting. Then it happened. An awkward step and then his body became buoyant. At that moment, Boomer and I entered a time machine. He swam with the same vigor, efficiency and grace as always. He actually swam with enough power to create a V-shaped wake behind him. And not a hint of regret or frustration, just pure joy at being in the moment.

He retrieved the tennis ball and swam back to me. His eyes were bright with the radiant spirit that always cried out, "How 'bout a little fun today?" My dear comrade in arms had his old life back.

I knew that Boomer's biggest apprehension about surgery had been his belief that he would no longer be Boomer. Today he now understood the Big Dog was still alive. The magic elixir was the same mystic potion we had used for years: one part human plus two parts Labrador plus one part lake, swish vigorously and have fun!

What pride I felt that this animal had reclaimed his life after losing a limb and having cancer moving through his blood. Pride in myself as well. I recalled that melancholy fall day last year when my magnificent friend bounded through the reeds and water as I considered whether we'd *ever* make it back to this swimming hole. I took these thoughts in through all of my senses. As his eyes met mine, I could tell Boomer sensed it as well. Our souls touched and we both knew the completion of a long journey back. Point earned.

I quickly promoted Boomer from the minor league and began to throw multiple tennis balls well out into the lake. Several people stopped to comment on Boomer's strong swimming and ability to retrieve two tennis balls simultaneously. These fans had no idea only three legs were paddling under the water. The Big Dog was immensely pleased with his performance.

Of course, a passing young lady observed Boomer and threw a tennis ball into the water while she directed her dog to join the game. The youngster splashed out about knee deep, turned, and headed back to Mom without the ball. Ever the showman, Boomer cocked his head and woofed once at the girl. "Boomer will take care of it," I read from my script for the umpteenth time. I tossed one of Boomer's balls in the vicinity of the now abandoned ball and let the birthday boy have the stage to himself.

"He can really get *both* balls?" she asked.

"Yeah, you can thank Rin Tin Tin yourself in about thirty seconds." Of course, the Big Dog lapped up the admiration and affection from his new girlfriend upon delivery of the missing ball.

The girl then kneeled down to thank Boomer and ventured a bit too close to Casanova's schnoz. I smirked, knowing what would come next. One precision lick, delivered with the speed and surprise generally seen in the reptile world when fetching a bug. I called them "sneaky kisses." Boomer snuck in a kiss and was embraced by the young lady. He looked over her shoulder at me during the hug, smiled, and said, "Betcha can't do that, huh?" I remarked to myself that very little had changed in the last year or so.

The birthday swim was shorter than we wanted. The ice had melted only a week or two before and Boomer was trembling cold. Even shivering, he would give me the "time for one more swim?" look. Finally we gathered our belongings and headed back to the car. I was glad I had saved the receipt for the life jacket. It was going back to the store. "You're still the best swimmer in this family," I reminded Boomer with a bit of sarcasm. He, in turn, had just a hint of a smirk on his face.

I loaded the dogs and prepared to close the hatch. Boomer was near and whimpered for me to come over. I leaned in and he gave me a series of kisses like never before. I started to laugh as I held him close. "Yes, I know, I know," I said. "Happy birthday to you and I'm so glad we are here too!" This went on for close to a minute. This was a borderline mushy violation for the Big Dog. "Your brother would be proud of you," I said, and did a double take on this scene. Beezer had had this same reaction to a special birthday walk here two years ago. In fact, we were parked in the identical spot.

A great lesson lies in Boomer's ability to swim—about finding the day's hidden treasure and appreciating the gift of today. Yes, Boomer had cancer. However, the disease was powerless that day. Boomer and I controlled it.

On the way home, I bought Boomer a rack of beef ribs and grilled them. He knew he was King for a Day as he waited by the grill. Leftovers and quality control checks were for another time. I cut up the rack and gave him a couple of big meaty smokies. I then sat down beside him and watched one contented dog go about his business.

CHAPTER THIRTY-NINE

Mets

WAS THE ARTY WORKING AT ALL? WE WENT TO BOULDER ONE morning for a routine chest X-ray to find out. Boomer hadn't had an X-ray since his diagnosis on December 15. Dr. Silver had hoped the new Arty regimen, now going on two weeks, would yield dividends. I was in the X-ray room and helped lift my three-legged pal onto the table.

Dr. Silver popped the films into the light and gazed at them. My intuition sensed a problem as no words were spoken. I somehow became cognizant of the ticking of my wristwatch as I stroked Boomer and stared at Rob's back for what seemed an eternity. "Well?" I finally stammered. Funny how you can stammer on a one-syllable word when you are stressed. Dr. Silver took out a pen and pointed at spots on the X-rays.

"Do you see these circles?" he said. I counted them to myself. One, a second, a third, a fourth. "They appear to be nodules or masses," Rob said. I recalled that the December films had been clean, showing no spots, so this *was* something new. It also signified the beginning of the final stage.

I could read the disappointment on Rob's face. He so wanted the Arty to work. He'd often told me how fond he was of Boomer, and we'd grown to become friends over the B Brothers' illnesses.

"I'm so sorry, Doug."

I asked him what I could expect in this phase. I was ready to hear it. He said the cancer had now metastasized to the lungs and would progressively cause breathing problems. I should be alert for difficulty with him recovering from exertion, for starters. There wasn't much else he could say.

The ride home was quiet. I examined my emotions. Sadness had entered the picture. I could now see the circle beginning to close as we came up toward the end. My very best friend on the planet would be departing soon. He had been at my side constantly for eleven years and would now be traveling on and leaving me behind.

I considered whether I was surprised at the events of today. Perhaps not. The oncologists had told me in December that I should expect two to four months. Today marked three and a half months. I also had worked hard at not tying an expectation to the Arty treatment. I did this because I knew disappointment follows when expectations aren't met. I reminded myself that the universe, in its infinite wisdom, still hadn't checked in with me to make sure its divine plans met with my approval. I had quit waiting for that phone call.

To me, hope could be dangerous because hope implied expectation of a specific result. For example, I "hoped" the Arty allowed Boomer to live healthy. I "hoped" we could enjoy summer 2007.

Instead, a better course would be to remind myself to live not with a specific hope but with *faith*. I view the word faith in more general terms. I have faith in the wisdom of the universe. I have faith that the outcome would occur exactly as intended. I was struggling with those concepts still. Perhaps the best I could do was remind myself that I attached very different meanings to these two similar words.

We got home and I prepared the dogs' suppers. I did stop off and get Boomer a bit of beef to add to his meal. I then lay down on the kitchen floor and watched him eat. Boomer was classic Lab. He just loved to eat. I propped myself up on an elbow and watched him scarf down his dinner. Occasionally, he'd shift his focus onto me as if to say, "Go get your own—this is mine."

I closed my eyes as Boomer ate and wondered what Beezer's wisdom might be about all of this. I emptied my thoughts, quieted my mind, and waited for my heart to hear something.

There is no need to hope for anything because everything you need and want is right in front of you. The key is to be happy in the present moment. Having faith is knowing how to remain present. You release a particular future outcome, or hope, and have faith that the universe will bring you exactly what you need right now. Hold this faith close and you'll never go wrong.

That evening was very quiet. Boomer had been looking quizzically at me the past few hours. He knew I was sad. I decided to sit down and have a talk with him. I explained that the cancer had gone to his lungs—the bone cancer group called it "mets." I couldn't do anything to stop it and I was sad.

Boomer looked at me and reminded me that this was all the more reason to enjoy today. All time together is special, but this time is extra special. "Do not be upset," I heard.

I gave him a hug and we agreed to go to the reservoir the next day. Then I sang him a silly little song with words I made up as I went along. He seemed amused, by the wagging of the tail.

Stroking him absentmindedly, I thought back to the fateful telephone call I'd placed to the hospice two years ago, the one where I'd heard the phrase *anticipatory grief* for the first time.

"No, Boomer, I have no intention of surrendering to grief or fear. I'm not *afraid* of your dying, but I *am* very sad.

"You see, my Big Dog, for people sadness and fear are separate emotions. I can't fear something in the present. I can only be afraid of something in the future. If I shift my focus to the future, I'll miss out on today. Now, especially this Saturday, today is the most valuable thing to us. I need to guard today with a heightened sense of resolve.

"Sadness, on the other hand, is present. For example, I didn't feel like working this afternoon because I was sad about your diagnosis. Sadness is both healthy and expected on a day like this. In fact, it is a great day to be sad. Of course, we'll have to be on guard for the

Dead End Kids' upcoming suggestion that sadness and fear are synonymous. We know better. Let's be okay about being sad and chase
those two and their fear back to their chairs. We don't have the time
or patience to mince words with them, especially today."

SEVERAL DAYS LATER, I POSTED BOOMER'S TEST RESULTS TO THE BONE
cancer list. Of course, the members responded immediately and en
masse with messages of sympathy—and suggestions. I was so thankful to have found both the kidney disease and bone cancer lists and
to have an opportunity to develop lifetime friendships with people I
haven't even met in person.

One of the ideas that I got from the bone cancer group that day
involved something called the "metronomic protocol," which is a
low-dose oral chemotherapy. The members of the list reported
instances of several dogs that had lived many months after discovery
of the first lung "mets" using this pill therapy. Several folks urged
me not to give up hope. There was that word again.

I talked over this new regimen with Dr. Silver, consulted with the
oncologist in Denver, and, of course, asked Boomer. I had the feeling
the Big Dog wasn't thrilled about more medication but would try it
if the medicine didn't interfere with his having fun.

The oncologist was pessimistic about the overall results, so I cautiously decided to give just a modified version a try for several days,
no more. If it later failed to serve Boomer's best interest, we'd alter
course. Just that fast.

I went to bed that evening with a bit of hope and a bigger question
running through my mind: What was I hoping for?

I lay there thinking about metronomic protocols, hospice and
dying. I was grateful that the human hospice programs had told me
to take a hike when Beezer was sick. This was too personal a decision
to rely on other people's definitions. The single important factor
was to quiet all outside noise, listen with my heart instead of my

mind, and determine what course of action was proper for me and my dogs. Nothing else mattered.

⌒

THE WORD "HOSPICE" IS DERIVED FROM THE LATIN HOSPITIUM, REFER-ring to a guesthouse of a monastery—a place of rest for weary travelers. The techniques the B Brothers and I used to avoid fear and guilt, which allowed me to remain present, were indeed like a rest stop for these weary travelers.

Human hospice is a pretty new experience in this country, starting around 1970. My hunch was that human hospice involves a clear line in the sand—that point where a dying patient is transferred usually from a hospital to a facility for end of life, palliative care. Alternatively, my plan with both my dogs had been to ascribe a "still fighting" attitude to treatment and doctor care versus a "no longer fighting" attitude to final care. Win or lose—all or nothing. It was how I used to look at my personal scoreboard of life. My story demonstrates how useless this philosophy was to me.

Looking back today, it occurs to me that when my dogs were sick I had combined my personal still-fighting approach with the hospice concept. I had no clear line, no set policies or procedures as you might have with a human model for end of life. My concept of integrating treatment and hospice care—starting at the earliest possible stage—worked better for me. I called it my Presence Plan™.

This plan evolved out of what I believed were shortfalls in traditional vet treatment plans. By definition a treatment plan demands being pulled out of the here and now. For example, with Beezer, plans were made for re-checks of blood tests times number of days down the road he was expected to have. With a treatment plan, I was left speculating and hoping that this future event would yield gains. My own mind already was racing forward in time, even without the suggestion of future tests. I also was retreating into the past by asking myself how this had happened. Was I negligent in previous treatments? In short, the existence of the treatment plan guaranteed that I would be everywhere in time except the here and now. Step one of my Presence Plan acknowledged that inherent tug on time.

Step two of the Presence Plan created a mechanism to counter-balance the "treatment plan." This is where my concept of hospice comes in. For me and my dogs, hospice is simply *living with balance.* My hospice belief begins with the statement, "Here's what's going on—we need to talk about it." I always felt better when I discussed the elephant in the living room that I'd been ignoring.

I'd actually been applying my Presence Plan for a long time. Our first fledgling step into pet hospice had come during the balancing sessions I called the Daily Appreciation. With Beezer, our Daily Appreciation conversations had concerned crossing over on his own if that was what he wanted or what was intended. These discussions pulled what I considered "traditional" hospice concepts back into untraditional time parameters. Our nightly discussions then had evolved into talks about happy times, sad ones and anything else on our minds. We talked about my uncertainty and later my inability to change the outcome of the disease, how to use what time we had left, and the landmarks in our intertwined lives. However, we had these discussions while treatment was *ongoing.* It became a way of keeping the checkbook of life in balance. I saw no need to change this successful tactic with Boomer.

Boomer and I *would* give the metronomic protocol a try. We'd also continue to layer in our own concept of hospice to provide a balance to our daily lives. We'd consider what we were hoping for and why. What was realistic? What was under our control? Most of all, how could we remain present given the challenging news of the day?

For us, it was never treatment versus hospice care. It was always both. Why choose between pepperoni and sausage on your pizza when the answer is to have both?

CHAPTER FORTY

Hope vs. Hopelessness

ONE DAY AT THE END OF MARCH I HAD TO BE UP EARLY FOR COURT and hadn't gotten much sleep. My nerves were frazzled. Prompted by nothing, I burst into tears on the drive downtown. Fortunately, I was able to compose myself before entering the federal courthouse. It did feel good to focus on something else for a little while.

I had been thinking a lot about hope and lack of hope. Although continuing with Arty, I knew it wouldn't arrest the cancer's progression, and so the questions persisted. Did this mean the situation was hopeless? Did this mean I was quitting on Boomer? Was I giving up and resigning myself to his death? Was I abandoning my best friend in his hour of need? I had to be sure.

The answer, I knew, had to lie in the concept of presence. Hope didn't always have to apply to the future, did it? Couldn't I have hope without creating an expectation?

Yes, I certainly could hope to live for the moment without interference from cancer. Therefore, I would lower my expectation from the nebulous future to a more manageable level: today. I would hope to have a happy day free of problems where Boomer and I could enjoy each other.

I thought about how my relationship with Boomer had developed much deeper meaning. Both the boys had taught me to appreciate the more mundane things in life, like simply enjoying their company. I returned the gift to Boomer by giving him the ability to swim in 2007. What a joy it must have been for him to feel like a full-bodied dog when he entered the water. I could also hope to set my fear aside and accept that Boomer's body was beginning to fail and there was nothing wrong or unfair about that. Boomer's eventual passing would be painful for me. However, suffering remained optional.

Hope wasn't an all or nothing proposition. Just because I don't hope for a magic bullet doesn't mean I don't hope at all. Just because I no longer hoped the cancer could be arrested doesn't mean I had quit on my best friend. Of course, guilt, and the little bastard shoveling that crap would argue otherwise, but I was wise to him now. I would hope for things that were realistic and attainable.

I also wanted to remind myself that somebody was inside that black fur. That somebody had cognitive function, needs and emotions. I hoped I was available to hear Boomer's voice and honor his wishes and nobility. I recognized this metronomic protocol could be a very short-term experiment, which I would be monitoring. I just would not spend my final days with Boomer obsessing about finding "cures." Our focus would remain on the journey and not the destination.

I now saw that, as options were closing on treatment or cures, new doors were opening. These doors led to a deeper meaning for my life with my dog. I hoped these lessons continued. I also hoped to honor my best friend's eleven years of devotion by attending to him during his final illness. A guy's guy is always there when his teammate needs him.

What a gift from the Boomer that, as his body weakened, his spirit and attitude taught me how to live healthier and happier. I recognized that the love and compassion I'd showered upon Boomer and his brother had always been a part of me. I had been unwilling to extend these emotions inward toward myself. Perhaps that was the greatest gift of all from the B Brothers.

It was then very clear. To lose hope for a cure or remission of a fatal disease was not to lose all hope. I wasn't without hope; I was adapting to the situation and changing what I hoped for. And, incredibly, many of the things I was hoping for I already had.

Boomer's Top Ten List On Hope

10. The greatest hopes come in the smallest packages. The progression of disease does not mean we are hopeless. Hope is not an all or nothing proposition.

9. I hope Doug doesn't obsess about trying to cure me. He'll miss the whole point of being together today.

8. Miracles happen! What if the miracle isn't that I get better, but that my brother Doug does? I hope he sees this possibility.

7. I hope we can look into each other's eyes every day for one minute without saying a word.

6. I hope Doug does not fear my death. Pain is mandatory, but suffering is optional. I'll be joining my brother and both of us will wait for him. We were sent to earth to teach him these lessons of hope, love and forgiveness.

5. I have opinions concerning further treatment. I hope he hears my voice and considers my needs and desires. I hope Doug can honor my nobility and even help me when it is my time.

4. I hope Doug has even and appropriate emotions. It helps both of us in many ways.

3. I hope Doug recognizes the days ahead are the icing on my cake of life and tries not to smear the frosting.

2. I'm alive today. I hope we can savor and linger in each precious moment.

1. I hope Doug realizes he cannot shower love, compassion and forgiveness on me unless he does the same on himself.

© 2007 B BROTHERS PRESS

Mahalia Norton hugs her favorite neighbor.

These are the memories I carry with me today.

Boomer's 11th birthday at Chatfield Reservoir was just plain special.

CHAPTER FORTY-ONE

Lights, Camera, Action!

APRIL 4. IT WAS 11:00 P.M. BOOMER WAS LYING IN HIS FAMILIAR SPOT at the foot of the bed. The same spot he had enjoyed for eleven years. He was kissing me goodnight, lying on his back to revel in tummy rubs. It was moments like this that validated our strategy not to focus on fighting cancer and kidney disease at home. This was why I went to the seemingly ridiculous positions of placing kid's chairs in my house and speaking to diseases as if they had campy villainous personalities. The absurdity of that circumstance allowed me to release my fear and focus on the day. For us, it was not about cancer; it was all about one more day of tummy rubs. That was all that mattered.

As we did every night, Boomer and I chatted before lights out.

"Boom, I want to thank you for your courage, especially this year. You never lost one bit of your fun spirit. That means so much to me. And as I've said on other days, you remember, you've always got my permission, whenever you feel the time is right, to just cross and go be with your brother. I want you to sleep well, dream fun dreams, and if we are lucky enough to have tomorrow, we will have a new adventure. Thank you for today, big doggy.

"I am adding one more thing, Mr. Boomer. I am trying very hard to learn your last lesson. I believe the last lesson you are here to teach me is humans don't need to fear death. I am going to try very hard to learn this lesson, so when you do leave, you and your brother will be so happy that all of the things you were sent here to teach me I learned. Goodnight, my brother."

As I listened to him snore, for some reason an incident from years ago popped into my head. When I was a freshman in college, one day on the ice rink I was playing center and went to swing at the puck at the same time the opponent did. His stick caught me full force on the nose; the impact broke my nose and orbital bone. But it happened so quickly, and, since I had taken so many other blows in this tough game, I kept on skating, not feeling anything. Then I happened to look behind me and saw blood everywhere. Wow, *somebody* got creamed, I thought. They made me get off the ice. All that blood. And everyone on the bench grimaced as they looked at my face. But it didn't hurt at all. That was what my dad had always told me about bloody noses. The thing is, you know you could get hurt playing hockey, but if you play anyway, you've beaten fear. I'd finally translated my hockey lessons to the rest of my life.

THE NEXT DAY I BOUGHT A VIDEO CAMERA. I DECIDED TO USE OUR TIME left to create a Boomer movie with scenes from our favorite activities together. My idea was two-fold. It would be fun for Boomer and me to have a little project so I would not be sitting around watching sand drop through the hourglass; the project would help me focus on how many adventures we still had left. Second, it memorialized the dog. Boomer would be the poster boy for how you can even have enjoyment after cancer metastasizes into the lungs. We were just a week into that discovery.

I also liked the challenge that this undertaking presented. I wanted to use the Boomer movie to show other people that you can, in fact, during the difficult days, have fun and also some introspection, some valuable quiet time with your buddy.

Boomer had started a new habit of barking for me to come upstairs and be with him during the day, so I brought my work upstairs to be close. I realized Boomer was recognizing we had a short earthly window left and the important thing was just to stay close. God bless him for that beautifully simple perspective and reminding me that this was the most special, magical time we would ever spend together and we would never get the opportunity back.

The next day I started on the list of activities for the Boomer movie. I lay in the pet bed of the upcoming best actor nominee as I went over the list. I kept waiting for the big ham to tell me to "have your people call my people." I'd make different recommendations and run them past Boomer, who seemed very amused by the entire exercise. We ended up with a list of all our favorite places to visit even though Boomer kept reminding me that what his public really wanted to see was him eating as many grilled meats as possible. Cancer was fading into the background where it belonged.

THE BOOMER MOVIE BEGAN PRODUCTION THE NEXT DAY. WHAT BETTER way to lead off than a trip to the bank? I parked the car, instead of going through the drive-through, and walked into the bank to speak with the tellers. Teresa, Evonne and Jessica had been so good to Boomer over the past few months. They genuinely cared about him and went to great lengths to make him feel like a valued friend of the bank. My intention was to have the tellers film from inside the bank out into the car. Well, they would have no part of that idea. Instead Boomer and Coral were both invited inside the bank. I replied that I didn't have leashes and they quickly assured me not to worry and just come on in, "We'll enjoy having Labrador retrievers running around the bank." One of them filmed us coming into the bank and Boomer was beaming. Boomer then made his way around the bank greeting everyone. Coral was a bit perplexed, but she was just glad to be part of the adventure as any good tag-along kid would be. Things got downright hilarious when the tellers invited the Big Dog back behind the teller line where their cookie "vault" was located. Boomer sat down and began to crack the safe. So Act 1, Scene 1 of the Boomer movie was titled "The Bank Job."

I sent a message out to both my dad and Beezer that night. I didn't know how much time we had and I wanted to make one last wish to them to the extent they had any pull in the heavens. I asked for a couple of weeks of good health so we could get the Boomer movie done. I hoped we had the time to finish.

CHAPTER FORTY-TWO

The Farewell Tour

I F YOU FOLLOW SPORTS, YOU KNOW THAT EVERY YEAR SOME AGING STAR
will announce that this will be his last season. The games begin
and each city visited by the soon-to-be-retiring veteran has some
type of ceremony. The ritual is collectively known as a "farewell
tour." The Boomer movie would include our own farewell tour.

Ours, of course, would be a bit challenging—not just a film about
a cute puppy or dog licks. Our goal was making a film that takes
place entirely in these final, challenging days. Could we do this? We
both enthusiastically answered "yes." Creation of the list and selec-
tion and priority of the scenes would force me to make choices,
along with my black dog's input, about how our time together would
unfold. We'd be staying present. We'd chase Team Fear back to the
Penalty Box. The remaining days would be the most special I'd ever
share with my beloved companion. I was done with bantering with

cancer and kidney disease. "A Trip to Chatfield Reservoir" was scheduled as scene two of the movie.

The next day we woke up to snow. You can always depend on Denver to help out with the most ridiculous weather completely unrelated to the calendar. This was April. There would be no trip to the dog park today. My mind switched over to plan B as I lay in bed and watched it snow. Well, time to improvise. Sunday mornings are good for one thing: being lazy. I asked Boomer if he wanted to have a morning chat in bed. Of course he did. I helped him into bed and he took his usual position at the foot. I rubbed him softly and told him what a great adventure we'd had together. I thanked him for the umpteenth time about the fine job of taking care of me his entire life, but especially after Beezer passed. Boomer would occasionally turn his head back to me for a few quick licks as he agreed with all my comments. I noticed he'd stretch out his front paws from time to time as he invited my tummy rubs. I buried my face in his fur, felt his heart beat, and gently rubbed his stomach. No words were necessary. Boomer didn't seem to mind the little camera focused on him a few feet away. The morning edition of our daily appreciation was now recorded and checked off the list. Boomer reminded me we won the daily point as well.

Later I whispered in Boomer's ear, "I'm so sad that these moments are coming to an end." So there I was, coming up on another fork in the road. A fork very similar to the one I'd found myself at some two years earlier with Beezer. The circle was closing rapidly now.

We got up a bit later that snowy day and made our way to the kitchen. The day before I had noticed Boomer's appetite waning. Then he didn't want his morning pills. I'd front-end loaded all his antioxidant pills in the morning in order to separate them from evening Arty treatment, which we were still continuing. Kidney pills, immune system, arthritis and joint relief—all tallied up to dozens of pills slathered in baby food.

I also noticed something else. The clanking of the plates and dumping out of the daily allotment of pills was now drawing vocal comments from the Big Dog. This was brand new. I ignored it for a couple of days, but Boomer kept up the barking. The next day he began to hop around the kitchen island as if to escape. His message was clear: "I don't want anymore of this." I stopped what I was doing and looked down at Boomer. "Stop!" I yelled at myself, "How shabby you are to chase down a three-legged dog and then force him to do this! Why am I not honoring his wishes? Enough is enough."

We made a pact. I would reduce the number of pills by about 80 percent. A couple of omega-3's, some hip/joint relief, and his two metronomic protocol pills, and that would be it. If I trusted Boomer with my life, then surely I ought to trust Boomer with his own life. Boomer had the right to make choices about his treatment and future and I needed to listen and abide. As Boomer watched, I opened the trashcan, leaned over and poured the rest of the pills into the can. The Big Dog immediately ambled over and gave me a big kiss. I clearly understood his vote.

"There," I said, "what do you think of that?" Boomer had a grin on his face as he sat and wagged his tail. There was something in that act that lifted my spirits as well, something intangible. Boomer and I had simply recognized what was important that morning. Down deep, I, too, sensed relief at stopping before it became madness. I decided to up the ante. "How 'bout we stop the shots, too?" The ensuing face wash made clear how the Big Dog voted on that issue. I thanked Arty for the strong effort at buying us a bit more time. I especially thanked Arty for fighting cancer for us so we could spend our time in peace.

I then put away some of the prep items collected on the counter. Boomer watched my every move as the mortar and pestle, scale, and other items were placed in the cabinet. The wagging tail indicated his approval.

STRANGELY, I FELT NO GUILT OVER POTENTIALLY "GIVING UP ON MY DOG."
I recalled how grief stricken I had been at these tasks during
Beezer's illness. It had been my resistance to change that brought
about my reaction. Today, I held change very close. I felt good
about my decision.

Later, as I walked past the penalty box, I smirked at the pink slip-
per brigade and remarked, "Whatdayathink of that?" and took great
pleasure at their silent response.

All our hard work on trying to stave off kidney disease was paying
off now. All dietary restrictions were removed and Boomer could eat
whatever he wanted on his Farewell Tour. I also made sure to fire
up the grill every day under the dutiful eye of my chief outdoor cook.

As the days wore on, I could feel the veil between my spirit and
Boomer's becoming more translucent. The beauty of the moment
between his life and mine was breathtaking. I could feel the separation narrow as our souls became closer. I felt honored to be
Boomer's earthly escort on those final days. And I could feel Beezer's
presence growing as responsibility for Boomer's journey was
entrusted more to him and less to me. I was awed at my awareness
of what was unfolding in front of my eyes and in my heart. All I had
to do was let it in.

Now I felt a sense of completion and a desire to move forward,
which meant finally letting go of my buddy.

"Hey Boom, I feel like a baby bird starting to outgrow its nest.
I've learned all your lessons and Beezer's lessons and the cramped
space tells me it's going to be time for one of us to leave very soon.
I don't feel bad about that. I've learned so much. I'm getting anxious
to test my wings. I want to see if I can fly..."

The following day was a watershed moment in the Farewell Tour.
The temperature warmed and we loaded up and went out to Chatfield.
My neighbor Pat offered to go with us to shoot the movie and I eagerly

accepted. Boomer walked without assistance and his smile clearly indicated how pleased he was. I'd read many Internet posts stating, "The dog doesn't know he's sick." I had come to believe just the opposite. What if Boomer knew exactly how sick he was and he didn't care?

What a life lesson in presence. Such a hypothesis does make sense. I am going to die of something at a future date. That unknown contingency has absolutely no effect on how I use the moment of today. Maybe it's just that simple.

The water was gaspingly cold, but neither of us cared. Boomer was happy to swim and I made sure to throw two tennis balls each turn to allow the ham to show off his most gifted fetching ability on film. Being able to video capture a dog park moment was very important to me and my seemingly endless lists. I can't fully explain why this was so important but now realize I don't have to.

Boomer swam for about ten minutes before his shivering made me call it a day. I'm not sure if the shivering was from cancer, cold water or both. Once again, it matters nada. For it's not about how much fuel you got in the tank, it's all about how you use the gas you got. We got back to the car and I lifted both dogs back in while Pat continued filming. Boomer then gave me a massive thank you and congratulatory face wash, which was captured in its entirety. I was grateful for this moment and happy to have this joyous exchange between two beings so deeply in tune with each other that a flood of tears followed. It was a release of recognition of years of joy, love and satisfaction of a job well done, on both our parts.

Later that week we made it to our Wednesday appointment at the swimming pool. This time my secretary came along to help with the movie. Boomer was classic. He'd swim out to fetch a tennis ball, grab it, turn, and stare straight into the camera as he swam back. What a beaut!

It occurred to me later that I was reaching the end of an odyssey that had begun in earnest two and a half years earlier, the day when canine illness entered our lives. All of the emotions, lessons, pain and joy were being compressed into those final moments with my second dog with a terminal illness. But I was tired of living and working in a dog hospital. Caring for these canine beings had been the greatest growth experience of my life, but I was exhausted. I hadn't been taking care of myself either. There just hadn't been enough time in the day. I wasn't sick, but lacked energy to do even routine activities.

Coral felt the changes, too. Normally placid, she now was jumping around the house, unable to be still. She seemed to be increasingly aware of goings on beyond the front door and would vocalize. When she was downstairs, she would leap to her feet and be off at the slightest alert from Boomer upstairs. I believe Coral was demonstrating to Boomer that she could be the Dog on Duty and things would be just fine left in her able paws. I so looked forward to the simple pleasure of taking her on a long walk. She deserved it.

In many ways, I felt that a catharsis begun years ago was close to completion, and I was eager to see what was next. It was like going through an adult adolescence. I half expected to wake up one morning with pimples and a surprising voice change. The passing of my remaining B Brother would complete the rebirth of Doug, a much friendlier, less fearful, less ego-based human. I could see how it was more important to embrace the entire human experience rather than just controlling my own little piece and shutting out the rest.

What a legacy from two little black dogs. I sit in awe that my B Brothers had taught me all that. I'm deeply appreciative of these two creatures coming into my life and showing me what was most important. They were the only teachers I'd ever have listened to.

We took a Nooner with Boomer early that day, an outing to the front yard. The sun was shining and Boomer lay down beside me. I felt the heat on the right side of my face. My right hand felt the radiance of the sun as Boomer's fur heated up. We sat and did absolutely nothing except enjoy the moment and each other's company. I closed my eyes and slowly stroked my gentle friend's body. "I can't see you, but I can feel your presence," I whispered to Boomer. He leaned up and gave me a short, slow kiss, no doubt thinking, "By George, I think he's got it."

CHAPTER FORTY-THREE

Surrender Does Not Mean Defeat

T HE WIND WAS HOWLING OUTSIDE. THE TEMPERATURE HAD DROPPED about twenty degrees since the day before. The schizophrenic Denver weather had U-turned again. Snow was expected on Thursday. Of course, Saturday would warm to 60. How grateful I was that we'd made one more trip to the dog park.

Boomer always had a difficult time with weather changes. It bothered his arthritis. So I tried to help him that morning with a couple of pain pills mixed in with baby food. I got a low muffled woof as I prepared the pills. I should have known better. I placed the dollop in his mouth and he fired it back at me as if discharging a bazooka. I was deservedly covered with goop and two deteriorating white tablets.

Actually, Boomer's steadfastness over medication of any type was of great help to me. At some point, more likely than not, the tumors would begin to impinge on his breathing. His panting would slowly increase. As much as I didn't want to see that, I remained vigilant. I knew what to do and I'd do it. I'd protect my buddy with my life.

Guilt would not be a problem. I could hear the "little bastard" whispering in my ear. He was reminding me of a quote from football coach Knute Rockne: "Show me a good and gracious loser and I'll show you a failure." Once again, before vanquishing counsel back to the penalty box, I chose to engage him at his own game: logic.

My ego suggested that I was abandoning Boomer because I had discontinued his meds. I was letting down my friend in his greatest hour of need, quitting on him, which made me a failure. This self-denigration particularly gnawed at me because the programming and practice over my entire life has been to buy into such self-abuse. Thank goodness I could flush this baloney down the toilet where it belonged.

Just because I didn't pump Boomer full of medication didn't mean I had quit on him. Quite the contrary, I loved Boomer so much that I would allow him the dignity to choose his own path. I had done all I could. Then responsibilities shifted. That is what teammates do. They pass the puck to each other. They move about on the ice, constantly in sync, having fun letting the other guys chase them around and never quite catching up. And I trusted my teammate.

An interesting paradox: I had learned to sacrifice my body when needed and do anything for my teammates on a hockey rink. Now, to serve my teammate best, I had to step aside. Sometimes the supreme effort remains confined to the inside. The blaze of glory occurs but takes place completely inside the heart and soul. No one ever sees it except the two entities involved when they share a touch or make eye contact. I didn't need the blaze of glory from others. It wasn't a hockey game or a prize fight. It was my life and I finally understood how to live in balance and harmony. I also realized that doing nothing is sometimes doing everything you can or should.

ON SATURDAY, APRIL 21, WE WENT BACK TO THE PARK. I HAD THE video camera rolling. It was quiet, I could hear birds chirping, some dogs in the neighborhood barking. It was an overcast day, so we had the whole area to ourselves.

Boomer was struggling to get to his feet now. It was hard to watch his life slip through his paws, but it felt good that he trusted me enough to let me care for him, and, quite frankly, I was glad that he wanted to stick around for one more day. I had been noticing a strange smell on his breath. I was not sure if it was uremic or what, probably just the smell of breath from life that was almost over, but I could tell it was different.

Boomer seemed to be cataloguing a few more smells on this earth. When cancer that has spread to the lungs gets serious, dogs get flu-like symptoms. I noticed an increased number of eye secretions—I called them sleepers—which I had to wash from his eyes every hour or so. His mouth and nose had been dripping as well. I could see small puddles beneath his nose when he slept in one spot.

"My Boomer, I'm going to be watching and listening to you very carefully today. I will continue to honor your wishes and place them first. I am calm and unafraid. Perhaps you and Beezer will soon be tumbling around together in a doggy embrace. My world will make a bit more sense when that happens. All our work of the past few years is coming to fruition. There is no fear."

And so, my education was now complete—I had learned all the lessons the dogs were sent to teach me. Well, one more…the beauty in the end of life process. I recognized how much I'd learned since Beezer passed. I no longer needed any formula or mathematical equation. I didn't even need counsel from my friends or Internet comrades. Just the opposite, I was spending no time on the computer or telephone. All I had to do was decide whether today was the day, and today was not. The fact that it was close didn't factor in a bit. I just trusted the process, trusted the life cycle, and trusted my dog. It was a time to relax into the moment and remind myself that there wasn't anything going on that was either unnatural or unfair.

A few days earlier, a friend had commented, "I just don't know what to say to make you feel better." I'd replied, "Why would I want to feel better?" It wasn't a time for me to feel better. My dog was dying. Feeling better would come later, but there was nothing the matter with feeling sad at that time.

I was working downstairs later that day; Boomer was upstairs snoozing on his bed by the front door. Suddenly I heard a puzzling wave of barking from the Big Dog. I left my work and went upstairs to investigate. Boomer didn't want to get up, but he was gesturing and directing his barks to the front door. I walked over and was surprised to see one of the neighborhood boys, maybe five years old, squatting at the edge of my front yard pond as he leaned over to play in the water. No other kids or adults were in the area.

The pond was small but deep enough for a little shaver to get into more trouble than he could get out of. I walked the little boy home and had a talk with his parents. "Boomer always keeps an eye on the little fella," I explained, "but Boomer will be leaving soon and the little guy won't have him around for protection." The family assured me that it wouldn't happen again.

I came home and sat down with the Big Dog. I stroked his head and thanked him. "I'm pretty impressed," I told him, "that you still wear the DOD armband even though you are sick. You'll always be the Dog on Duty around here."

⌒

I HAD THOUGHT BOOMER'S WORSENING BREATHING PROBLEMS WOULD ultimately cause me to make the final decision. I was wrong again. I began to realize the final issue I would deal with would be Boomer's ability to get up and move.

Being Sunday, I mentioned Chatfield Reservoir, which transformed my dog as it had for eleven years. I merely mentioned the words and again his tail started wagging and his ears went to alert. He got a big smile…but he couldn't get to his feet. I helped him up and we gingerly moved toward the car and I lifted him in. Arriving at the Chatfield parking lot, his breathing was becoming more labored. I opened the hatch and looked at my magnificent friend. He no longer had the energy to move to the gate. The eyes said yes while the body said no.

I made an easy yet difficult decision then. I was not going to ask Boomer to do something that he was just not capable of doing. Nor did I want to break his spirit by showing him the water and then having him not be able to go enjoy it. His last swims had been successful and fun. In fact, eleven years at this reservoir were an unshakeable barometer about our fellowship in fun. That day, the barometer told me everything I needed to know. Our Chatfield excursions would remain forever successful and untainted by failure. Most of all, my great dog would not have his last memory of this special place be tarnished with pain, frustration and disappointment. It was now time for those great swims to become part of our memories. So I closed the hatch, turned around and headed back home.

Lying in bed that night, we talked about decisions. God bless Boomer for sucking it up and finding the strength to come to bed.

"Boomer, you've been the best dog in the world. You've been my best friend. I just want to tell you what a good job you've done taking care of me since your brother left. I'm not going to let this go on any longer. There's no way out. I know your tail is still wagging, but it comes at a pretty high cost. Let's sleep tonight and perhaps call the doctor tomorrow. I'm sad about moving forward without you, but I'm looking forward to trying."

The Sunday Morning Picture

I WOKE UP AND FOUND BOOMER AT HIS FAMILIAR PLACE AT THE FOOT of my bed. I could see his chest rise and fall rhythmically every few seconds. Silently, I exhaled deeply and sank back into my pillow as I contemplated what this day might bring.

My first thought was how far I had come over the last two years. On May 1, 2005—it had been a Sunday—I lay in exactly this spot with my two sleeping brothers seemingly fused together at the back and head. I had interpreted that picture as creating pain and fear in my mind. In many ways, I had a mulligan today: an opportunity to replay that picture from the same spot and do it without the pain and fear. I reached over and began to pet Boomer as I surveyed my thoughts and emotions: I was sad but I was also at peace. I knew the frantic phone calling of 2005 to the doctors for advice was not going to happen today. Whatever this day brought, it would be discussed and decided by Boomer and me. There was no need for any outside counsel.

It was evident today would be more difficult for Boomer than yesterday. I had been seeing steady, daily decline, measured over the past three days. Yesterday, Boomer could move about if I lifted him to his feet. Today, he was even unable to push himself back to a sitting position. He'd just tap the floor with his front paws as if playing patty-cake with the ground.

Even a few steps were exhausting once I got him to his feet. My first task was to take the sling and support him so he could go outside and tinkle. Boomer was teetering a bit, but we were able to accomplish this function with a bit of teamwork. I got him back inside and into his dog bed. He was winded by even slight movement, and the sleepers were accumulating in his eyes constantly. I needed to take a warm washcloth and clean him up every ten minutes.

I sat and talked with the Big Dog and expressed my opinion. "I think you and I are at the end of the road," I said as I searched his eyes for a response. "I think it's time for you to go on ahead and I'll be along directly." My heart heard him say, "I'm tired and it's time for me to move to the other side of the circle."

I went over to the bookcase, the one with a couple dozen three-ring notebooks, and grabbed the one with all the telephone numbers. The numbers I never wanted to use. My first call was to Boulder and Dr. Silver. He had been nice enough to offer to come to my house on "the day." His schedule was such that he was unable to get to my house until Thursday, though—three days away. I thanked him but replied that I didn't think we had three days. Boomer was deteriorating on a daily basis. We *might* make it to Thursday, but at a higher price than I was willing to pay.

I next called Dr. Christensen. She had a full Monday as well but could come Tuesday after work. She had come over to the house the

Friday before and thought Boomer looked pretty good. However, the decline had started the next day. I agreed to a Tuesday appointment, although my heart wasn't really into that idea. I couldn't fathom reaching such a momentous decision and then sitting around not implementing it. That seemed cruel to both dog and human. Fortunately, I had redundancies for this situation that NASA would even be proud of.

I called a backup, Dr. Brandenburg. She and I had never met, but I was well familiar with her practice. Dr. Brandenburg is a vet who has redirected her entire practice to providing in-home euthanasia for pet owners. She has created a transition experience aimed at a peaceful resolution when the body has said enough. I called and got a late afternoon appointment.

Next, I called the funeral guy, Scott, who had helped me out with Beezer's cremation. I mentioned on the telephone that he helped me out with my black Lab a couple years before, but, of course, he didn't recall. I went over the timing for the day and Scott said he could be out early evening to pick up the body. "Um," I stammered, "I'd prefer to bring the body to you." A long pause ensued and Scott said, "Now I remember you." I got a chuckle out of that.

Next, I called back Dr. Christensen and left a message to cancel the Tuesday appointment. She immediately called me back and said she could come after work today, but she would need help transporting Boomer's body back to the clinic for pickup by Scott. Of course, Dr. Christensen had forgotten about our unusual protocol, so the transport was unnecessary. She professionally and a tad emotionally informed me that she needed to be the one for today's task. She had begun to treat Beezer in fall 2004, and, I'm sure, needed the same closure that both Boomer and I did.

So I called back Dr. Brandenburg, thanked her for being available and willing to help, and told her plans had changed and Dr. Christensen would be there. I then called Scott and told him we wouldn't be done until later in the evening, which proved too late for delivery to the crematorium. I actually was relieved. This experience had created a spiritual awakening inside of me. I knew end of life procedures were very important to the journey. I had a great desire for Boomer to pass at home, in his own bed, and enter whatever world lies next with a fixed compass bearing behind him. It would be the last thing I could do for him. I also would spend the day calling Beezer to come forward and be available to receive his brother. I told the Beez that I'd be transferring care of Boomer to him as my job would soon be completed.

Equally important was my desire to have Boomer's body lie undisturbed for a period of time. I have no idea or belief about timing of the exit of a spirit from a body. I just wanted to make sure Boomer was given enough time. And in any event, the entire country runs on a Madison Avenue rush for every friggin' thing touching our lives. This just didn't strike me as one of those commodities.

Lastly, and just as importantly, I wanted to give Coral ample time with the body, so she could both say goodbye and come to grips with the change in her life. She and Boomer had gotten very close. Ever the gentleman, Boomer had invited Coral in and made her feel welcome. I knew today would be difficult on this gentle little soul, and I wanted to make decisions that took her feelings and needs into consideration.

So that was it. A bunch of telephone calls, plans, changes and general chaos. That's the way life and death is: unpredictable, imprecise and untidy even under the most deliberate circumstances. I was glad to have all my telephone numbers and contingency plans. My earlier organizing allowed me to take care of business and refocus on spending this most special day together with my Boomer.

The one thing that was still working very well on Boomer was his stomach. The day would be filled with one tasty treat after another. Since it was still morning, our first yummy of the day would be a stop at the donut shop.

Donuts had a particular pull on the Big Dog, and this adventure was strictly a spectator sport for me. Traditionally, when my coworker Dave would show up with a cup of coffee and a donut, Boomer would immediately follow him downstairs to the office, sit near his desk and stare at the donut. Not a hopeful look, not a pensive look, but a steely-eyed stare of uncommon focus. The long, single strand of drool would start next, which, by then, was the only hint that an actual living animal, and not a taxidermist's creation, was sitting by Dave. I always enjoyed quietly watching these two haggle through their serious negotiation and the difficult allocation of a single donut. Dave cared deeply about the B Brothers and I knew this would be a difficult day for him. So I decided we'd get a box of twelve and I'd let those two have a nice long talk.

Around noon I could tell Boomer wanted to go outside. He was arching his head back and slowly playing patty-cake on his dog bed with his front paws. That's all the strength he had, but it was more than enough information for me to step in and help. I hadn't recalled seeing him go outside to defecate in the past couple of days as his mobility was limited. I had a hunch it might be time.

I grabbed the sling, reached beneath him, lifted Boomer to his feet and ran the sling around his abdomen. Boomer took the lead and headed toward the back door. I was surprised at how out of breath he was in just ten feet. We got out the door and I noticed his front legs were very unstable as we went down the single stair to the grass. This was even true where I was supporting a significant percentage of his body weight via the sling. Once on the grass, I shifted the sling a bit forward so he could urinate and straddled his hind section, holding each end of the sling independently. This allowed Boomer the most freedom of movement to find a spot and squat. Sure enough, moments later, Boomer evacuated. I recall this story for several reasons.

First, it was a special moment for Boomer and me, working as a team to the very end. Boomer gave me a great thank you face wash.

Coming back inside, as Boomer and I waddled past the Time-Out Center, I announced that we just got today's point from a little known category: mixed-doubles team dump. I defiantly told Moe and Curly to top that.

Second, it was important to watch for signs about today's final decision. It had taken all Boomer's and my strength to maneuver into position to address this bodily function. I don't think we could have accomplished the task if Boomer lost the ability to use his front legs. That would be next, perhaps with other difficult surprises. I'm 100 percent sure Boomer would have been crushed if things progressed to where he was soiling himself inside or in his bed.

Third, our last backyard outing summed up the past several years in about a ten-minute experience. I've never been so humbled by and appreciative of the privilege to take care of my two best friends in their final illnesses. The simplest of acts took on the greatest of meaning, both to the dogs and to me. Our ability to work together toward the common goal of living today has been one of the most profound learning experiences of my life. Finally, the awe I experienced as my animal teachers took me by my tear-stained hand and showed me how to set aside my fear and guilt was the greatest tutorial. I never set out to change anything in my life. However, by immersing myself in the experience, I've allowed change to occur in a way I'd never imagined. In fact, if I could turn back the clock two years to a different scenario, I wouldn't.

The morning progressed and I spent a quiet couple of hours with Boomer upstairs. My office mates were so quiet I scarcely knew they were working. Lunchtime meant a pizza order. Boomer's thumping tail clearly revealed his approval as I walked in the door with a hot pie. I have no idea what goodies are waiting at the Bridge, but I felt reasonably certain that sausage and pepperoni were decidedly earthly experiences. I sat down next to Boomer, munched a piece, cut hunks for him, and asked him what he wanted to talk about. "What unfinished business do we have?" I asked. I was initially surprised because neither one of us said anything. Upon reflection, the silence made perfect sense. We had been diligently working on this project for about two and a half years. There wasn't any unfinished business to talk about because there wasn't any unfinished business. We left every bit of soul and energy out on the ice rink of life and were now sitting exhausted in the locker room.

I lay down on the bed next to the Big Dog, placed the pizza box on my chest, and intermittently munched on slices and handed tastes to Boomer. We just looked at each other, said nothing, and drank in the moment. I remember that afternoon for its utter simplicity. Just a couple of the fellas enjoying a pizza. It was as good as it gets.

I also took time here and there to go downstairs and leave Boomer alone. I wanted to give him time to collect his thoughts and ready himself for birthing into whatever came next. I used this time to sit quietly and call Brother forward along with my father. I closed my eyes and focused on Beezer as my mind drifted back in time, back to when he and Boomer would carom off each other as we walked on leash so many years before. I remembered my obsession with finding the reason Boomer insisted on walking to the left of his brother. The riddle was answered during an early animal communication session when Beezer was ill. The dogs explained that during their mother's pregnancy, Boomer was located to Beezer's left inside the womb. Walking on Beezer's left just felt natural. I was astonished and dumbfounded at the time. I released the need for proof and chose to consider *what if this were true?* Today, the solution to the riddle puts a smile on my face. It's just a nice way to live, with habits imprinted in the womb. In several hours, the circle would connect and my dear B Brothers would be side by side in the womb of the universe. I did, of course, remind Beezer today to position himself to Boomer's right. No sense taking any chances.

Later in the afternoon I fired up the grill and made burgers. Boomer stayed in his dog bed the whole time, but his eyes and head carefully recorded the event. Ears at alert and tongue smacking gave me a last few glimmers of the old Boomer. His body was broken, but his spirit was alive and well. I'll always cherish that afternoon together as we both faced the inevitable with a focus on today and each other.

Dr. Christensen arrived about 7:00 p.m. The doc and I shared a tearful embrace and exchanged words. It was a difficult day for her and I thanked her for her attention and care for both dogs over the past few years. Her house calls, constant care and devoted bedside manner were a source of much reassurance. Privately, I was relieved that she was the one to come over. I'd discussed final arrangements with Boomer days before and asked his permission to bring in Dr. Christensen if the situation required. Boomer agreed. He liked Dr. Christensen very much, although he never understood why she liked to look at his tongue so much.

Boomer lay in his dog bed as Dr. Christensen examined him. She noted his deterioration and explained that the next progression of the disease would be deadly. I had been comfortable in my decision to make today the day, but her opinion reassured me.

Meanwhile, little Coral had retreated to the kitchen and was occasionally peeking around a corner to see what was going on. I walked over to her and sat down. "Boomer is going to have to leave us tonight," I explained. "His body is broken and he needs to go to the invisible place. You can stay here or go outside, whatever you choose. Don't be afraid; we both knew this was coming. You and I are going to be all right." I petted her, briefly pondered why I still thought I needed to explain things like this to my dogs, and returned to Boomer.

Now I lay down next to my Big Dog and wrapped my arms around him. I could feel his heart beating. Dr. Christensen had shaved a portion of the leg and inserted a catheter. I looked into Boomer's eyes and told him how much I loved him and how lucky I was to have him be my dog. He leaned over and gave me one last long, slow, not-so-sneaky kiss. Dr. Christensen then gave him the first shot and my buddy was soon snoring.

Out loud, I began to speak to Beezer. I knew he was there. I told him that his brother was ready and I was relying on him to come get Boomer. My job was done and it was his turn to take care of his brother. I then told the Big Dog to be at peace and instructed the doc to give the second and final injection.

Dr. Christensen soon told me she was beginning the second shot and I could feel Boomer's heart begin to slow. Just at that moment, Coral rushed into the room and stood beside Boomer as I felt the final heartbeats and then nothing. Boomer just went to sleep in my arms. I buried my head in Boomer's fur and sobbed. It was 7:49 p.m., April 23.

The doc helped me move Boomer's body onto an adjacent dog bed. I had placed several blankets underneath him to make movement the following morning a bit easier. I put Boomer's favorite friend, Big Duck, between his paws and wrapped the blankets around him. He looked very peaceful. I thanked Dr. Christensen and she left.

Coral's actions during Boomer's passing had reinforced my faith that he would be okay. The only possible explanation for her behavior is that she sensed Boomer's spirit leaving his body and ran over to attend as part of an animal ritual, something ancient that, perhaps, we humans have forgotten, if we ever knew. Still, her reaction was intentional and unmistakable. I reflected back to that Sunday morning picture from two years ago, with the boys lying on the bed back to back the morning Beezer left. I was very sad tonight, but part of me rejoiced. My beloved B Brothers were back together and, in a way I couldn't fully comprehend, the Sunday morning picture had been reinstated.

Boomer lay in his bed one last night. Several hours after Dr. Christensen left, I noticed Coral curled up sleeping next to Boomer's body. Outside, the first spring rainstorm made tiny pitter patter sounds. All was otherwise quiet and peaceful.

IT SNOWED THE FOLLOWING DAY. A DEEP, WET, SPRING SNOW THAT would be gone in several days, but cold and messy for the time being. I wondered how difficult a time Boomer and I would have had in the event he lingered past Monday. I was glad neither of us had to extend our teamwork experiment into a blizzard.

Several days later, once the weather cleared, Coral and I ventured out for a walk. Initially, she seemed happy to be walking down the street toward our bike path. However, I noticed her gait begin to slow as we approached the end of the street and the grassy path. We took several steps and she seemed insistent on smelling each blade of grass individually. I let her be and walked ahead. After a bit of futile encouragement to come along, I walked back to her.

"It's okay," I said. "I miss Boomer, too. It's going to be hard for a while without him around. We don't have to go any farther today. How 'bout we go back home and try again tomorrow?" Just then I heard a strange rustling sound behind me.

I turned and was amazed at what I saw. Two birds, two identical black birds, were side-by-side hovering in the air, at the same altitude, staring directly at me. They were about eight feet off the ground, about six feet away from me. The birds were stationary but for their flapping wings, hanging in midair. You've got to be kidding, I thought.

The lessons of the past few years went through my mind in a millisecond: fear, guilt, control and my small place in the universe. Dogs as teachers, humans as pupils, proof versus belief. But mostly, in that split second I thought about love. The love I showered upon the B Brothers was the same love I had withheld from myself. The messengers also suggested that perhaps less had changed in my life than my normal worldly senses suggested. I realize that now. I thanked the birds for stopping by and just like that they vanished.

I chuckled as I dismissed the argument within myself over what the birds meant. There was no need for any judgment or earthly resolution to what many might claim was a strange coincidence. The boys had taught me that everything happens for a reason. Precisely what happened with those two birds was unimportant. All that mattered was my new found permission to dream *what if* the birds were exactly what they appeared to be? It sure was a nice way to begin the day. All I had to do was release resistance and settle into the moment. Just because I couldn't explain it didn't mean it didn't happen.

Coral and I gave each other a wink and a nod and we walked back home. Happy for today, happy to be together, happy to win today's point. The B Brothers never got better from their illnesses, but I sure got better from mine. I always did enjoy a good paradox.

Epilogue

I HAVE MUCH TO BE THANKFUL FOR AND REMAIN STEADFAST IN MY belief that everything happens for a reason. In November 2007, just seven months after Boomer died, I had the opportunity to once again mull over that concept. Coral, my shy nine-year-old yellow Lab, was diagnosed with early stage kidney disease. Once again, the B Brothers notebooks were dusted off as I reacquainted myself with doggy illnesses. The concepts of fairness, why and what hadn't I learned the first two times jumped into my head as well.

My initial reaction had been to suspect some problem in the house for the prevalence of kidney disease. This couldn't be a coincidence...three dogs, three kidney diseases...all taking place within these walls. What gives? Chemicals, fertilizers, radiator fluid? That seemed like a stretch. None of my dogs ever had access to that stuff so I just let that notion float away. But what then? I was headed down that perilous path again.

Thankfully, I caught myself in time. The difficulty with this line of thinking—of trying to find blame and reason—would have been once again projecting ego into the equation. If something fixable under my control explains the condition, it would follow that I have the ability to control and fix it. I also could see Mr. Guilt warming up on the sidelines. No, I thought, as I sat on my couch pondering life: been there, done that.

Then I'd considered what other possible alternatives explained the need for yet a new journey, this time with Coral. It was so strange to do this again that I almost could see a certain beauty just out of reach at the horizon line.

Mulling this over, I have to chuckle. The B Brothers' journey was about *my* growth. What if this was about something else? What if it was time for me to give back? Maybe this was about Coral, not me. What if this was a reward as opposed to punishment? After all, where else would a dog with kidney disease in Denver be better served than at my house? Being entrusted as human caretaker for another animal with this difficult disease is very humbling. Perhaps Coral's presence meant I did a pretty good job with the boys and the universe is comfortable passing me the puck again.

Coral had a rough life before she came home with Boomer and me that Valentine's Day in 2006. She had been a breeding female who had used up her usefulness after a caesarian section and being spayed. Perhaps Coral, as she dozed off at night, made a wish upon a star. A wish to some day experience life as that most special of pets—a cherished family dog.

I also consider whether Coral's kidney disease is nothing more than a mirage. The carrot on the stick I'm not supposed to reach for. After all, I'm aware that Coral and I will one day both join the B Brothers. That is okay by me.

I am beginning to notice changes in this shy dog's behavior. Recently I was sitting on my couch removing my shoes. Coral came over and planted a dainty, ladylike kiss on the end of my nose. Then a couple more. She smiled at me as if accomplishing a great feat of dogdom—a pooch peck! She had never given me a kiss before.

I laughed and petted her gently (she's still not comfortable being hugged) and said, "You're letting your inner Labrador come out, Coral. Good girl."

Another day I was barbecuing a rack of beef ribs—Boomer's favorite. I gave Coral a rib to gnaw on, knowing her jaws were not strong enough to break the bone. Coral typically would take any treats outside to eat. Even the smallest morsels, which faced immediate disintegration, were transferred out the doggy door. Apparently, Coral associated treats in the house with a felony.

However, that evening we had a rainstorm of tropical proportions. Coral had gone out with her bone, like I'd figured, and stood on the covered patio with it jutting out of her mouth like a five-dollar cigar. I sat down in the living room and decided to let her work it out. Moments later, I heard chewing sounds from the kitchen. She had brought her prized bone back in the house and was comfortably lying on the kitchen floor gnawing away. I was so proud of her. "Way to go, girl—it's your home and you are entitled to eat your bone in the kitchen."

These are the memories I now hold close. This frightened little dog's awakening into her true self is the gift we both cherish. I'm honored to assist in her transformation and deeply appreciative of my new ability to sort out the noise and focus on what is happening right in front of me.

I think Coral's wish for a better life came true. It doesn't matter whether she lives a week, a month or a year or more. She is a beloved family member, and what greater gift could a human provide to a pet? It's magical to watch her emerge.

By the way, in 2007 I was made a moderator on the Yahoo.com kidney group list. It was one of the richest moments of my life. I feel honored to help others and recount the blessings and perspectives that my pet teachers instilled in me. I'm still not a wizard, but I made my peace with that long ago.

Commemorative brick outside
Colorado State University Veterinary Teaching Hospital

Index

– A –

acceptance, 108, 120
acolyte, 117–118
acupuncture, 28
airplane crash story, 125–128
albumin, 123, 140
alternative treatments, 28, 38,
   194, 201
Amiee (Boston friend), 37
amputation
   animal communication and,
      210–211
   Boomer and, 176–177, 195–197,
      202–205, 207–212
   decisions regarding, 194–197, 201–
      202
   fear and, 197
   fiduciary relationship and, 194
   procedure briefing, 203
   process during/following, 204
   questions surrounding, 171, 172
   recovery period following,
      207–212
   Silver and, 197, 202, 204
   swimming following, 230–232, 254–
      255, 256
   traveling to, 202
Ana (doctor), 209–210
anemia, 3, 139
animal communication
   after amputation, 210–211
   Boomer's cancer, 175–179
   Boomer's inclusion in, 87, 112–113
   Boomer's kidneys and, 167–168
   circle of life session of, 112–114
   listening heart to heart and, 65
   ninth birthday, 96–100

   spending quality time and, 93
   during sub-Q, 125
   writing books and, 72
animal communicator
   Callahan's approach as, 63–64, 93,
      96–100
   first sessions with, 64–65
   Goldstein, Robert, recommending,
      57
   O'Hara's approach as, 63, 65, 72,
      112–114
   proof regarding, 63
anticipatory grief, 51–52, 259
arteminisin (Arty)
   administration of, 241, 242–243, 245
   character of, 240
   continuation of, 257, 258, 272, 273
   instructions for using, 241, 243
ashes, of Beezer, 148, 151, 154

– B –

B Brothers
   author's smell and, 98
   Chatfield Reservoir birthday and,
      100–102
   Cleo/Homer and, 10
   commemorative brick for, 298
   on fear, 99
   fiduciary duty regarding, 194
   litter mates' kidney disease, 167
   manners of, 15–16
   ninth birthday of, 95–103
   pact with, 3–4
   relationship of, 96–97
   Saturdays with, 21–23
   snobby character of, 15
   story times with, 85–86, 91–93

unity of, 5, 19–21, 283
walking pattern of, 20–21, 289
balance, 162
bank deposits, 225–226
"The Bank Job" (Boomer movie scene), 269
Becky (rehab therapist), 231, 232
bed footage, 272
Beezer. *See also* B Brothers
　alternative treatments for, 28, 38
　animal communicator and, 64
　ashes of, 148, 151
　Beezer's Top Ten Reasons Not to Feel Guilty and, 162–163
　Bonus Coverage and, 137
　Boomer reunion with, 12
　Boomer's last day and, 286
　Boomer's salute to, 147–148
　caregivers' honoring of, 121–122
　ceremony honoring, 150–151
　chasing balls and, 15
　clostridium and, 129
　as comedian, 19
　communication session/ Boomer and, 87
　conference call dump by, 16
　death of, 6–7, 149
　diet, 43, 73–74. *See also* phosphorus, protein
　disposition of, 10, 14, 15, 49–50
　eating challenges with, 105–106, 111–112
　evenings with, 47, 48, 49–50
　female Lab biting, 16–17
　final steps and, 142
　funeral home and, 7–8
　getting, 11–12
　glomerulonephritis and, 27, 167
　guilt list by, 162–163
　IBD and, 123–124, 133, 139, 141
　improvement in, 28–29
　in-patient treatment for, 84–86
　kidney disease diagnosis, 26–27
　last days regarding, 81, 139–142
　law practice and, 33–34
　letter to author by, 88–90
　letters to, 3–8, 26–27, 67–69, 100–102, 149–151
　names for, 14

as office dog, 17–19
paintbrush incident of, 133–137
poodle incident with, 22–23
relapse of, 29
senses of, 20–21
story time, 86
spiritual presence of, 150, 176, 202, 274
sub-Q for, 30–31, 35–36, 46, 47–48, 49
syringe sessions with, 105
teacher/pupil lesson from, 67–69
tennis balls and, 15, 101–102
terminal diagnosis of, 30
throwing balls to, 15, 101–102
treatment goals for, 80–81
weakened state of, 152
Beezer's Spot, 166–167, 168–169
Beezer's Top Ten Reasons Not to Feel Guilty, 162–163
biologic value, 43
birds, black, 292–293
birthday
　Boomer's, 253–256
　cake for, 10–11
　Carolina and, 107
　first, 9–11
　games at, 10
　ninth, 95–103
　Suzette and, 9, 10
black birds, 292–293
blizzard, Christmas, 181–182
blood pressure, author's, 53–55
bone scan, 189, 190
Bonus Coverage, 137
Boomer. *See also* B Brothers
　"The Bank Job" and, 269
　"The Daily Point" game and, 219–221, 225–228
　amputation and, 176–177, 195–197, 202–205, 207–212
　animal communication and, 87, 112–113, 167–168, 175–179, 210–211
　ball rescue operations of, 166
　basement stairs and, 230
　Beezer's ashes and, 148, 151
　Beezer's communication sessions and, 87

Beezer's in-patient treatment and, 86
Beezer's reunion with, 12
Beezer's spirit and, 150
birthday celebration of, 253–256
Boomer's Top Ten List on Hope, 265
cancer diagnosis of, 170–171,
    257–258
Christmas wishes for, 183–184
companion for, 154
Coral regarding, 178, 286,
    290, 291
death of, 290–291
disappointment of, 176
disposition of, 10, 14, 15
as Dog on Duty, 17, 279–280, 196,
    220, 227
fading health of, 278–281,
    284, 287
fear and, 175, 197, 230
fiduciary duty and, 193–197
final signs from, 179
final wishes of, 177, 178–179
as flirt, 190–191
as food mop, 106–107
friends, 227, 228, 243.
    See also stuffed animals, toys
Hang with Boomer Club and,
    207–208
heart-to-heart with, 174, 200
hope list by, 265
kidney disease denials by,
    167–168, 178
kidney disease prevention for,
    153–154, 167
last day of, 283–291
last meals of, 286–287, 288–290
on lessons, 178
letters to, 182–184
limping of, 169–170
lump and, 250–252
mixed-doubles team dump and,
    287–288
mystery throws and, 168
names for, 14
Nooners with, 239–240, 276
office and, 147–148, 161
pain and, 175–176, 177, 178
park outings with, 237–239,
    249–250

poodle incident with, 22–23
putting author to bed, 200
radiation treatment on, 188,
    190–191
root canal surgery for, 152, 153
salute by, 147–148
strength of, 152
sub-Q and, 47–48
surgery recovery and, 207–212,
    229–232
tennis ball retrieving by, 15, 101,
    166, 168–169, 232, 253–255
toys and, 15, 19, 134, 226–228
Boomer's Top Ten List on Hope, 265
Brandenburg, Dr., 285

– C –

Callahan, Sharon
    communication approach of,
        63–64
    first session with, 64
    ninth birthday communication via,
        96–100
    spending quality time and, 93
cancer, bone. *See also* Yahoo bone cancer
    group
    "The Daily Point" and, 218
    animal communication regarding,
        175–179
    author's attitude regarding, 251
    as con artist, 215–216
    diagnosis of, 170–171
    diet and, 245, 249
    embracing, 182–183
    fear and, 216–217, 218
    fiduciary relationship and,
        193–197
    goal of, 215
    guilt surrounding, 245–248
    vs. kidney disease, 171, 187,
        245, 249
    messages and, 214–215
    radiation and, 188, 190–191
    Team Fear and, 222–224
cancer, lung
    diagnosis of, 257–258
    metronomic protocol and, 260

Canine Rehabilitation Center,
   230–232
Carolina (ex-wife)
   birthday comment by, 107
   foundering marriage with, 23
   getting dogs and, 11–12
   non-slip runners and, 207
   tough love talk by, 209
ceremony, for Beezer, 150–151, 166
change
   acceptance of, 120
   Beezer's passing and, 149
   fear regarding, 118
Chatfield Reservoir
   B Brothers' birthday at, 100–102
   Beezer's Spot at, 166–167,
      168–169
   Boomer's birthday at, 253–256
   Boomer's last trip to, 280–281
   filming at, 274–275
   mystery throws at, 168
   present moment and, 102
   throwing balls at, 101–102
chemotherapy, 129, 171, 172, 188, 189,
   246–247, 260
Cherry Creek Reservoir, 21–23, 105
Chihuahua, eighty-five pound, 14
Christensen, Hannah
   alternative treatments and, 28, 38
   Beezer's passing and, 6–7, 128, 129,
      130
   Boomer's desires regarding, 177,
      179, 195
   Boomer's passing and, 250,
      284–285, 290–291
   methadone and, 195
Christmas
   Beezer and, 32, 36
   blizzard, 181–182
   letter to Boomer, 182–184
   night, 188
   wishes for Boomer, 183–184
chronic renal failure (CRF), 119
church, 117–118
circle of life session, 112–114
Cleo (B Brothers' mom), 10
clipper ship story, 120
clostridium, 129

coincidence. *See* Rule of
   Coincidence
Colorado State University Veterinary
   Teaching Hospital, 188–189,
   190–191, 298
Colorado weather, 9–10, 181–182
comedian, 19
commemorative brick, 298
con artist, 215–216
conference calls, 16, 203
Coral (yellow Lab)
   background of, 296
   at bank, 269
   black birds incident with,
      292–293
   Boomer's desire regarding, 178
   Boomer's last day and, 286, 290,
      291
   disrupted routine of, 210
   as Dog on Duty, 276
   emergence of, 297–298
   kidney disease of, 295–296
   rolling in poop, 238
   swimming and, 166
   temperament of, 154, 166
creatinine, 28, 29, 39, 119, 141, 153
creditor law, 33. *See also* creditor's
   attorney
creditor's attorney, 18, 175
cremains, 151, 154
CRF. *See* chronic renal failure
cyclosporine, 124, 139, 140

– D –

"The Daily Point" game
   establishment of, 218
   examples of, 219–221, 225–228,
      230, 272
   rules in, 223–224
   Team Fear and, 222–224
Dave (coworker), 18, 33, 287
death. *See also* hospice care
   The Needs of the Dying and, 108
   acceptance of, 108
   anticipatory grief and, 51–52
   of Beezer, 6–7
   Beezer's presence following, 176
   of Boomer, 290–291

day following Beezer's, 145–146
discussions about, 107–109
  of Dutch, 125–128
  fear and, 267
  of Koktavy, 125
  worry and, 98
decision processes, 201–202
diagnosis
  cancer, 170–171, 257–258
  kidney disease, 26–27
  terminal, 30–33
diet
  Beezer's, 43, 73–74
  cancer/kidney disease paradox of,
    245, 249
  fear and, 45
  guilt regarding, 44–45
  kidney disease and, 42, 139,
    245, 249
  lessons on, 73–75
  protein/phosphorus in, 42–43
  supplement reductions in,
    272–273
  syringe sessions and, 105
  water/snow in, 74
  Yahoo kidney group and, 42
disappointment, 54, 176, 257,
  258, 281
Dog on Duty, 17, 276, 279–280
doggie door, 19–20
doggie trek, 15–16
donuts, 286–287
dump
  Beezer's conference call, 16
  mixed-doubles team, 287–288
Dutch (author's friend), 125–128
Dutch (Onalee's dog), 155–157

– E –

eating
  Beezer's challenges with, 105–106,
    111–112
  frustration surrounding, 137
  syringe sessions and, 105
  water/snow, 74
ego
  faith and, 76
  fear and, 151

lesson on, 75–77
my inner self and, 118–120, 130,
  171, 212, 242, 247, 276, 277
paradox and, 185–186
projecting, 296
proof, control and, 61
ego-based, 55
EPO. *See* epoetin alfa
epoetin alfa (EPO), 139–140

– F –

failure, 277–278
faith
  ego and, 76
  hope and, 258–259, 263
  leap of, 55–56, 58, 64
  lesson on, 72–73
  in O'Hara, 175
  present moment and, 259, 263
family life, 115–118
family reunion, of dogs, 9–11
Flanagan, Dr., 53
farewell tour
  author's transformation during,
    275–276
  Chatfield filming during, 274–275
  movie regarding, 271–272
  Nooner during, 276
  supplement/shot reductions and,
    272–273
  swimming pool during, 275
fatal disease
  "The Daily Point" and, 218
  as con artist, 215–216
  fear and, 216–217, 218
  goal of, 215
  messages and, 214–215
father, *see* Jack Koktavy
fear
  amputation and, 197
  B Brothers on, 99
  basement stairs, 230
  Boomer's, 175, 197, 230
  cancer and, 216–217, 218
  change regarding, 118
  diet and, 45
  embracing cancer regarding,
    182–183
  hockey and, 268

pain/suffering and, 72
sub-Q, 32
Team Fear and, 218, 222–224, 225, 242, 271
Fentanyl patch, 194, 195
fiduciary duty
  B Brothers/author's relationship and, 194
  Boomer's leg regarding, 193–197
  definition of, 193
focus expands, 162
fork in the road, 59–60, 142, 187, 216, 272
freedom, 98–99, 185, 287

– G –

Geoffrion, Bernie, 14
GFT. *See* glomerular filtration test
Glawe, Dr., 170–171
glomerular filtration test (GFT), 189, 190
glomeruli, 30
glomerulonephritis, 27, 167
Goldstein, Martin, 37
Goldstein, Robert, 37, 63
  animal communicator and, 57
  supplements prescribed by, 38
grief, anticipatory, 51–52, 259
guilt
  Beezer's lesson on, 68
  Beezer's Top Ten Reasons Not to Feel Guilty, 162–163
  cancer/kidney disease and, 245–248
  Christmas wishes regarding, 183
  diet and, 44–45
  pain/suffering and, 72

– H –

Hang With Boomer Club, 207–208
happens for a reason, *see* reason
helmet, leather, 159, 160
hockey
  Bonus Coverage and, 137
  fear and, 268
  Koktavy and, 117, 158–160, 195, 199
  leather helmet and, 159, 160

lessons learned from, 39, 158–160, 195
as life microcosm, 158–159
stories surrounding, 117–118
Thumbelina and, 159
whistle during, 160
homeopathy, 30, 38
Home-Prepared Dog & Cat Diets (Strombeck), 42
Homer (B Brothers' dad), 10
hope, 258–259, 263–265
  Boomer's Top Ten List on Hope, 265
Horizontal Bowel Disease, 134
hospice care
  anticipatory grief and, 51–52
  death discussions and, 107–108
  human hospice, 51–52, 260, 261
  Presence Plan and, 145, 261–262

– I –

IBD. *See* inflammatory bowel disease
ice hockey. *See* hockey
Ichabod (Chesapeake Bay retriever), 157–158, 161
Indiana Jones and the Last Crusade (movie), 55–56
inflammatory bowel disease (IBD), 123–124
  paintbrush incident and, 133–137
  protein loss and, 139
  worsening of, 133
in-patient IV treatment, 84–86
interpretation, 213–215
IV treatment, 47–48, 84–86

– J –

Jason (massage therapist), 250
jin gu shen qi san, 28
Jody (Yahoo kidney group member), 157–158, 161
juxtaposition, 141–142

– K –

Kessler, David, 108
kiddy pool, 13–14
kidney disease.
  See also Yahoo kidney group

"The Daily Point" and, 218
alternative treatments, 28, 38
animal communication and,
    167–168
attempts to control, 39–40
author's business and, 33–34
author's handling of, 26–33
B Brothers litter mates and, 167
blood test numbers, 29
cancer vs., 171, 187, 245, 249
cleaning up after, 145–146
as con artist, 215–216
confirming, 189
coping with, 27–28
Coral's, 295–296
creatinine and, 28, 29
CRF and, 119
daily routine resulting from, 48–49
denials of, 167–168, 178
diagnosis of, 26–27
diet and, 42, 139, 245, 249
early stage, 190
fear and, 216–217, 218
four undisputed facts, 246
glomeruli and, 30
glomerulonephritis and, 27
goal of, 215
guilt surrounding, 245–248
in-patient IV treatment, 84–86
insidious nature of, 120
litter mates', 167
messages and, 214–215
muscular deterioration from,
    121–122
Myer's Cocktail for, 84–85
prevention of, 153–154, 167
progressive nature of, 43
protein loss and, 139, 242, 245
rallying against, 37
sub-Q for, 30–31
Suzette and, 25–26
Team Fear and, 222–224
Koktavy, Jack
    character of, 158
    communication with, 113–114
    death of, 125
    ice hockey and, 117, 158–160,
        195, 199
    leather helmet and, 159, 160

short temper of, 116
stroke recovery of, 211
summer vacations and, 115–116
on teammate protection, 195
Thumbelina and, 159
on toughness, 199
whistle of, 160
Koons, David
    advice from, 57–58
    on faith, 72

– L –

Langova, Dr., 188–189, 190
law practice. *See also* creditor's attorney
    amputation/conference call and,
        203
    author's, 75–76, 190
    Beezer's disease affecting, 33–34
leap of faith
    animal communicator and, 64
    coincidence vs. reason and, 58
    doctor and, 38
    health forcing, 55–56
    paradox and, 187
leather helmet, 159, 160
Leslie (friend of author), 141
letters
    Beezer blood test, 26–27
    Beezer, honoring,149–151
    Beezer, reminiscing with, 17-19
    Beezer to author, 88–90
    Beezer's passing, 3–8
    Boomer and Christmas, 182–184
    Chatfield Reservoir birthday,
        100–102
    teacher/pupil, 67–69
limping, 169–170
Lisa (kidney group moderator), 119
listening to animals, 63–65, 112, 279
Lombardi, Vince, 39

– M –

Mark (UPS man), 240
metamorphosis, 87
methadone, 195, 197, 201
metronomic protocol, 260
mixed-doubles team dump, 287–288
monster, 171, 214, 216, 217, 223, 251

mother (Louise), 29, 117, 134
movie
 "The Bank Job" scene from, 269
 "A Trip to Chatfield Reservoir"
  scene in, 274–275
 bed footage and, 272
 farewell tour and, 271–272
 motivations for making, 268–269
 swimming pool scene in, 275
Mr. Potato Head, 14
Myer's Cocktail, 84–85
mystery throws, 168

– N –

The Nature of Animal Healing
 (Goldstein), 37
The Needs of the Dying (Kessler), 108
Neely, Dr., 169–170
Nellie (B Brothers' sister), 11, 167
nephrons, 42
new territory, 100
newbie, 43–44
nicknames, 14
Nooners with Boomer, 239–240, 276

– O –

office
 author's business and, 18
 Beezer's dump in, 16
 Boomer's salute and, 147–148
 Boomer's time in, 161
 dog, 17–19
 fun in, 18–19
O'Hara, Terri, 63
 Beezer's ashes and, 148
 Beezer's final moments and, 142
 Boomer's amputation and, 210–211
 Boomer's cancer and, 175–179,
  188, 194
 Boomer's kidneys and, 167–168,
  245
 circle of life session with, 112–114
 first session with, 65
 Koktavy and, 113–114
 Spook U and, 175
 writing books and, 72
Old Place, 88, 90

Onalee (Yahoo kidney group participant),
 155–157
osteosarcoma, 170–171

– P –

pact, with B Brothers, 3–4
pain
 Boomer's, 175–176, 177, 178
 cancer vs. kidney disease and, 171
 Fentanyl patch and, 194, 195, 196
paintbrush incident, 133–137
paradox, cancer/kidney, 245, 249
paradox resolution
 ego and, 185–186
 happy life and, 187
 judgment/freedom and, 185
 mystery solving and, 184
 soul and, 186–187
 steps in, 185–187
paramedics, 44
Pat (neighbor), 209, 274, 275
pathologic fracture, 170–171, 193–194
peace, 136
philosophers, 44
phosphorus
 guilt regarding, 44–45
 kidneys and, 42–43
photos, xiv, 46, 62, 66, 70, 78, 104, 110,
 132, 138, 172, 192, 206, 236, 244,
 266, 298
pizza, 288–289
poodle incident, 22–23
Presence Plan, 261–262
present moment
 author opening to, 212
 Beezer's Top Ten Reasons Not
  to Feel Guilty on, 162
 Chatfield Reservoir and, 102
 Dutch's story regarding, 127
 faith/hope and, 259, 263
 lesson about, 130–131, 259
 trust in, 99–100
process-driven decision, 201–202
protein
 diet and, 42–43
 IBD and, 139
 kidney disease and, 42, 129, 139,
  141, 153, 167, 242, 245, 249

– R –

radiation, 171, 188, 189, 190–191, 193, 194, 210
reason, 58-60
    happens for a, 73, 113, 217, 245, 293, 295
recordings, during sub-Q, 49–50
results-driven decision, 202
Rhonda (paralegal assistant), 18, 33
Rockne, Knute, 277
root canal surgery, 153
Rule of Coincidence
    fork in the road and, 59–60
    leap of faith and, 58
    reason vs., 60
running away, 15–16

– S –

sadness, 71, 184, 250, 258, 259–260
Safe Harbor Labrador Retriever Rescue, 16–17
salute, Boomer's, 147–148
Scott (funeral guy), 7–8, 285
self-employment pressures, 33
self-judgment, 72
Silver, Robert, 37
    amputation and, 197, 202, 204
    animal communicator and, 63
    arteminisin and, 240–241, 257
    Beezer's last visit to, 121–122
    lung cancer and, 257–258
    Myer's Cocktail and, 84–85
    qualities of, 79
    treatment goals and, 80, 260
sister (Kris), 29, 32, 36
sneaky kiss, 255, 290
snow cone, 74
soul, 7, 12, 15, 27, 64, 65, 67, 90, 97, 102, 105, 108, 186–187, 197, 228, 254, 274, 278, 289
spirit, 15, 88, 108, 113, 114, 147, 150, 151, 157, 162, 174, 264, 274, 286, 291
Spook U, 175
stalled traffic, 213–214
story times, 85, 86
    off the hook and, 91–92
    participants in, 92–93

philosophical discussions and, 92
    setting of, 91
stroke, 211
Strombeck, Donald R., 42
stuffed animals, 15, 19, 86, 226–228.
    See also friends
subcutaneous treatment (sub-Q)
    administration of, 36
    animal communication during, 125
    author's trepidation before, 35
    Beezer preparing for, 46
    clipper ship story and, 120
    communion during, 49, 124–125
    description of, 30–31
    fear surrounding, 32
    IV placement for, 47–48
    love and, 72
    needle placement in, 48
    recordings during, 49–50
    steps in, 35–36
sub-Q. *See* subcutaneous treatment
suffering, 72, 130–131, 264, 265
supplements, 38, 272–273
surrender, 89, 178, 179, 217, 259
Suzette (former legal secretary)
    dog litter and, 11–12
    dogs' birthday and, 9, 10
    kidney disease and, 25–26, 27
swimming
    amputation and, 230–232, 254–255, 256
    on Boomer's birthday, 254–255, 256
    Coral and, 166
    pool scene, 275
    triathlon and, 232–234
syringes, 145, 146, 241, 243.
    See also syringe sessions
syringe sessions, 105

– T –

Team Fear, 218, 222–224, 242, 271
tennis ball
    Beezer and, 15, 101–102
    Boomer and, 15, 101, 166, 168–169, 232, 253–255
    cremains and, 151
    rescue operation, 166
terminal diagnosis, 30–33

three brothers, 97, 174
Thumbelina, 159
tightrope, 248
Tootsie Rolls, with feet, 13
traffic, stalled, 213–214
trailhead, 248
treatment, 261–262.
   See also subcutaneous treatment
     alternative, 28, 38, 194, 201
     goals, 80–81
     in-patient, 84–86
     radiation, 188, 190–191
     reduction of, 272–273
triathlon, 39, 76, 232–234

– V –

vacations, summer, 115-116
Vanbiesbrouck, John, 14

– W –

walking pattern, 20–21, 289
weather, Colorado, 9–10, 181–182
What the Bleep Do I Know? (movie), 67
wizard, 44, 73, 74, 119, 162, 298

– Y –

Yahoo bone cancer group
   Ana and, 209–210
   metronomic protocol and, 260
   paradox resolution and, 186
Yahoo kidney group
   author as moderator of, 298
   Beezer's Top Ten Reasons Not
     to Feel Guilty, 162–163
   complex discussions on, 155
   dietary information from, 42
   discovery of, 41
   disease information from, 42, 43
   e-mail from, 57–58
   helping others on, 157–158,
     161–163
   Jody/Ichabod and, 157–158, 161
   Lisa and, 119, 120
   member labels, 43–44
   Onalee/Dutch and, 155–157
   paintbrush incident and, 133–137
   problem outsourcing to, 140–141
   protein/phosphorus and, 42–43

I Need Your Help...

To honor the memory of Beezer and Boomer
To support our nonprofit animal organizations
To spread the word about a charitable B Brothers project

⌐

I HOPE YOU FOUND *THE LEGACY OF BEEZER AND BOOMER* TO BE A worthwhile read. Now, I'd like your help with a charitable project dear to my heart. I have developed a partnership program exclusively for nonprofit animal organizations. My plan, called The B Brothers Project, invites nonprofit organizations to participate and earn 40% of book sales. The nonprofit group does not need to buy anything or invest even one dollar.

Why am I doing this? Over the years I have learned about these wonderful organizations. I know that many are now struggling financially. Some even have had to close their doors. As you know, all the lessons I learned were taught by Beezer and Boomer. They were the teachers—I was the pupil—and I believe that teachers should be paid. The B Brothers are gone, but I am certain they would approve of their share of book proceeds going to charitable organizations that support companion animals.

The B Brothers Project will help animal groups, large and small...shelters, humane societies, pet adoption centers, animal advocacy organizations, rehabilitation sites, clinics and more. Please tell your nonprofit friends about this unique fund-raising opportunity. Ask them to visit *BeezerAndBoomer.com* for details. I am proud to offer this project—the dollar percentage nonprofits will earn *can* make a difference, and I cannot think of a more worthy cause. Complete details are located at our website:

BeezerAndBoomer.com

Stay Connected...

M ANY WONDERFUL WEBSITES OFFER ASSISTANCE TO PET owners and guardians *after* the animal has passed. My concern, and the reason I wrote the book, was to help pet owners *during* the illness. I have created an online forum where individuals going through this difficult part of the journey with a companion animal can congregate in a place of compassion and caring. At this forum you will find:

- a blog where thoughts and ideas, fears and triumphs can be exchanged

- an inspirational page where you can share your favorite stories and photos from your journey

Complete details are located at our website:

BeezerAndBoomer.com

Coming Soon...

A LSO ON THE WEBSITE YOU WILL FIND INFORMATION ABOUT upcoming products from B Brothers Press.

Beezer & Boomer Legacy Workbook

A step-by-step guide and journal to create your own Legacy with your pet. Each of our experiences with our companion animals is unique. When the B Brothers were ill, I found it so helpful to have notebooks for diet and medicine information, funny and touching notes about the dogs, names and contact information of vets and support people, and day-by-day activities. The workbook includes all the steps I took and pages to tailor to your journey. It also will make a welcome gift.

E-Books

A series of single-topic guides on a variety of issues covered in *The Legacy of Beezer and Boomer*. These downloadable mini-books include *Creating a Presence Plan*, *Dealing with Guilt when Your Pet Is Ill*, *Home Hospices for Pets*, *Dealing with the Monsters* (cartoons) and many more.

CDs, DVDs, Webinars & Downloads

Hear directly from veterinarians and experts on hospice care and animal-human relationships. These videos are like attending private symposiums on the latest information on companion animals.

Please also visit the website to order additional copies of *The Legacy of Beezer and Boomer* and learn all the details about The B Brothers Project to help animal nonprofit organizations.

BeezerAndBoomer.com

Jay Simon

About the Author

DOUG KOKTAVY GRADUATED FROM THE UNIVERSITY OF DENVER Law School. He is a self-employed creditor's attorney in Denver who has played ice hockey for years and competed in triathlons. He enjoys volunteering for pet organizations, biking, running and taking quiet walks with his yellow Labrador, Coral. Doug can be reached at *BeezerAndBoomer.com* and (888) 906-BEEZ (2339).

C. SMITH '09